SUSTAINING THE NEW ECONOMY

Sustaining the New Economy

*Work, Family, and Community
in the Information Age*

Martin Carnoy

RUSSELL SAGE FOUNDATION

New York, New York

HARVARD UNIVERSITY PRESS

Cambridge, Massachusetts

London, England · 2000

10 9 8 7 6 5 4 3 2 1

Martin Carnoy is professor of education and economics at Stanford University.

Library of Congress Cataloging-in-Publication Data

Carnoy, Martin.
Sustaining the new economy : work, family, and community in the
information age / by Martin Carnoy.
p. cm.
Includes bibliographical references and index.
ISBN 0-674-00373-X
1. Employees—Effect of technological innovations on. 2. Work and family. I. Title.
HD6331.C279 2000   00-027030
306.3'6—dc21   CIP

For Jean and Juliet

Contents

Preface

For the past thirty years, I have lived and worked in Silicon Valley's new economy. I have watched it transformed from the innovative edge of American industry to an engine of global growth. Around 1975, I began interviewing chief executive officers of technology-based firms and the workers building the chips and electronic devices that were the Valley's mainstay. In those days, we were still in the modern industrial age—Silicon Valley firms were focusing on hardware and manufacturing. Yet the essence of high-tech work was not very different than it is today. People changed jobs often and looked for start-ups where they could get a piece of the company. The eighty-hour work culture was in place, but it was not as ubiquitous as it is now. Fortunes were made, but not nearly as rapidly as they are today. The new gold rush was just beginning, and each decade has brought success on an ever greater scale.

In 1984, I ran for the U.S. Congress in California's 12th District against Ed Zschau, a high-tech entrepreneur and a popular incumbent. The primary issue in that campaign was not *whether* high technology, but how it was affecting life in the Valley. Zsachau argued that the new economy would not only leave everyone better off economically but would generate minimal social costs. My campaign emphasized the need for well-organized public interventions in transportation, schooling, family services, and job networking and training. Zschau won, but judging by the Valley's traffic jams, stressed families, and struggling schools sixteen years later, I had the right idea.

Today, the "idiosyncrasies" of Silicon Valley in the 1970s are becoming the dominant culture of work in America and are rapidly spreading to other countries. I feel them in my everyday life even though I do not work in a dot-com or business networking company. My children and my friends' children move from job to job without blinking an eye. The workforce is as detached from their workplace as they are from their government and community. Our world is moving at a faster pace. Thanks to a communications and software revolution, we are more "connected" than ever before—by cell phone, email, and video conferencing—yet more disconnected than in the past from social interaction.

The fruits of a rapidly growing economy based on innovations and hard work are patently obvious. Less obvious are the costs absorbed by individuals as they take on the attributes required to succeed in the new economy. And, even less noticeable is what happens to those who are marginal to society. Yet, unless these costs are dealt with and the underlying fabric of the new society reconstructed, economic growth will be threatened. Sustaining the new economy means building a new set of social institutions to support it. This book tries to lay the groundwork for the process of rebuilding.

I am indebted to Manuel Castells, my intellectual brother, who like the proverbial phoenix, rose from the ashes of a life-threatening illness to create his greatest work, *The Information Age.* Many of the ideas we shared over a period of years appear in these pages. Much of the research for the book took place in the mid–1990s during a sabbatical year at the Center for Advanced Study in the Behavioral Sciences in Palo Alto, California. Anyone who spends time at the center is inspired and grateful for the opportunity, and this certainly includes me.

Many others contributed to this work. Eric Wanner and the Russell Sage Foundation have been very supportive, both intellectually and financially. Eric made suggestions early in the project that shaped the direction of my research. My good friends in France, Jarl Bengtsson and Jean Louis Reiffers, helped me get feedback on my ideas from key people in Europe and Japan. Michael Aronson of Harvard University Press persuaded me to make many important changes. Suzanne Nichols, my editor at the Russell Sage Foundation, and Katherine Kimball were tireless in putting the manuscript into shape. David Haproff, also at Russell Sage, guided me through the review process.

Although writing is not great for family life, my wonderful family makes my writing possible and meaningful. Like the families I describe in this book, mine is complex and lives with a great deal of stress. Yet, my wife Jean, my young daughter Juliet, my two grown children from an earlier marriage, David and Jon, my mother, my mother-in-law, and my wife's many siblings are a real blessing. They give me support by just being my family.

Martin Carnoy

1

Our Work in a
Changing Economy

Alan Burke works for a small company in North Carolina's booming Research Triangle. His firm processes discount coupons, bills the product manufacturers for the discounts, and refunds the money to the supermarkets that collected them. This is the third job—all in the Research Triangle—Alan has had in the last eight years. The last two were in software sales, but Alan had jumped at this opportunity because he had been a Latin American studies major in college. Alan's company ships the coupons to Mexico, where their codes are keypunched, and the files are then electronically transferred back to North Carolina. He monitors the Mexico operations and is exploring ways to speed up the process. The faster the coupons can be turned around in Mexico, the more business his company can do. Between trips south of the border and the twelve-hour days at the office, Alan does not get to spend much time with his wife, Helen, who also works, and his five-year-old son, Darrin. Alan also worries whether this job will last; but he likes its intensity, and he sees the time he gives up at home as an investment in his future, hoping the sacrifice will lead to more challenging jobs in the future.

The new economy that gets Alan to work so hard and rewards him so well is more than the bourgeoning internet, dot-com companies, and inter-firm networking. It is a way of work and a way of life. Its core values are flexibility, innovation, and risk. As the new economy becomes the main source of wealth creation worldwide, it infuses old industrial cultures with these values. It requires a workforce that is not only well educated, but also ready to change jobs quickly and to take the risks associated with rapid change.

Alan Burke is just a short step away from social isolation. He has friends at work, but when he changes his job, chances are his friends will change as well. His urban-suburban-sprawl neighbors are, like him, totally engrossed in their work lives, so he knows them only to say hello. His parents are in Minnesota, his only sibling in Arizona. Should he lose his job before securing another one to replace it, there is really no one to count on locally except his wife, and the loss of his job could knock that already stressed relationship over the edge.

The institutions that tie Alan and other workers to one another—jobs, family, community—do not work the way they used to. Because of globalization and changes in technology, firms today need to be flexible in how they structure jobs and employment. This means that workers cannot count on working for the same firm, or even doing the same kind of work, for very long. Workers like Alan and those he employs need to network in the job market to hedge against job loss and to move ahead. They also need the quality education that enables them to perform many different types of tasks related to their career, to adjust to constant change, and to get and use the information required to make complex decisions affecting their economic and social lives. However, the two-adult, one-breadwinner family structure that was instrumental to the education of earlier generations has changed. Now, many households are headed by a single adult, and if there are two adults in the family, they are both likely to work, and there is little time to invest in their children. There is a real question of how well today's children will be prepared to cope with tomorrow's flexible work environment. Communities that integrate adults and children in neighborhood support organizations are also a thing of the past. The time needed for community involvement is dispersed in long commutes, transporting children to and from school, and networking and studying for that next job. With less stable and less supportive communities, adults are forced to rely on their own resources when adversity strikes. When those resources exist, all is well and good; when they do not, it can be all the more difficult to climb back.

If new institutions do not emerge to compensate for these fundamental transformations, the flexible production essential to high productivity in the global new economy will be that much less efficient, with disastrous effects all around. Men's and women's work is being transformed by globalization, new information technologies, and women's fight for equality, but the social institutions needed to support this change lag far behind.

The Individualization of Work and the Erosion
of Social Institutions

Alan Burke's work, social relations, and self-definition are the product of historical changes that are transforming our everyday lives. Our national economies and even our national cultures are globalizing. Globalization means more competition, and not just with other companies in the same town or the same state: even flower growers in California have to vie with Costa Rican and Chilean imports, flown up the same day from thousands of miles away. Globalization also means that a nation's investment, production, and innovation are not limited by national borders. Everything, including the way we relate to our family and friends, is rapidly becoming organized around a much more compressed view of space and time. Companies in Europe, the United States, and Japan can produce microchips in Singapore, keypunch data in India, outsource clerical work to Ireland, and sell worldwide, barely concerned about the long distances or the variety of cultures involved. Even children in school or watching television are reconceptualizing their world in terms of the meanings they attach to music, the environment, sports, and race or ethnicity.

People's work has shifted from the production of agricultural and manufactured goods to the production of services and to increasingly sophisticated services at that. The main ingredient in these new services is knowledge—knowledge that increases productivity, provides a closer fit between a client's specific needs and the services delivered, and creates possibilities for the development of new products and new services. With more competition, knowledge also becomes increasingly important in manufacturing and agriculture. Quality of production, design, efficient organization, new products, customized production, and just-in-time delivery are the knowledge-intensive aspects dominating today's manufacturing and agricultural activities in both developed countries and the export sectors of developing countries.

Our lives are being transformed by a massive diffusion of new information and communication technologies. Thanks to computers and internet communication, large firms can restructure around different product lines, and even small firms can now go international and customize production for a vast variety of clients. Each one of us can correspond with people around the world instantaneously on the World Wide Web. We can get the daily news, search encyclopedias, make travel arrangements, do our banking, and buy merchandise directly from our homes. To those who know how to use it, telecomputing gives access to huge amounts of information.

The Changing Workplace

The transformation of work has been misinterpreted and mystified by writers who claim that new information technology means a massive and growing shortage of jobs, particularly good, high-skill jobs. Their claim that the new technology restricts the number of jobs, though seductive, is not supported by facts. New technology displaces workers; but it simultaneously creates new jobs by raising productivity in existing work and making possible completely new products and processes. As postindustrial economies and governments adjust to new realities, employment growth, not displacement, dominates. There will be plenty of jobs in the future, and most of them will be high-paying jobs.

Technology-caused job shortage may be a false alarm, but profound changes are occurring in the workplace. In the future, a job may not mean the same thing it does today. More intense competition on a worldwide scale makes firms acutely aware of costs and productivity. The solution arrived at by employers has been to reorganize work around decentralized management, work differentiation, and customized products, thereby individualizing work tasks and differentiating individual workers in relation to their supervisors and employers. This has made subcontracting, part-time employment, and the hiring of temporary labor much easier, because a lot of work can be narrowed down to specific tasks, even as other "core" work is conducted by teams and is organized around multitasking. Socially, workers are gradually being defined less by the particular long-term job they hold than by the knowledge they have acquired by studying and working. This knowledge portfolio allows them to move across firms and even across types of work as jobs get redefined.

The effect of individualization and differentiation is to separate more and more workers from the "permanent" full-time jobs in stable businesses that characterized post–World War II development in Europe, Japan, the United States, and other industrialized countries. Just as an earlier factory revolution drove a wedge between workers and the products they made, the new transformation is dissolving the identity that workers developed with industrial organizations such as the corporation and the trade union.

Workers are being individualized, separated from their traditional identities, which were built over more than a century, and from the social networks that enabled them to find economic security. The job and everything organized around the job—the group of friends in the company, the after-work hangouts, the trade union, even the car pool—lose their social function. They are as "permanently temporary" as the work itself.

Some, mainly highly educated professional and technical workers such as Alan Burke, are building new networks. Instead of just talking to colleagues within the companies they work for, they develop electronic mail and informal information relations across companies. Network technology such as the internet helps; the exchange of information among professionals from a broad range of firms in upscale after-work hangouts serves the same purpose. The main question is what happens to the vast majority of workers who do not have easy access to information about other companies or to workers in other firms, or those highly skilled workers who have fallen out of the communications loop. They tend to be left in an individualized limbo, "disaggregated" from traditional networks but not "integrated" into new ones. New, private networks, such as temp agencies, are emerging to fill this void. With a few striking exceptions, however, such as construction unions that traditionally allocate temp jobs among their members, these networks are not organized for or by workers. They fail to satisfy the need for social integration served by stable jobs, unions, and professional associations.

Changing Families and Communities

Besides workplaces and job-centered social networks, families and communities are the traditional social integrators. In times of transition, whether it be from an agricultural society to an industrial one, industrial to postindustrial, or now local or national to global, families and communities are called upon to bear most of the responsibility in preserving social cohesion. Families also transmit much of the skill and knowledge needed by children to make their way in the adult work world. Thus, it is not surprising that whenever these workplace transitions occur, families and the communities that form around new work organizations are put under a lot of stress. The "industrial family" that emerged in the shift from agriculture to factory work beginning two hundred years ago often worked together in the factory, as if they were still on the farm. That system gradually broke down, however, and women were put in the unenviable position of feeding, caring for, and educating their children on wages controlled by their husbands. Neither did women have much control over the number of children they bore. Mothers were often too old to work for themselves by the time their last child reached working age. Working-class family life in nineteenth-century factory towns was therefore hardly idyllic, and women in these highly stressed families were called on to play a key role in maintaining moral and social cohesion. Middle-class women were better off financially, but if Jane Austen's characterization of nineteenth-century life is accurate, they too were bound tightly by strict, male-ordered conventions.

Families have changed profoundly in the past hundred years. Women have gradually rejected the burden of single-handedly maintaining social cohesion and educating the next generation. They began in the late nineteenth century by reducing family size through sexual abstinence. Middle-class women worked out their menstrual cycles and made themselves unavailable to their husbands during periods of fertility. This practice eventually spread to working-class women. The invention of the condom also helped. Smaller families made social cohesion easier, gave more time for community building, and allowed women to create a social life for themselves outside the family—even, increasingly, in the workplace. However, the latest round of women's revolt, starting in the late 1960s, struck at the underlying gender relations in family and work. Women rejected the identity of "homemaker" that was assigned them by industrial society. Masses of married women entered the workplace, part time at first and then full time. Many women ended up going it alone, heading families without men. All this happened before and independently of globalization and new information technology.

Yet when workplace restructuring did come along a short decade later, employers could not help but be influenced by women's new willingness to work and hired them in great numbers as a new source of relatively highly educated labor. However, the nuclear family with a full-time mother doing the home work—the family that had sustained and nurtured the Industrial Revolution—had been transformed. Moreover, the new organization of work that was successfully responding to the competitive pressures of a globalized economy had come to depend on the relatively cheap, highly productive, and highly flexible labor supplied increasingly by these wives and mothers. This constellation has occurred just when a strong, cohesive family with time and energy to invest in the education and well-being of both adults and children is most needed during the difficult transition period toward new forms of work and personal life.

In addition to the meaning and structure of the family having changed, the communities that had emerged from the Industrial Revolution, such as the factory towns and industrial cities with their ethnic and other highly organized suburban enclaves, had broken down in the postindustrial flight to the new urban formations François Ascher calls "metapoles"(Ascher 1998). A wave of accelerated territorial urban and suburban sprawl has by and large undermined the material base of neighborhood sociability. Globalization produces less secure and more dispersed work arrangements than earlier organizations of production. Families with two working adults are the norm, and parents and children tend to build networks within the variety of institutions in which they spend their time rather than socializing with neighbors. This makes these already semitransitory communities even less relevant to the integration of the disaggregated workers of the globalized age.

The transformation of work and the family is also dissolving the political relations that developed in the industrialized countries between working people and government through publicly provided social services, such as social security and medical insurance, provided mainly to people with full-time lifetime jobs and through civic and political groups organized around traditional communities and families. Government social transfers emerged from nineteenth- and early-twentieth-century industrial worker movements responding to the new work conditions in factories. Once workers had been pulled from their farmhouses and put into factories (and factory towns), they were able to organize, and targeted the workplace as a target for bettering their social conditions. Such organizing spread to broader political organizing based on working-class interests and the fight for workers' benefits.

The very notion of government as linked directly to the needs of people in communities and workplaces also emerged from civic organizations based in local communities. They counted on participation by individuals whose conception of time and space were defined by particular notions of community and family. As those notions change, however, civic life also changes, undermining political and social relations that once integrated individuals into a national state.

The Failure of Current Public Policy Responses

With the current economic transformation—every bit as important as the last one in the nineteenth century—trade unions and governments, accustomed to the last industrial Revolution, are not responding to the new conditions. Indeed, under pressure from both right and left, government reactions are generally off the mark, reverting to models that no longer function very well. The system of work that underlies the very concept of these social programs has changed. Flexible work and flexible employment have difficulty coexisting with rigid social entitlements. The individualization of work and the shrinkage of the public safety net create additional stress for families and communities as they try to help their members adapt to the new requirements of work life. Certain definitions of the company, the job, the family, and the community were all essential to the form of government social programs that emerged in the twentieth century; but these definitions are going through major change, making these programs much less effective.

Today's free market conservative models do not work either. Ironically, they rely on family and a civic culture that reached its high point in the heyday of the welfare state, when the "little woman" stayed home taking care of the kids while Dad earned a wage that could support the family, and this family "team" was extensively involved in voluntary civic activities. These institutional structures existed in the developed countries largely because of a partnership between government and working individuals in the context of a particular work system. Free market conservatives now want to hark back to that family and the civil society it nurtured, but they do not want the kind of government intervention that made it possible. In any case, the current work system does not warrant that kind of partnership between government and individual. The free market conservatives believe that markets in and of themselves will create a society in which high technology and high productivity flourish. This belief is plainly wrong.

Because neither political model works effectively, families, communities, and public institutions are less and less capable of restoring social equilibrium to lives knocked off balance by the individualization of work and drastically changing gender relations. In and of themselves, work and family changes do not necessarily have negative consequences. The resurgence of the individual, with greater freedom and self-directed initiative, frees people from bureaucracies, from the often excessive constraints of work-place microsocial networks, and from the grossly unequal relations dominating families. Such newfound freedom can only be enjoyed, however, if alternative forms of social organization provide people with a web of relationships that can serve as both psychological support and a basis for interaction. The whole system of relationships among these cornerstones of our societies is at stake.

Not every society faces the same problems in confronting these changes. Like all transitions, this one has caught each society at a particular historical moment in its development. Family relations, relations between labor and employers, the individual's relation to government, and community structures are all the product of this history, and they differ from one society to another. To the degree that globalization, increased competition, the new technologies, and changes in relations between men and women have universal dimensions affecting everyone, every society must react, but each may, and probably should, react differently.

A Global Approach

This book addresses the question of how societies can reorganize themselves to meet the new conditions of "flexible production" required for high productivity in a global economy in the context of societies undergoing massive social change. Piecemeal measures destined to increase the number of jobs or to educate and better train workers are not enough. They do not address the interactions triggered by the processes of change at the root of globalization and the new organization of work. Public policies, business strategies, and community organizing strategies need to be changed, and before this can be done we must first understand the connection between labor markets and the simultaneous (and related) changes taking place in families and communities. Once these changes are understood, policies and practices can move to make societies more socially coherent and economically productive in the new context.

These phenomena can be understood from two different vantage points. The first looks at the institutions—the workplace, the family, and community—in which individuals organize their social relations. These social sites are highly interconnected and change simultaneously. No one site takes the lead in the change process. Workplace transformation is still crucial to the change in people's lives. Economic globalization, with its increased competition, and the new information and communications technology, with its massive impact on space and time and the way people connect with one another, are pervasive influences on social relations. However, other changes originate outside the workplace and are as important for grasping the overall process of change. Women's rejection of their male-assigned identities as primarily wives and mothers profoundly affects our social world. It also interacts with globalization and new technology to transform the workplace and family life. Finally, increased individualization and rising levels of education influence identity and the reformation of community, and these, too, interact with globalization, changes in work, and women's redefinition of family to produce an even more complex set of changes in social relations.

The second view is across societies. Contemporary societies are similar in many ways, but they also differ socially, politically, and culturally. Their institutional histories are particular to each. As a result, they react differently to global change across social spaces: workplaces, families, and communities. The "Anglo-Saxon" highly developed countries—Australia, Great Britain, Canada, New Zealand, and the United States—tend to follow more "open," free market economic policies. Their labor markets are most "flexible." Women's movements within these countries have been parallel, and family changes similar. Even in this similarity, however, there is much variance. Canada, so like the United States in many ways, is much more protective of its workers as it engages in the new global economy. Canada provides more public support to families and has much less poverty, but unemployment rates are higher. Great Britain also differs from the United States despite years of neoconservative economic and social policies that paralleled the Reaganomics of the United States in the 1980s.

These differences among the more flexible labor markets are small compared with those between the Anglo-Saxon countries and continental Europe, Scandinavia, and Japan—and there is considerable variance within that second group as well. Women are more likely to divorce, and women with children more likely to work, in Scandinavia than in Italy, Spain, or Japan. Families and labor markets in the latter societies are much more "traditional" than those in the former. Unemployment rates are much higher in Italy and Spain, so young people marry later and have fewer children—so few, in fact, that populations in both countries are in danger of declining. Other societies provide support to families through major government subsidies for child care, as in France and Scandinavia, which seems to have an effect on the number of children couples are willing to have. Although youth unemployment rates are as high in France as in Italy or Spain, women in France have about the same number of children as British women or Anglo women in the United States, where youth unemployment rates are much lower and labor markets more flexible.

These varying institutional histories mean that people in different societies have reached high standards of living by somewhat different routes. Today, all societies face a changing global economic and social environment and changing gender roles. People accustomed to certain lifestyles have to make personal and collective decisions on how to adjust. They do not want to abandon these lifestyles; after all, over the past fifty years, the Western way of life has been associated with vast economic and social improvements. Many Americans cannot understand why the French, Italians, and Germans, facing high unemployment rates, do not deregulate their economies to look like that of the United States, with its massive job creation but stagnant wages and increasing work hours. In turn, Europeans, despite unemployment and other problems, cannot understand how Americans can tolerate such high rates of child poverty and the stresses of constant work with little if any vacation time. The United States is also pressuring an economically troubled Japan to reduce regulation, to jumpstart their economy by freeing up markets. The Japanese used these same regulations, however, to become a global high-tech powerhouse in just two generations, and it did so with low unemployment and poverty, a high degree of job security, and almost no social strife.

Because of these institutional differences, each nation, or group of nations, is likely to choose different ways to adjust to the same transformative forces. Even with these differences, all nations will have to rely to one degree or another on their public sector or the state to successfully reintegrate individuals socially. To reintegrate individuals as they are buffeted about by the reorganization of work and family, nation-states, regions, and local communities will have to focus on enhancing knowledge, especially for those groups least able to participate effectively in flexible labor markets.

This is not going to be easy. A major shift is occurring in the way people regard the traditional source of leadership on such policies—their national governments—and in the way they participate in politics. This change has occurred because, with globalization, nation-states have become steadily less able to satisfy the varied economic interests of diverse groups living within their boundaries. In 1964, almost 80 percent of Americans agreed with the following statement: "You can trust the government in

Washington to do what is right just about always, or most of the time." This proportion declined to about 27 percent by 1980 and, after rising back up to 45 percent in 1984, continued a steady decline to 20 percent in 1994 (Inglehart 1997, figure 10.2). Until the latest recession of the early 1990s, Western Europeans did not show a similar trend in attitude toward their political systems, but the reaction to this recession seems to have been much more negative than in the past (Inglehart 1997, figure 10.5).

Under these conditions, it is no accident that nation-states are looking for low-cost social policies that simultaneously enhance growth and reincorporate "disaggregated" workers. Economists have long argued that a major source of economic growth is a society's investment in learning (Schultz 1961). Whatever its contribution to the creation of wealth in the past, human knowledge is an even more important ingredient in the information economy. A primary characteristic of flexible production in the new global environment is that it is human capital intensive, new knowledge intensive, and networking intensive. Relatively low labor and materials costs alone are no longer enough to assure a firm or nation a place at the global table. The importance of knowledge is accentuated as innovation becomes increasingly endogenous to firms and firm networks. The globalization of innovation also means that even at the peripheries of global firms, the production of information technology depends on a knowledge-enhancing environment. Because of this defining feature, the production of information technology and the quality of information itself inherently depend on a society's members' access to knowledge, particularly the kind that help them integrate into the new flexible, global environment.

This fact may seem obvious, but it poses a fundamental problem bound to dominate societies for years to come. In the past, even the recent past, much of the knowledge creation required for social integration occurred in workplaces, families, and local communities, and this process needs to continue in the future even more intensively. However, if employers want just-in-time knowledge, if families are leading just-in-time lives, if communities are increasingly disparate and spatially ill defined, how can the creation of knowledge take place? It is not just an issue of providing the same educational and information services now available. A high proportion of children in developed societies are being born into less educated families. In the past, this was not a significant problem because these children could expect to find decent, relatively high-paying jobs in an expanding manufacturing sector. That, however, is no longer the case. The amount and diversity of knowledge demanded in higher-paying jobs are increasing; yet, more important, the knowledge base required just to function effectively in flexible labor markets, no matter what the job, is also becoming more complex.

This means that institutions' abilities to integrate individuals around access to knowledge—institutions ranging from local organizations to nation-states to even supranational organizations—define the boundaries of the new communities. I make the case in chapter 5 that this is already happening in many different forms, and it is not just happening among highly educated, highly networked individuals. In some instances, the most innovative responses to the new flexible economy are coming from the most marginalized sectors of society.

On the other hand, any traditional organization unable to deliver the various kinds of broad-based education needed for individuals to cope successfully in the new global environment—what I call "integrative knowledge"—will become superfluous to individuals' conception of community. The most obvious candidate for such superfluousness is the state, because it is the state, especially the nation-state, that has borne the greatest responsibility for socially integrating workers during the late industrial age. If governments prove unable to organize institutions successfully around integrative knowledge and a "livable" form of economic development, they will cease to be central to citizens' lives. Individuals will seek other institutions and communities that they believe will do a better job in delivering integrative knowledge to them and their children. So the stakes are high: those nations and localities without coherent reintegrative institutions will be marked by gradual social disintegration and social conflict. Not all developed societies will adjust quickly to the change taking place, and some will suffer serious consequences as a result. Yet I am optimistic, and the analysis in this book reflects my optimism. Political leaders who see the handwriting on the wall early will be able to organize delivery of integrative knowledge and livable economic development to create the conditions in which flexibility and economic competitiveness can be sustained. I believe that all the member countries of the Organisation for Economic Co-operation and Development (OECD) have the capacity to sustain flexible production and at the same time be enjoyable places to live. Those nations and localities that pull themselves together politically to do so will thrive in the global economy. Those that do not, however, face a difficult future.

2

New Technology
and Job Markets

The U.S. economic boom of the 1990s was the first truly global high-tech expansion, fueled by an explosion in computers sales, software development, the internet, telecommunications, and multimedia. Not only is the production of these products expanding at a dazzling pace, their use in the traditional manufacturing and services of developed countries is becoming ubiquitous. The technological transformation of the economy has been greater in the United States in the 1990s than in any major country of the world.[1] Employment growth is also dazzling. From the beginning of 1993 to the beginning of 1999, the U.S. economy created more than 14 million new jobs, increasing employment from 119 million to 133 million. Unemployment dropped below 4 percent to its lowest level since the late 1960s, and the ratio of employment to population, which measures the percentage of all people between the ages of sixteen and sixty-five who have jobs, was 64 percent, higher than at any time since World War II. More than half of these new jobs in the 1990s were considered "high paying"—professional and managerial jobs across industries and technical and sales positions in high-paying industries, such as electronics, manufacturing, communications, and utilities.

The United States is not the only economy riding the high-tech wave. In Asia, and also in many countries of Latin America, many new manufacturing jobs were created in the 1980s and early 1990s to replace those lost in Europe and the United States. Before financial problems hit the Asian economies in 1997, overall employment in the region expanded much more rapidly than in the United States. The bottom line is that in much of the world, globalization and new technology have been associated with continued job growth. In the developed countries, the growth of "good" high-skill jobs is outpacing the growth of lower-skill jobs. Many jobs have been destroyed, but even more have been created. Continental Europe, the one developed region of the world in which job growth has been slow and high unemployment was pervasive in the 1990s, is technology intensive, but much less so than the United States; and the highest unemployment rates in Europe are in Spain and southern Italy, areas of relatively low technology intensity.

Employment growth, however, depends on much more than technological change. A broader set of variables that affect economic growth and frame technological change and increase firms' willingness to hire new workers—including macroeconomic policies, political climate, and public investment in human capital—are crucial to shaping the way technological change impacts the number of jobs.

Not everyone is willing to accept the proposition that investing in new information technology is compatible with job growth. For example, Richard Barnet, the codirector of the Institute for Policy Studies in Washington, D.C., wrote a long piece in *Harper's* in 1993 titled "The End of Jobs." Barnet argues that, thanks to the new technology, plenty of goods and services can be produced, but there has not been enough work to go around, because fewer workers are needed to make the additional amount of product. He cites the massive number of people worldwide who were unemployed or underemployed (in 1993) and the growing number of people in the developed countries who were considered superfluous. According to Barnet, many new competitors in Asia and Latin America have been fighting for a piece of the global job pie that, if not shrinking, has not been growing fast enough to satisfy all of the demands for jobs (Barnet 1993).

Barnet sounds an old alarm. Two persistent beliefs resurface in periods of economic change. One is that new technology replaces workers, leading to reduced demand for labor and, hence, a shortage of jobs. The second is that new technology de-skills most work, leading to lower wages and the degradation of working men and women. These beliefs come from observations of a single firm's behavior in the short run or the effect of innovations on the skills needed in some production processes. When a firm installs new technology, it generates cost reductions or product innovations that allow it to expand. Most new technology, be it in agriculture, manufacturing, or services, has been labor saving: in the short run, the firm generally reduces its labor force even as it produces more output. From that point of view, new technology appears to reduce employment. Many technological innovations aim not only at eliminating unskilled labor but also at reducing a business's reliance on highly skilled and highly paid employees. For example, early automobile production used skilled bicycle workers. Henry Ford introduced the assembly line in 1912 to routinize and speed up production. In the process, he was able to de-skill car manufacturing and take control of the speed of work away from his workers. He was also able to hold down his workers' wages, at least for a while. Similarly, more recent innovations in the manufacture of machine tools have practically eliminated highly skilled lathe operators and replaced them with much less skilled workers keypunching computer instructions for programmable lathes.

Technology's destruction of jobs and degradation of work have been popular notions throughout the generations, beginning in the early nineteenth century. New technology definitely did either eliminate or de-skill the jobs of workers in this period. With new technology, firms were able to produce as much or more product with far fewer workers per unit of output. To that extent, the stories were true and the ideas valid.

The larger picture, however, is very different. In the past, new technology made it possible to produce products for less, pushing prices down and increasing real incomes of consumers at home and, in turn, raising demand for these and other products and increasing the potential for export, which also expanded demand. As production increased, the overall demand for labor increased, not only in the firm that adopted the new technology but in other industries as well. The effect on real income raised demand for other products, and the expansion of the firm increased the demand for the new technology, increasing employment in the supplying industry. Perhaps even more important, new technology meant the arrival of new products at affordable prices, products that satisfied unfulfilled wants. The assembly line used fewer workers per unit of output than bicycle-style production but lowered the price of an automobile to a level at which an average worker could afford one. A major new industry developed worldwide, greatly increasing the demand for skilled and semiskilled workers, not only in auto production but also in steel, tires, rubber, petroleum, road construction, and tourism. Thus, despite the constant flow of labor-saving innovations in the nineteenth and twentieth centuries, employment grew rapidly in the most technology-intensive countries, and more output in those industries generated even more employment in other industries associated with them.

The International Labour Office commissioned two separate studies to synthesize available data on these effects—one by the British political economist Raphael Kaplinsky, the other by the economist John Bessant—which independently reached similar conclusions. Kaplinsky (1987) analyzed the impact of technological change on employment and skills at seven different levels: individual processes within a plant, production in the plant as a whole, and production in the firm (which may have several different plants), in the industry, in the entire sector, in the economy, and in the economic region. He observed that technological innovation may reduce employment and skills at the level of individual processes, at the plant level, and sometimes even at the firm level; but these same innovations play out differently at the level of industry, sector, economy, and region. "It would appear that the quantitative macro and micro studies are drawn to fundamentally different conclusions. Process and plant level investigations generally seem to point to a significant displacement of labour. On the other hand, national level simulations more often reach the conclusion that there is no significant problem on hand" (Kaplinsky 1987, 153). Bessant concurs: "Across the whole spectrum the pattern is one of both losses and gains, with overall relatively small change in employment" (Bessant 1989, 27). For Kaplinsky, who was one of the first to argue that information technology has different properties from previous technologies, the employment effects of computers, software, and telecommunications at the industry level and above are still positive, mainly because of their significant positive impact on productivity.

This is not just a theoretical rationale for technological innovation. Over the past two centuries, industrialization absorbed massive numbers of agricultural workers into factories and offices despite the simultaneous adoption of new labor-saving technologies. The agricultural workers who constituted the overwhelming majority of our population in the nineteenth and early twentieth centuries have been all but phased out of national production. Their children took jobs in manufacturing and services. Workers today work much less than those of a century ago, produce more, earn substantially more, and have access to a greater variety of jobs. Technology displaced workers but also contributed to much higher labor productivity and the production of new products, which helped create new jobs, economic growth, and higher incomes.

The de-skilling argument revolves around a similar misunderstanding. Many new technologies are consciously de-skilling, but others eliminate both low- and high-skill jobs and require their replacement with jobs for semiskilled workers. For example, thanks to Andrew Carnegie, the steel industry went through a major, highly conflictive transformation in the 1890s. Skilled master puddlers and their unskilled laborers were knocked out of work, and semiskilled operators went to work on the new steel production technology.[2] The Ford assembly line reduced the demand for skilled bicycle craftsmen but created a host of other skilled and semiskilled jobs. They were filled by relatively unskilled first- and second-generation immigrants from rural areas in the United States and Europe. Although it is harder to make the case that in the industrial countries, workers doing any particular task (for example, building a house) in 1920 were more skilled than comparable workers in 1870—and less skilled than comparable workers in 1950—each succeeding generation was certainly expected to perform a greater variety of tasks than their predecessors and could perform them faster, given the technology at their disposal. On average, they also produced much better and more sophisticated products.

Today's version of the "technology destroys and degrades jobs" argument acknowledges that eventually the labor market was able to absorb the workers displaced by previous rounds of technological innovation. Service activities successfully absorbed workers from the automation of agricultural and industrial jobs; but this time, the argument goes, there is a difference: information technologies strike at the heart of these very service activities so that the previous history of technological innovation will not be repeated (Barnet 1993; see also Rifkin 1995 and Aronowitz and DeFazio 1994).[3]

> The universal use of computers has increased exponentially the "multiplied productive powers" of labor. In this regime of production, the principal effect of technological change—labor displacement—is largely unmitigated by economic growth. That is, it is possible for key economic indicators to show, but only for a short time, a net increase in domestic product without significant growth of full-time employment. On the other hand, growth itself is blocked by two effects of the new look to working in America. Labor redundancy, which is the main object of technological change, is, indirectly, an obstacle to growth. In the wake of the shrinking social wage, joblessness, the growth of part-time employment, and the displacement of good, full-time jobs by badly paid part-time jobs tend to thwart the ability of the economic system to avoid chronic overproduction and underconsumption. (Aronowitz and DeFazio 1994, 21)

Jeremy Rifkin claims that "as all these sectors [manufacturing and services] fall victim to rapid restructuring and automation, no 'significant' new sector has developed to absorb the millions who are being displaced." The new knowledge sector, he continues, staffed by symbolic analysts such as engineers, managers, consultants, teachers, and media professionals, will continue to grow but will remain elite and small compared with the "number of workers displaced by the new generation of 'thinking machines'" (Rifkin 1995, 35). Rifkin predicts a jobless future resulting from the new technology. Of those who have work, the vast majority will be in "mindless" jobs: "While earlier industrial technologies replaced the physical power of human labor, substituting machines for body and brawn, the new computer-based technologies promise a replacement of the human mind itself, substituting thinking machines for human beings across the entire gamut of economic activity" (Rifkin 1995, 5).

These are powerful, almost hypnotic predictions. To any worker downsized out of a job, they must be persuasive. For American and Japanese workers and for most European workers, however, they have proved to be completely wrong in the 1990s. Employment in the service sector shows no signs of slowing down and, at least until the currency devaluations in Asia in 1997, exports have surged. Even manufacturing employment staged a mini-comeback in the United States. The new knowledge sector is hardly remaining elite. The computer and telecommunications sectors, including the host of software and other services booming around computers, is providing the same kind of new dynamic for the economies of developed countries as did the automobile industry in the first half of the century. Soon, the biotechnology and pharmaceuticals sectors, also knowledge based, will add to this high-skilled job creation machine. Are computers replacing the human mind itself? Again, the prediction seems totally off base as we begin a new millennium. University enrollment is expanding all over the world, and the number of graduate students in the developed countries is growing even faster. In fighting for a lessening of immigration controls, the computer industry argues that they face a shortage of almost four hundred thousand computer scientists. Even if overestimated, this figure suggests that, if anything, computers are increasing the demand for brainpower rather than reducing it.

The technophobe analysts misguide us because they observe changing patterns of employment and interpret these to be the end of employment. The two are simply not the same. One reason they fall into that trap is that they look only at male employment. In *The End of Work*, for example,

Rifkin spends pages and pages discussing automation of sector after sector, yet in only one chapter does he mention women. He predicts that jobs such as cashiers and secretaries are being "automated out." But what about the masses of women moving into the service professions? The growth of the female labor force is the most important labor market event of the past thirty years everywhere in the postindustrial world. It has only been accelerated by the new technology, a development Rifkin chooses to ignore.

Yet, Barnet's and Rifkin's arguments have had great impact because changing patterns of employment are disruptive and, combined with other changes in the workplace, promote insecurity. The fact that highly skilled professionals and managers are not immune to job loss, and that downsizing seems to have become a feature of economic expansions, not just contractions, has drawn a lot of attention. White-collar downsizing and computers seem connected in the public mind, and so the argument is persuasive. It is especially persuasive in European countries with high unemployment rates and slower job growth, and so it has to be taken seriously. Indeed, the end-of-jobs message is popular enough and seemingly populist enough that wings of political parties on both the left and the right have made it a central part of their economic message. However, the message is false.

What is worse, it diverts attention from the real changes taking place in labor markets—changes that call for a very different set of macroeconomic and social policies than those implied by the antitechnology analysis. Instead of blaming new technology for whatever labor market woes exist, we need to take a realistic look at how the labor market is shifting and how we can create more and better jobs in this new environment.

Information Technology, Jobs, and Skills

Contrary to dire predictions, the spread of computer technology is producing rapid job growth. These are new kinds of jobs, but as they generate income, traditional service jobs increase. The economic expansion generated by the new technology is also driving unemployment rates down in the United States and most other OECD countries. Although some groups, such as older male workers and, in some countries, youthful workers, have difficulties finding employment even as economies expand, there is little connection between these difficulties and the spread of computer technology.

Neither is the spread of technology associated with the de-skilling of work. The relationship between technology growth and skills demanded is complex, not unidirectional. Many of the new jobs require high skills, and managerial and professional jobs are the fastest growing occupations throughout the OECD countries. However, middle-level jobs seem to have declined, and economic growth has produced many new unskilled jobs, often filled by new immigrants.

Job growth and changing employment structures are typical of periods of technological change. The new computer technology may be very different in many ways from earlier machine technology, but it is having a similar impact on these broad dimensions of labor markets.

Employment Growth

The most obvious question is whether the widespread diffusion of information technologies in factories, offices, and services has reduced job growth or resulted in increased unemployment. In the past twenty-four years (from 1975 to 1999), the United States created about 48 million jobs and Japan about 10 million. The much smaller Australian and Canadian economies created more than 2.5 million and almost 5 million jobs respectively. In the seven years of recovery following the recession of 1990 to 1992, the U.S. economy created 16 million new jobs. Even in the problem economy in Japan from 1994 to 1997, 2 million jobs were created. Australia and Canada also recovered from their recessions of 1990 to 1993 with rapid employment growth in the next six years. By contrast, job creation in the countries of the European Union (EU) was about 11 million from 1975 to 1999, and, until the late 1990s, the overwhelming majority of these were in public sector employment. The absolute number of jobs in the EU declined between 1990 and 1996 but began to increase again from 1997 to 1999.[4] Yet Europe's slow employment growth is more the exception than the rule (figure 2.1).[5]

A subtheme of the "jobless future" argument is that technology is also to blame for a global decline in manufacturing jobs. Since 1970, about 11 million manufacturing jobs have been lost in the European Union, and another seven hundred thousand in the United States. The absolute number of manufacturing jobs in the world, however, is increasing, not declining. The number of manufacturing jobs in Japan increased during this same period, although they declined in the recession of the late 1990s. These,

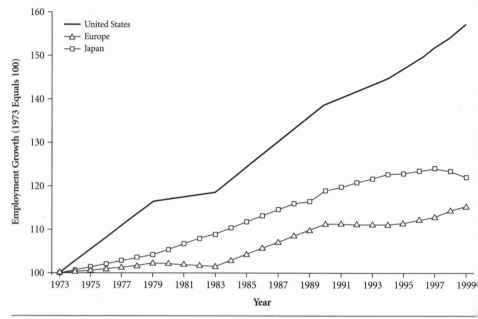

Figure 2.1 Index of Employment Growth by Region, 1973 to 1999 (Percentage).
Source: OECD 1998b; OECD 1999a.

added to the large gains in manufacturing jobs in the newly industrializing countries, more than offset the losses in Europe and the United States. New manufacturing jobs created just in the People's Republic of China, India, Brazil, Mexico, and South Korea since 1985 total more than 14 million, of which 12 million were in the People's Republic of China alone (see table 2.1).

Unemployment

If the developed countries are headed for a jobless future, we should be seeing broadly increasing unemployment rates in the United States, Japan, and throughout Europe, particularly since the early 1980s, when companies began to invest heavily in computer technology in the service industries. The data indicate that unemployment rates were much higher in the 1980s than in the 1960s but declined in a number of countries in the 1990s (table 2.2). In the United States, for example, the average unemployment rate (7.2 percent) from 1980 to 1989 (the expansion under Ronald Reagan

Table 2.1 Employment in Manufacturing in Major Countries and Regions, 1970 to 1997 (Thousands)

Year	United States	European Union	Japan	Brazil	Mexico	China	India[a]	Republic of Korea
1970	19,367	38,400	—	2,499	2,169	—	4,594	887
1975	18,323	36,600	13,400	3,953	—	42,840	5,087	2,678
1980	20,285	35,200	13,670	7,425	2,581	67,140	5,872	2,955
1985	19,245	30,700	14,530	7,907	—	83,490	6,183	3,504
1990	19,076	30,200	15,050	9,410	3,275	96,970	6,118	4,911
1993	18,075	30,344[b]	15,300	8,539	3,310	92,950	—	4,652
1995	18,468	28,000	14,560	8,548	3,067	98,000	6,767	4,773
1997	18,657	29,919	14,420	8,407[c]	3,290[c]	96,100	—	4,474

Source: ILO, *Statistical Yearbook,* 1986, 1988, 1994, 1995, 1996, 1997; OECD 1993b; OECD 1998b; INEG 1998, table 9.7. The European Union includes the Europe 15 (Sweden not included).

[a]Public and private employees in firms with ten or more employees.

[b]In 1991, the German series changed to include workers from the former Democratic Republic of Germany. This increased the number of manufacturing workers by 2.8 million in 1991. This implies a "real" number of manufacturing workers in the European Union (without the DRG) of about 28.8 million by 1993 and about 28 million by 1997.

[c]1996.

and George Bush) was higher than it was from 1960 to 1969 (4.6 percent) or in the 1970s (6.2 percent), which included the recession of 1974 and 1975. Unemployment from 1995 to 1999 (the expansion under Bill Clinton), however, was about the same (4.9 percent) as it was in the 1960s (4.6 percent), despite corporate downsizing and continued rapid diffusion of computer technology during the 1990s. The United Kingdom's unemployment rate also fell sharply in the 1990s, although it was much higher than in the 1960s. Japan's official unemployment rates rose in the 1990s during the long recession. Japanese unemployment rates were much higher in the late 1990s than in the 1960s (3.8 percent versus 1.3 percent), but unemployment was still low. Canadian and Australian rates were much higher in the 1980s than in the 1960s and reached 10 percent levels in the recession of the early 1990s, but rates declined in both countries as their economies began to recover after 1993.

Europe's core-country labor markets are the main exception to stable or falling unemployment rates in most industrialized economies. Unemployment crept up in France, Germany, and Italy despite growth in the gross

Table 2.2 Unemployment Rate, by Country, Various Years (Percentage)

Country	1960 to 1969 (average)	1970 to 1979 (average)	1980 to 1989 (average)	1990 to 1994 (average)	1995 to 1999[a] (average)	1990 to 1999[a] (average)
Australia	1.8	3.7	7.3	9.6	8.3	9.0
Austria	1.6	1.8	3.3	5.4	6.3	5.8
Belgium	2.2	4.3	11.1	10.6	12.2	11.4
Canada	4.6	6.7	9.3	10.3	8.9	9.6
Denmark	1.4	4.1	8.1	11.0	7.7	9.5
Finland	1.9	3.5	4.9	10.9	12.9	11.9
France	1.8	3.8	9.0	10.5	11.9	11.2
Germany[b]	0.7	2.4	6.8	7.8	10.6	9.2
Ireland	4.3	7.5	14.3	14.7	9.7	12.2
Italy	5.1	6.3	9.9	9.6	12.1	10.8
Japan	1.3	1.6	2.5	2.4	3.8	4.1
Netherlands	0.7	3.8	9.8	6.2	5.5	5.8
New Zealand	0.1	0.6	4.5	9.2	6.8	8.0
Norway	1.1	1.4	2.8	5.6	4.1	4.8
Spain	2.5	4.2	17.5	19.1	20.4	19.8
Sweden	1.7	2.1	2.5	5.2	7.2	6.2
Switzerland	—	0.3[c]	0.6	2.7	4.2	3.4
United Kingdom	1.4	3.8	9.5	8.8	7.3	8.0
United States	4.6	6.2	7.2	6.6	4.9	5.8

Sources: The years 1960 to 1969 and 1970 to 1979 are estimated from ILO 1981, table 10, and OECD 1997b, table 2.15. The years 1980 to 1989 and 1990 to 1999 are from OECD 1999b.

[a] Unemployment rate in 1999 based on projected rate.

[b] Unemployment rate from 1960 to 1993 is for West Germany, 1994 to 1999, for Germany including former German Democratic Republic.

domestic product (GDP) per capita from 1993 to 1997. Although unemployment in France began to come down in 1998 and 1999, the rates in those three countries have hovered around historic levels, near 12 percent, with even higher rates for youths in France and Italy. In 1994, 25 percent of males age twenty to twenty-four and more than 30 percent of females of the same age were unemployed in France and Italy, compared with 17 percent for both groups in the OECD as a whole (OECD 1996a, chapter 4). Youth unemployment rates continued to rise from 1994 to 1997 (OECD 1998a, appendix table C). Other countries such as Spain and, until recently, Ireland also have high youth unemployment rates. What is more telling, less than 60 percent of males and less than 50 percent of females age twenty to twenty-four in France and Italy participated in the labor force compared with 74 percent and 64 percent in the entire OECD (OECD 1996a, chapter 4). Even so, unemployment rates in much of northern Italy are low. If anything, there is a shortage of labor in the North and young people have little trouble getting jobs. On average, firms are small, but technological innovation is much more advanced than in the South.

Neither does every country in Europe have rising or even high unemployment rates. In addition to northern Italy, the United Kingdom, the Netherlands, Norway, Denmark, and Sweden are the most significant exceptions to the European "exception." The Netherlands, Germany, Norway, Sweden, and Denmark also have relatively low youth unemployment rates. Since 1983, the Dutch have managed to increase employment at the rate of 1.7 percent a year, roughly equivalent to the 1.8 percent yearly increase in the United States. Although many more of the new jobs in Holland are part time than is the case in the United States, the Dutch ability to create new jobs stands out as a bright spot in the European landscape—all the more so because, unlike the United States, Holland has been able simultaneously to increase both jobs and real wages (OECD 1998c).[6] Thus, based on unemployment numbers, it is fair to say that joblessness was much more of a problem in Europe in the 1990s than in the 1970s, but not all European countries are failing to employ their workers. Certain regions, in fact, have been successful inside national economies with high overall employment rates. Like the Netherlands, these regions are technologically advanced, are especially entrepreneurial, and have been able to find niche markets in the world economy, sometimes without flexible conditions in labor markets (Stella 1996).

Discouraged Workers

Official unemployment rates may not tell the whole story. When unemployment rates rise, workers lose their jobs and, if they fail to get another job quickly, they can get discouraged and stop looking. If not actively looking for work, these unemployed do not get counted in the official unemployment statistics. They are known as discouraged workers. In those countries with high unemployment rates, the number of discouraged workers should also be large, because high official unemployment rates indicate that jobs are hard to find. If official unemployment rates greatly underestimate the number of workers who would work if only they could find jobs, that would give greater credence to the idea that changes in the world economy (increased use of new technology, for example) are creating a job crisis.

The OECD did a detailed study of discouraged workers in 1993, covering the years 1983 to 1991, a period during which firms throughout the developed countries were investing in computer and telecommunications technology (OECD 1993a). It was also a period of economic recovery from the worldwide recession of the early 1980s and, for some countries, the beginning of another recession in 1990 and 1991. The study found that discouraged workers in most OECD countries represented about 1 percent of the labor force in 1991 (table 2.3). Counterintuitively, in many countries with relatively low unemployment rates, such as Japan, Norway, and Sweden, the number of discouraged workers is a high percentage of the number of unemployed workers. When the economy hits a downturn in Japan, women tend to leave the labor force rather than remain unemployed. This dampens the rise in the unemployment rate but increases the number of discouraged workers relative to the unemployed. Yet this negative relation between discouraged workers and unemployed workers does not hold for Belgium and Italy, where unemployment is high and so also is the proportion of discouraged workers.

The majority of discouraged workers are women, ranging from 77 percent or more in Australia, France, Italy, the Netherlands, Portugal, and Spain to just more than 50 percent in Canada, Sweden, the United Kingdom, and the United States. Moreover, in most countries the proportion of discouraged workers rises in economic downturns, as the unemployment rate rises (OECD 1993a, chart 1.1).

Table 2.3 Discouraged Workers as Proportion of Labor Force and of the Unemployed, by Country, 1991 (Percentage)

Country	As Percentage of Labor Force	As Percentage of Unemployed	Unemployment Rate Including Discouraged Workers	Percentage Females Among Discouraged Workers
Australia	1.5	15.5	10.9	79
Belgium	1.7	18.2	10.8	56
Canada	0.7	6.5	10.9	52
Denmark	0.2	2.4	10.6	71
France	0.1	1.5	9.5	82
Ireland	0.5	3.3	16.2	71
Italy	2.6	23.7	13.3	79
Japan	1.9	90.8	3.9	78
Netherlands	0.8	12.8	6.7	83
New Zealand	0.9	8.6	11.1	—
Norway	1.4	24.8	6.8	58
Portugal	0.4	9.6	4.5	85
Spain	0.1	0.6	16.4	77
Sweden	1.5	54.1	4.1	52
United Kingdom	0.4	4.8	8.7	57
United States	0.8	12.1	7.5	54

Source: OECD 1993a, table 1.5, chart 1.1.

When discouraged workers are added to the unemployed, the adjusted unemployment rate in most OECD countries in 1991 was high, above 8 percent. In many countries, such as the United States, the United Kingdom, the Netherlands, Australia, Canada, and Japan, the adjusted rate fell by 1997, but in others, such as France, Germany, and Italy, it rose.

The most important conclusion drawn from an analysis of changes in the circumstances of discouraged workers over time is that what happens to these adjusted unemployment rates (which include discouraged workers) is almost entirely a function of changes in official unemployment, not changes in worker discouragement. Discouragement appears to be much more related to business cycles than to secular trends. In terms of its absolute level, the proportion of discouraged workers is apparently caused not only by high rates of overall unemployment but by other factors as well—

for example, the ability of the economy to absorb women into the labor market.

Older Workers

A general feature of highly developed economies in the past three decades is the steady decline in the labor force participation of male workers older than fifty-five years of age. Studies by French sociologist Anne Marie Guillemard show that in most advanced societies, labor force participation for fifty-five- to sixty-four-year-old men fell rapidly in the past twenty-five years. By the early 1990s, the typical proportion of older men working or seeking work in developed countries was 45 to 65 percent, down from 75 to 90 percent levels in 1970 (see figure 2.2) (Guillemard 1993). Almost 40 percent of the male workforce in most of these economies now leaves the labor market by the age of fifty-five, because of early retirement, disability, or permanent unemployment.

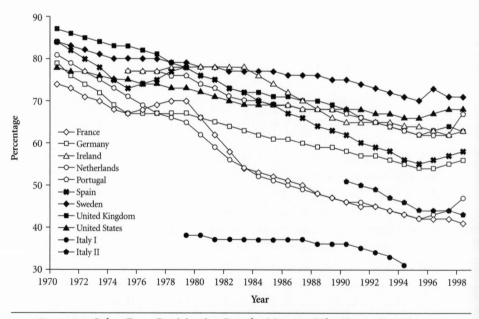

Figure 2.2 Labor Force Participation Rate for Men Age Fifty-Five to Sixty-Four, by Country, 1970 to 1998 (Percentage) *Sources:* Guillemard 1993; OECD 1996a; OECD 1999b. *Note:* Italy I, earlier OECD series; Italy II, later series.

Have older male workers been pushed out of active participation because jobs are getting scarcer? Yes and no. Yes, because in many European countries, rising unemployment rates have hit older male workers as hard as other workers, and older workers are much more likely to retire when they encounter longer-term unemployment (OECD 1992, 1998a, chapter 4); and yes, because some European governments have lowered the official retirement age (the age at which a person can begin receiving a pension) specifically to open up jobs to younger people facing high unemployment rates.

There is evidence, however, that many workers want to stop working and start collecting pensions earlier rather than later. The retirement age was lowered in Europe and the United States in the 1960s because it was politically popular to do so, not because unemployment rates were high. Even when the job market was expanding, older workers wanted to retire earlier.

Any analysis of this problem also needs to differentiate between an overall scarcity of jobs as a reason to move older workers out of the labor force and shifts in demand for education and skills, which would tend to affect older (male) workers more because of the sectors they work in, their level of education, and their relatively high salaries. Older (male) workers may lose jobs and be driven into retiring earlier because their jobs become obsolete even as the total number of jobs increases or because they become relatively expensive compared with younger, better-educated workers or female workers. Data show that with the decline in manufacturing, older, less-educated male workers in manufacturing production jobs were replaced in the labor force by younger, better-educated male workers in rapidly expanding high-end service sector jobs and in the marketing, finance, and sales side of manufacturing. The increased availability of female workers in the OECD countries beginning in the late 1960s also encouraged employers to replace older male workers with younger women, who generally work for lower wages. Neither of these cases illustrate an "end" to jobs that pushed out older male workers from the labor market. Another piece of evidence that supports the gender-substitution thesis is the much smaller drop (and, in most countries, even a rise) in labor force participation rates of older women workers (age fifty-five to sixty-four) during this same period (OECD 1998a, appendix table C).

Was it the new information technology that made older workers obsolete? Figure 2.2 suggests that new technology probably had little to do with the decline in the labor force participation of older workers. Most of the drop in the participation rates of older male workers in the United States, the United Kingdom, Sweden, Germany, and Japan took place in the early 1970s, before firms began using computers. In the 1980s, participation rates generally leveled off, with certain exceptions, such as France, the Netherlands, and Spain. In Italy, the participation rates for older male workers have been relatively low (about 50 percent or less) since at least the mid-1970s.

Women's Labor Force Participation

Huge numbers of married women entered the world's labor markets in the 1970s and 1980s. The increase in women's labor force participation in the past generation was one of the most important changes in labor markets worldwide and was a main feature of labor markets in the highly developed countries. From 1973 to 1997, for example, the participation rates of women age fifteen to sixty-four rose about 10 percentage points in France, Germany, and Italy, even though the three countries had only small increases in overall employment (see table 2.4). The ratios of employment to population for women rose less rapidly than participation rates because of increased unemployment rates overall, yet they rose nevertheless (table 2.5). In those three countries, the rise in women's participation and employment-to-population ratios was matched by large declines in men's labor force participation and employment-to-population ratios. In France and Germany, these declines were mainly owing to the earlier retirement of older male workers. Thus, even though no net new job growth occurred in the core of the European Union, jobs shifted. Older male workers were retired earlier from the labor market, and younger women workers were brought in.

In OECD countries that have created a significant number of jobs, such as Australia, Canada, Japan, the Netherlands, Norway, Switzerland, and the United States, the participation of women in the labor force increased much more, 16 percentage points in Australia, more than 20 percentage points in Canada and the United States, 25 percentage points in Norway, and more than 30 percentage points in the Netherlands. The ratio of employment to population—that is, the percentage of the population that have jobs—rose somewhat less. At the same time, the participation of men in the labor force fell much less in these countries, and in some, such

Table 2.4 Labor Force Participation Rate, by Gender, Various Years (Percentage)

Country	Men			Women		
	1973	1983	1998	1973	1983	1998
Australia	91.1	85.9	82.1	47.7	52.1	63.9
Austria	83.0	82.2	80.2	48.5	49.7	62.5
Belgium	83.2	76.8	72.5	41.3	46.3	53.8
Canada	86.1	88.5	81.8	47.2	62.2	69.0
Denmark	89.6	87.6	83.5	61.9	74.2	75.0
Finland	80.0	82.0	76.6	63.6	72.7	69.7
France	85.2	78.4	74.1	50.1	54.3	60.8
Germany	89.6	82.6	79.2	50.3	52.5	60.9
Greece	83.2	80.0	77.2	32.1	40.4	48.2
Ireland	92.3	87.1	77.8	34.1	37.8	52.1
Italy	85.1	80.7	72.0	33.7	40.3	43.9
Japan	90.1	89.1	85.3	54.0	57.2	59.8
Luxembourg	93.1	85.1	76.0	35.9	41.7	47.6
Netherlands	85.6	77.3	82.8	29.2	40.3	62.9
New Zealand	89.2	84.7	83.5	39.2	45.7	67.1
Norway	86.5	87.2	85.5	50.6	65.5	75.9
Portugal	—	86.9	79.0	—	56.7	61.9
Spain	92.9	80.5	77.7	33.4	33.3	48.7
Sweden	88.1	85.9	80.7	62.6	76.6	75.5
Switzerland	100.0	93.5	90.1	54.1	55.2	74.2
United Kingdom	93.0	87.5	83.9	53.2	57.2	67.8
United States	86.2	84.7	84.2	51.1	61.9	70.7

Source: OECD 1996a, table K; OECD 1999b, table B; Japanese series changes for 1998 from OECD 1996a, 1997a, 1998a.

Note: Data are for men and women age fifteen to sixty-four.

as the United States and Norway, hardly at all. Although Japanese women's participation rose only 5.8 percentage points, less even than in the low-employment growth countries of Europe, the labor force participation rates for Japanese men also declined less between 1973 and 1998, from 90.1 percent (in the old series) to 85.3 percent (in the new series) among males age fifteen to sixty-four (see table 2.4). Thus, many of the new jobs in the highly developed countries in the 1970s, 1980s, and 1990s have gone to women. Even in economies with little job growth, such as those of France or Germany, the number of jobs held by women increased steadily. Part of the explanation for the shift to hiring women is that the kind of job avail-

Table 2.5 Ratio of Employment to Population, by Gender, Various Years (Percentage)

Country	Men			Women		
	1973	1983	1998	1973	1983	1998
Australia	89.9	77.5	75.2	46.4	47.0	59.2
Austria	82.4	79.4	75.9	47.7	47.1	59.0
Belgium	81.6	69.2	67.0	39.9	39.8	47.5
Canada	81.9	77.8	74.7	44.1	55.0	63.3
Denmark	89.0	78.3	80.2	61.2	65.0	70.2
Finland	78.1	77.4	68.2	62.3	69.0	61.2
France	83.8	73.4	66.5	47.9	48.3	52.3
Germany	88.8	76.6	72.5	49.7	47.8	55.6
Greece	81.8	75.3	71.0	31.2	35.6	39.6
Ireland	86.5	73.8	71.4	32.8	33.6	48.2
Italy	81.6	75.7	65.1	29.9	34.2	36.7
Japan	88.8	86.7	81.7	53.4	55.7	57.2
Luxembourg	93.1	84.0	74.6	35.9	40.9	45.6
Netherlands	83.5	69.1	79.9	28.6	34.7	59.4
New Zealand	89.1	80.3	77.1	39.1	42.8	62.1
Norway	85.6	84.4	82.7	49.3	63.0	73.5
Portugal	99.2	82.8	75.8	30.5	49.8	58.1
Spain	90.5	67.9	67.0	32.5	26.5	35.7
Sweden	86.2	83.0	73.5	60.8	73.9	69.4
Switzerland	100.0	92.7	87.2	54.1	54.7	71.0
United Kingdom	90.3	75.9	78.1	52.7	52.6	64.2
United States	82.8	76.5	80.5	48.0	56.2	67.4

Source: OECD 1996a, table A; OECD 1999b, table B. Japanese series changes for women in 1998 from OECD 1996a, 1997a, 1998a.

Note: Data are for men and women age fifteen to sixty-four.

able in the economy changed. The absolute number of manufacturing production jobs declined significantly in Europe (but not in the United States or Japan), whereas the number of service jobs during the same period increased. The other part of the explanation is that many more women, especially married women, became available to work both part time and full time. Women's view of the marriage contract went through a sea change in most developed countries, beginning with the United States and Scandinavia in the 1960s. As that change occurred, many married women began to work in paying jobs. Employers took time to adjust to this change, but adjust they did, even in male strongholds such as the professional and managerial side of the electronics industry (Carnoy and Gong 1996).

Those who argue that the new technology leads to the end of jobs totally ignore the massive job growth for women: problematic as the decline of jobs for men may be, especially for older men, and the failure of job growth in the private sector to absorb youthful workers in the major continental European economies, it is also true that even there large numbers of "new" women workers have entered the labor market. When the end-of-jobbers do deal with the issue of women's work, they tend to regard it as low-end work and as less meaningful than the traditional jobs held by men in the past. There is no doubt that women get many of the least desirable jobs in most economies, but they are increasingly getting many of the better jobs as well. Arguing that low-end jobs have little meaning for women also misses the point. Women work for lower wages than men; they are more likely to work in part-time jobs than men, and they tend to move in and out of the labor market more often than men. That does not make them less valuable as workers or their jobs less meaningful. Indeed, the increasing advantage that women seem to be gaining in the labor market may tell us more about the future than the declining participation of older men.

Is New Technology to Blame for Differences in Net Job Growth?

The major countries in Europe have had low job growth since the 1970s, but most developed countries have experienced the creation of a considerable number of new jobs in the past two decades. Are these differences a result of investment in new information technology? Do economies that use more information technology per worker have higher unemployment?

The best indicators for the diffusion of information technology (IT) would be the stock of computer hardware and software per worker. Such data are not widely available.[7] We can, however, get information for most OECD countries on annual spending for IT hardware, software, and computer business services. Because computer hardware and software have rapid depreciation rates, such annual spending data over a period of several years can approximate the stock of IT in an economy. Prices of these products also vary from country to country, and this may bias estimates. Nevertheless, comparative spending data give a fairly good picture of how much IT countries are using and how much they increased IT use in the late 1980s and early 1990s.

The OECD regularly estimates IT spending in member and nonmember countries. Using purchasing-power parities (PPP), the data show that twenty-one OECD member countries spent $358 billion in 1994, 81 percent of which was spent by only five countries: the United States, Japan, Germany, the United Kingdom, and France. On a per worker basis, the United States spends more than any other country, about $1,500 per worker in 1994. France, Belgium, Switzerland, the Netherlands, and Australia spend less, but still a high $800 to $1,000 per worker. In the same year, Germany spent about $700 per worker if the total labor force is included but $900 per worker if the labor force in the former East Germany is excluded; Japan and Italy spent about $600 per worker. At the lower end of the spectrum, Spain's IT spending in 1994 was only $440, Portugal's about $200, and Greece's only $80 per worker (table 2.6).

Table 2.6 Spending on Information Technology per Worker, Employment Growth, and Unemployment Rate, by Country, Various Years

Country	Spending per Worker (U.S.$ PPP)[a]		Employment Growth 1987 to 1994 (% per year)	Unemployment Rate 1995 (% per year)
	1987	1994		
Australia	647.9	949.4	1.9	8.5
Austria	303.0	540.5	0.8	5.9
Belgium	469.6	945.9	0.5	13.0
Canada	525.0	772.7	1.6	9.5
Denmark	395.2	717.1	0.2	10.0
Finland	414.9	650.0	−1.6	17.2
France	540.5	871.6	0.1	11.6
Germany	519.2	722.2	0.7	9.4
Greece	54.9	79.2	0.5	10.0
Ireland	272.7	341.9	0.4	12.9
Italy	428.6	606.1	0.0	12.0
Japan	350.0	604.6	1.2	3.1
Netherlands	578.9	873.0	1.8	7.1
New Zealand	431.6	833.3	0.3	6.3
Norway	410.2	750.0	0.3	4.9
Portugal	186.0	204.5	0.3	7.2
Spain	294.1	440.7	0.6	22.9
Sweden	559.4	891.3	−0.6	7.7
Switzerland	497.1	981.4	1.5	4.2
United Kingdom	595.2	873.0	0.6	8.2
United States	973.0	1487.8	1.8	5.6

Source: OECD 1996a; OECD 1996b, figure 2.1; OECD 1995.

[a]PPP = purchasing power parity.

Growth rates of IT spending per worker from 1987 to 1994 also varied greatly among OECD countries, from a high of more than 10 percent annual growth in small countries such as Switzerland and Belgium, to 7 or 8 percent in Japan, France, and Germany (if only workers in the former West Germany are included) to 6 percent in the United States, the United Kingdom, and Spain, and to very low rates in Ireland and Portugal.

Another measure of IT diffusion is the percentage of total households with personal computers (PCs). Again, the United States is far ahead of the pack. In 1994, 37 percent of U.S. households had PCs. In Denmark, 30 percent of households had PCs, in Germany 24 percent, in the United Kingdom 24 percent, in France 15 percent, and in Japan only 12 percent (OECD 1996b, table 2.2).

A third measure of technological diffusion—more a measure of the capacity for using IT through telecommunications—is the number of main telephone lines per capita; and a fourth measure, related mainly to the number of households with PCs but also related to the availability of telephone lines, is the number of internet hosts per capita (see table 2.7). In terms of both measures, the United States is near the top of the list. Japan has many telephone lines per capita but hardly any internet hosts, reflecting the relatively low number of households with computers but also the apparent de-emphasis on individual computing in Japanese schools and even in the Japanese workplace. The Scandinavian countries are relatively high in the number of telephone lines and internet hosts, but Germany is low on both. France has many telephone lines but has almost as few internet hosts as Japan.

Taking any one of these measures or all of them together, there appears to be little, if any, relation between technological diffusion and employment growth or the unemployment rate. For example, the growth of IT spending per worker in OECD countries from 1987 to 1994 is completely unrelated statistically to the growth of employment in that same period. Neither is growth of IT spending related to the unemployment rate. The unemployment rate in 1995 appears to be related, but not to the point of statistical significance, to the level of IT spending per worker in 1994; yet the single best statistical estimate of the relation is negative. This means that the higher the level of IT spending per worker in 1994, the lower the unemployment rate in 1995.[8]

Failure to find any statistical relation between the diffusion of information technology and employment is consistent with almost all studies done on this subject in the past decade. In Germany, the so-called Meta-Study,

Table 2.7 Use of Communications Technology, by Country, Various Years

Country	Telephone Lines[a] 1987	Telephone Lines[a] 1996	Cellular Phone Subscribers[b]	Internet Hosts[c]
Australia	42.8	51.9	20.8	28.1
Austria	38.4	46.9	7.4	11.0
Belgium	34.5	46.2	4.7	6.4
Canada	51.2	60.2	11.4	20.1
Denmark	52.9	61.8	25.0	20.3
Finland	48.0	54.9	37.0	61.3
France	44.6	56.4	4.2	4.0
Germany	44.1	53.8	7.1	8.9
Greece	34.7	47.7[d]	—	2.0
Ireland	22.5	39.5	8.2	7.6
Italy	33.3	44.0	11.2	2.6
Japan	39.3	48.9	21.4	5.8
Netherlands	42.4	54.3	5.2	17.4
New Zealand	41.1	49.9	13.8	23.7
Norway	46.4	55.6	28.7	34.2
Portugal	16.1	37.5	6.7	2.4
Spain	26.2	39.2	3.3	2.9
Sweden	65.1	68.2	28.2	26.9
Switzerland	52.9	64.4	9.3	18.7
United Kingdom	45.5	52.8	12.2	12.4
United States	48.8	64.0	16.3	37.9

Sources: International Telecommunications Union (ITU) 1995, 270–75; ITU 1998, tables 2, 10, and 19; Paltridge 1996, 201.

[a]Number of main telephone lines per 100 population.
[b]Number of cellular phone subscribers per 100 population, 1996.
[c]Number of internet hosts per 1000 population, 1996.
[d]1994.

commissioned by the minister of research and technology, concludes that it is "the context" that counts for variation in observed effects of IT. The study forecasts that in the short term unskilled jobs will be displaced, although enhanced productivity will probably result in more jobs created in the long term (Schettkat and Wagner 1990). In the United Kingdom, a study by William Daniel (1990) on the impacts of technology on employment in factories and offices concludes that it has had a negligible effect. Research on Spain conducted by Cecilia Castaño (1994) and by Felipe Saez

(Saez et al. 1991) has found that, if anything, higher technological levels in sectors and firms have helped preserve employment against downsizing tendencies. In the United States, an analysis by Steven Miller (1989) on the impact of industrial robotics concludes that most displaced workers will be reabsorbed in the labor force. Similar conclusions showing modest effects of technology on employment levels in the United States are found in studies on factories and offices commissioned by the U.S. Congress's Office of Technology Assessment (U.S. Congress 1984, 1986). In an international comparison, Japanese economist Susumu Watanabe (1986) provides an interpretation for the wide variation of effects of information technology on employment in the automobile industry, examining the impact of the introduction of similar microelectronic machines in the United States, Japan, France, and Italy. Whereas U.S. and Italian firms reduced their labor force, in France, as a result of union bargaining, it remained stable; and in Japan, employment actually increased because new technologies were used to retrain workers and increase productivity and competitiveness, thus enlarging market shares and expanding demand and employment (Watanabe 1986).[9]

According to the OECD's 1994 *Jobs Study,*

> empirical evidence available suggests that, overall, the current wave of technical change has had a positive—albeit limited—impact on employment. But this evidence is not sufficient in itself to allow unqualified generalizations. This is so because positive and negative effects do not coincide either in time or in space; adjustment takes time, and the industries and types of workers that will benefit from technological change are different from the ones that lose from it. Also, institutional and systemic factors affect the capacities of countries to efficiently generate employment through development, acquisition, and diffusion of technologies. (OECD 1994b, 164)[10]

What about the future of employment? Critics can always argue that the effects of information technology on employment have not yet had time to make themselves felt. That argument, however, is not very convincing. Large changes have already taken place in OECD workplaces, and employment projections for these countries are not particularly pessimistic. Although projections should always be taken with a grain of salt, simulation models projecting future employment lend no support to the "end-of-jobs" idea. In the United States, the most widely cited simulation study is the model elaborated by Wassily Leontief and Faye Duchin in 1984 for the period from 1963 to 2000 (Leontief and Duchin 1985). According to their results for the year 2000, diffusion of computers will result in an 11.7 percent reduction in required labor for a given output. However, this projection is based on the unlikely case of fixed aggregate demand. They argue that if productivity increases as expected, demand will also increase, resulting in new job creation sufficient to absorb displaced labor. This is precisely what has occurred since the Leontief and Duchin study was published. The simulation model developed by Jurgen Blazejczak, George Erber, and Gustav Horn for the German economy to project employment growth between 1987 and 2000 concluded that "at the aggregate level demand effects do in fact compensate a relevant part of the predicted employment decrease" (Blazejczak, Erber, and Horn 1990). Finally, employment projections for OECD countries made by the OECD Secretariat in 1994 predicted a significant increase in jobs for the United States and moderate employment growth for Japan and the twelve countries (at the time) of the European Union (Stevens and Michalski 1994). For the period from 1992 to 2005, the net projected increase of jobs totals 24 million in the United States (an increase of 19 percent), 4 million in Japan (an increase of 6 percent), and about 10 million for the European Union (an increase of about 7 percent). However, these projections are highly sensitive to variations of the assumptions on which they are based (for example, migration and labor participation rates).

This is exactly my argument. The absence of a relation between IT intensity and employment growth or unemployment suggests that the evolution of the level of employment is a result of factors other than the rate of IT diffusion. Technology does not destroy overall employment. Employment growth depends mainly on socially determined decisions regarding the uses of technology, immigration policy, the evolution of the family, the institutional distribution of working time in the life cycle, the new system of industrial relations, and economic policies.

What Kind of Jobs Are Being Changed?

According to the end-of-jobs argument, new information technology not only reduces job growth but also de-skills most of the jobs that are left. The new job market is one in which a few good "boutique" jobs are created developing computer software and other information and communications technology, but most jobs are de-skilled and increasingly eliminated. In

Rifkin's words, "While some new jobs are being created in the U.S. economy, they are in the low-paying sectors and generally temporary employment. In April of 1994, two thirds of the new jobs created in the country were at the bottom of the wage pyramid" (Rifkin 1995, 4).

The data do not support this argument either. As manufacturing production jobs decline in the highly industrialized countries, it is a fact that many "middle-paying" jobs are eliminated. Bennett Harrison and Barry Bluestone have called this the "disappearing middle" (Harrison and Bluestone 1988). Workers who lose those jobs, especially older workers, are likely to fall into lower-paying jobs or, facing long-term unemployment, retire from the labor force (OECD 1992, chapter 5). If we look only at what happens to those workers, we would conclude that jobs are being deskilled and eliminated. However, in the economy as a whole, a lot more is happening. All kinds of new jobs are being created as the old ones disappear. Younger workers have much higher average levels of education than older workers. The "disappearing middle" jobs are "replaced" mainly by higher-paying jobs, not by low-end jobs—although few workers who lose the middle-level production jobs get these higher-paying jobs. Rather, the new jobs go to new entrants or younger workers moving up the job ladder.

The United States labor market is a good example of the way this happens. Most of the massive number of new jobs created in the United States over the past twenty years have gone to women, who first flooded the labor market in the 1970s, largely in part-time work, and then increasingly shifted in the 1980s to full-time work. However, the number of jobs for men has also increased substantially. The increase of middle-level jobs declined rapidly after 1970, mainly because of the slowdown in growth in manufacturing production jobs. Especially after the recession from 1980 to 1982, the new jobs becoming available in the economy as a whole were largely higher-paying jobs (mainly professional and managerial jobs but also sales and technical jobs in higher-paying industries, such as manufacturing and utilities) for higher-educated workers.[11] That does not mean that average real wages in higher-paying jobs were rising. Indeed, for much of the period from 1970 to 1998, real wages declined for men in all levels of jobs, with a sharper decline for those in lower-paying jobs than in higher-paying jobs. For women, real wages rose in higher-paying jobs and fell in lower-paying jobs. The movement "up" for white males, however, resulted in an overall small rise in average earnings in the 1980s (*Economic Report of the President* 1999, table B33).

Tables 2.8 and 2.9 illustrate another aspect of the dichotomous growth

Table 2.8 Employment Shares by Pay Scale, Gender, and Ethnicity, United States, Various Years (Percentage)

Ethnicity/Gender/Pay	1960	1970	1980	1988	1990	1998
Total employed						
High wage	24.6	25.5	28.2	32.4	32.9	33.0
Middle wage	44.7	43.8	34.4	38.1	38.2	34.6
Low wage	31.6	30.8	37.4	29.5	28.8	32.4
White males						
High wage	28.4	29.4	32.3	37.2	39.5	37.7
Middle wage	48.0	45.8	43.6	39.7	37.2	36.2
Low wage	23.6	24.9	24.2	23.1	23.2	26.0
Black males						
High wage	7.9	9.1	13.8	16.3	18.0	20.6
Middle wage	36.2	45.2	47.9	42.8	40.9	40.5
Low wage	56.0	45.8	38.2	40.9	41.0	38.5
Latino males						
High wage	10.5	13.9	16.2	16.9	15.6	16.7
Middle wage	42.2	45.8	44.2	43.1	38.2	37.9
Low wage	47.2	40.2	39.6	42.0	46.2	45.0
White females						
High wage	19.2	20.2	24.6	30.5	32.1	35.5
Middle wage	47.5	46.0	43.7	39.4	38.8	31.9
Low wage	33.2	33.8	31.7	30.4	29.1	32.3
Black females						
High wage	9.1	13.5	17.8	18.8	20.4	24.0
Middle wage	19.0	33.3	42.2	41.1	40.7	33.9
Low wage	71.8	53.1	40.0	40.2	38.9	40.5
Latina females						
High wage	5.2	11.5	13.6	17.3	18.2	19.8
Middle wage	50.0	52.3	46.1	42.5	43.0	34.1
Low wage	44.9	36.2	40.3	40.3	38.9	45.6

Source: U.S. Department of Commerce, Bureau of the Census 1981a, 1981b, 1984, 1988, 1990, 1995.

Notes: In this formulation, Construction Industry sales, clerical, craft, and operatives defined as middle wage. The total percentage figures for 1998 include the percentage distribution for Asian-origin males and females. Since that distribution is very similar to that of white males and females, including Asian-origin Americans changes the overall distribution by less than 0.2 percentage points in each category. But because, by 1998, Asian-origin workers represented about 2.8 percent of the labor force, we included them. Their impact on the percentages in early years was much smaller. Percentages of jobs by category were estimated separately by year for each gender-ethnic group. Thus, percentages for each year for a gender-ethnic group add to 100 percent.

Table 2.9 Employment Gains by Pay Scale and Ethnic-Gender Group, All Workers, by Decade, 1960 to 1998 (Thousands of Additional Jobs)

Pay Scale/Gender/Ethnicity	1970 to 1960	1980 to 1970	1990 to 1980	1998 to 1988
High wage				
Total employment gains	3,500	7,600	10,450	7,700
Males	11,850	3,650	4,700	2,350
White	1,600	3,100	4,000	1,000
Black	100	300	400	450
Latino	150	250	300	900
Females	1,650	3,950	5,750	5,350
White	1,400	3,400	5,000	3,600
Black	200	350	400	750
Latina	50	200	350	1,000
Middle wage				
Total employment gains	5,500	7,450	1,600	600
Males	2,000	2,650	−750	900
White	1,000	1,600	−1,600	−1,100
Black	600	500	150	300
Latino	400	550	700	1,700
Females	3,500	4,800	2,350	−300
White	2,700	3,500	1,300	−1,800
Black	600	800	550	200
Latina	250	500	500	1,300
Low wage				
Total employment gains	4,000	5,300	4,650	10,000
Males	1,600	2,300	2,300	4,750
White	1,500	1,800	500	2,000
Black	−100	—	600	250
Latino	200	500	1,200	2,500
Females	2,400	3,000	2,350	5,250
White	2,300	2,400	1,300	2,200
Black	−50	50	550	750
Latina	150	550	500	2,300

Source: U.S. Department of Commerce, Bureau of the Census 1981a, 1981b, 1984, 1988, 1998.

of jobs in the 1980s: the better new jobs went disproportionately to non-Latino white males and females, and low-paying jobs went disproportionately to less-educated African Americans and Latinos. The 1990s economic boom saw continued and somewhat slower growth in the number of high-paying jobs, a resurrection of upward mobility for African Americans, and huge growth in employment for Latinos in both lower- and middle-paying jobs, but the decline of the middle overall.[12]

Changes are also occurring in job growth in other developed countries. Professional and managerial jobs as a share of total employment have increased rapidly in the past fifteen years as the share of production jobs has declined (see table 2.10). Clerical jobs in Europe and Japan continued to increase in the 1980s (although not in the United States or Canada), but this growth slowed in the late 1980s and 1990s (ILO 1996, 27, table 2.7).

If investment in new technology had any effect in this period, it was to reduce the number of middle-level production jobs and to expand the number of higher-paying jobs and, to a lesser extent, lower-paying jobs. In the majority of countries, there were also many more higher-paying jobs created than middle-paying jobs destroyed. Changes in the labor markets

Table 2.10 Managers and Professionals in the Total Labor Force, by Country, Various Years (Percentage)

Country	1980	1987	1996
Australia	20.88	23.18	24.92[a]
Canada	22.95	28.94	32.78
Denmark	25.03[b]	26.92	19.56
Germany	16.76[c]	18.55[c,d]	17.67
Italy	—	—	10.60
Japan	11.89	14.06	16.10
Netherlands	22.20	26.60	27.49[e]
Spain	8.29	11.29	19.41
United Kingdom	—	—	26.32
United States	27.30	27.65	31.90

Source: ILO 1990; ILO 1997, table 2C.
[a]1993.
[b]1981.
[c]Data refer to Federal Republic of Germany.
[d]1986.
[e]1995.

of developed countries, then, do not conform either to the traditional conceptions of limited job opportunities and wholesale de-skilling (Braverman 1974) or to the reskilled labor, high-consumption future predicted by
Daniel Bell (1973).

Even if more jobs are being created at the high end than at the low end,
de-skilling or reskilling could be taking place within levels of jobs. The
promoters of the end-of-jobs argument are convinced that technology is
reducing the skills of most workers. The more prevalent view is that jobs
are requiring more skills, not less, that higher levels of technology are associated with increased demand for higher-skilled labor.[13]

Most of the research analyzing the effects of information technology on
work in a variety of countries comes to a similar conclusion: new technologies increase the importance of the human mind in the work process. For
example, Harley Shaiken (1985, 1994), Marc Guillaume (1983), Maryellen
Kelley (1990), Cecilia Castaño (1994), Guido Martinotti (1984), Shoshana
Zuboff (1988), Larry Hirschhorn (1984), and Paul Adler (1992) have argued that the broader and deeper the diffusion of advanced information
technology in factories and offices, the greater the need for increasingly
autonomous and educated workers who are able, willing, and motivated
to program and decide entire sequences of their work. This research suggests that information technology has not induced a shift toward indirect
work at the expense of direct work that has become automated. To the
contrary, the role of direct work has increased because information technology can empower direct workers at the level of the shop floor in factories and offices, be it in the process of testing chips or underwriting insurance policies. What tends to be displaced through integral automation are
routine, repetitive tasks that can be precoded and programmed by machines. Although low-skill routine tasks are still the daily experience of
millions of workers, these researchers suggest that the work in advanced
societies is headed toward jobs dominated by the performance of intelli-
gence-intensive tasks. This does not mean that everybody will be a software writer or a financial analyst. At the same time, however, nursing, security, and cooking might well become highly trained, information-rich
activities.

That said, the debate on de-skilling in the United States—where the dis-
cussion has been documented most with actual data—has stalemated.
Technology seems simultaneously to de-skill and reskill the labor force.
The actual impact of technology on skills depends on the characteristics of

the labor force and on the relation between the economy and the educational system (Spenner 1985; see also Freeman and Soete 1994).

A number of studies before and during the 1980s questioned whether improved technology—even computer technology—upgraded the average level of skills required in jobs. A comparison of skill requirements of jobs between 1960 and 1976 with changes in the skill composition of U.S. workers has found that the number of jobs requiring the highest level of skills diminished in that period, whereas the number of workers who had such credentials increased dramatically (Rumberger 1981). A review of studies in the United States and Europe concludes that

> there is no evidence that jobs, taken as a group, are experiencing dramatic upgrading and downgrading in terms of their skill requirements. This does not mean an absence of upgrading and downgrading changes but rather an approximate balancing in the direction and quantity of changes of an approximate conservation of total skill. . . . It is intriguing that there are more hints of downgrading in studies of skill as autonomy-control and more hints of upgrading in studies of skill as substantive complexity, suggesting the possibility of divergent aggregate trends in the two dimensions of skill. (Spenner 1985, 141)

The review goes on to note that "the impacts of technology on skill levels are not simple, not necessarily direct, not constant across settings, and cannot be considered in isolation" (Spenner 1985, 146). The same innovation in different firms can alter skill requirements in different ways.

Later analyses of changing skill requirements also show mixed results. One study concludes that employment shifts within a particular industry are the crucial element explaining increased income inequality in the 1980s, and that these shifts toward more educated workers accelerated in the 1980s (Bound and Johnson 1992). This, the study claims, is indirect evidence of the increasing impact of technological change on the demand for higher-level skills. Another study argues that the large increase in the nonproduction share of manufacturing employment in the 1980s (employment of production workers fell 15 percent from 1979 to 1989 and nonproduction employment rose 3 percent in the same period) means that the manufacturing sector experienced substantial skill upgrading and that "biased technological change is an important part of the explanation" (Berman, Bound, and Griliches 1993). Yet almost all the shift in production labor as measured in this study took place before 1983, and almost all the investment in computer technology took place after 1982 (Howell and Weiler 1996).

Data from the Hay compensation consulting firm, which rates the skill requirements of jobs at a nonrandom sample of U.S. firms, suggest for production jobs "strong evidence of systemwide upskilling in job requirements combined with some tendency to shift the composition of employment toward job families with greater skill growth" between 1978 and 1988 (Cappelli 1993, 527). Peter Cappelli also finds changes for clerical jobs, but these vary significantly by function (Cappelli 1993, 524). Half the clerical jobs experienced an upgrading of skills, and the other half (for example, office equipment clerks and telephone operators), associated with new office technologies, were characterized by significant de-skilling. Thus, some clerical jobs apparently became more complex during this period and others, with the introduction of advanced technologies, were routinized and reduced in scope.

Lawrence Mishel and Ruy Teixera (1991) compared sixteen hundred jobs that were rated in 1977 and rerated in 1991, and found little change in skill requirements. They estimate only modest job-related upgrading of skills in language and math, and requirements in specific vocational preparation and interpersonal skills were virtually unchanged or slightly diminished. Similarly, David Howell and Edward Wolff (1991), using *Dictionary of Occupational Titles* data to measure indexes of cognitive, interactive, and motor-skill job requirements, estimate shares of occupation groups in total employment by industry, the use of new technology in various industries by the value of computer purchases per dollar of output, the share of new investment in total capital stock, and the share of engineers in the total workforce. They have found that a more intensive use of new technologies is associated with an increase in the levels of cognitive skills of the labor force and with a higher share of professional and technical workers but also with lower shares of managers and clerical workers as well as low-skilled operatives and laborers.

Yet another study analyzes employment shares of low-skilled blue-collar and white-collar workers as compared with computer investment per worker in five industries from 1979 to 1992. That study finds little relation between the employment share of blue-collar workers and investment in computer technology in any of the industries but a consistent negative relation between technology and employment of low-skilled white-collar workers. "These results suggest that if there was skill restructuring across occupations during the period of large-scale investment in computers, it was away from administrative support jobs, and toward professional, managerial, and technical jobs at the end of the decade" (Howell and Weiler 1996, 10–11).

In sum, these studies suggest that there has been a gradual increase in the demand for highly skilled workers and that this trend is expected to continue. There is little evidence, however, that the trend is accelerating as the result of increased investments in information technology. Indeed, the rate of skill growth seems to have declined with each decade since the 1960s (Howell and Wolff 1991; Mishel and Teixera 1991). Apparently, investment in earlier technologies negatively impacted mainly low-skilled production workers, particularly in the 1970s and early 1980s, whereas investment in new information technology negatively impacted mainly lower-skilled white-collar workers in the 1980s and 1990s.

Higher Wages Versus More Employment?

Information technology may not be ending job growth, but is it possible that job growth under the new conditions of global competition can only be achieved by keeping wages from rising in real terms? Labor markets did not operate this way in Europe and the United States in the twenty-five years after World War II. For a generation, productivity, employment, and real wages rose in tandem. Now things seem to have changed. Many OECD countries traded off lower employment growth for higher wages in the 1980s and 1990s, and some, lower wage growth for higher employment growth.

The highest productivity growth from 1983 to 1995 among the major OECD economies took place in Italy, Germany, Japan, and France, followed by the United Kingdom and, trailing behind, the United States and the Netherlands. The greatest employment growth was in the United States and the Netherlands, followed by Japan. The United Kingdom, Germany, France, and Italy had very low employment growth (0.6 percent or less annually). Italy posted negative job growth in this period. However, these low job-growth countries generally saw steady increases in real wages for those who held jobs, anywhere from 1 percent (France) to 2 percent (Germany) annually. This contrasted sharply with low average wage increases in high job-growth countries such as the United States and the Netherlands. Japan was the exception, with reasonable employment growth and high wage growth (see figure 2.3).

Did voters consciously choose higher wage increases at the expense of job growth in countries such as France, Italy, and Germany? The 1997 legislative elections in France and the latest elections in Germany, where Socialists and Social Democrats won on pledges to increase employment (implicitly, without sacrificing high wages or social benefits) made clear that the French and Germans are not sold on the American model of job growth at the expense of wage increases, a host of social benefits, and job security, nor on the English model of deregulation of social benefits and job security. A majority of the French and German public apparently still believe that they can recreate the earlier post–World War II period, in which workers got wage increases and the economy was able to create enough new jobs.

Within the context of preserving the welfare state and permanent jobs,

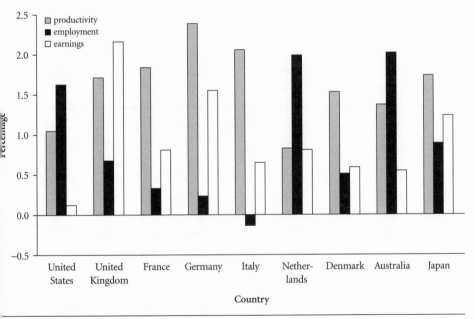

Figure 2.3 Annual Growth of Productivity, Employment, and Earnings, by Country, 1984 to 1998 (Percentage) *Source:* OECD 1999a. *Note:* Productivity is defined as GDP/worker.

and under the assumption that there is a "fixed" number of private sector jobs, the French government is trying to create employment by sharing a limited number of full-time jobs among a larger group of workers by lowering the number of hours in what is considered a full-time workweek. The essence of the French, and now the Italian, legislation is to reduce the work week to thirty-five hours with a "negotiated" reduction in pay. Production is to be reorganized around several shifts that will more fully utilize existing capital equipment, raise productivity, and increase employment.[14] Under the current law, when French employers agree to a reduction of hours, they are rewarded with lower social charges on the pay of their less-skilled employees plus a subsidy (six hundred to eight hundred dollars [U.S.] annually) for every worker included in the plan. The state is willing to induce employers to participate in the scheme because, allegedly, less money will be needed to pay unemployment compensation and because production, productivity, and hence profits will presumably rise, raising tax revenues (Aznar 1993).[15]

There are serious problems with the idea of job sharing as a national policy. Despite its claims, it does not solve the problem of job creation. In practice, cutting hours of work without or with cuts in pay (even if those cuts are partially made up by the state) may save jobs, but it does not create them. The mid-range projection of the number of jobs created under the French law, should a large number of firms comply, is about 80,000 per year. A 3 percent growth rate creates 350,000 jobs annually. In any year, a significant fraction of the labor force loses its employment, and an equally significant proportion is hired. The best that can be expected from job sharing is that it will curtail job losses. Companies have traditionally used approximately the same number of workers more efficiently over a greater number of shifts and simultaneously reduced the ratio of labor to capital. For example, one French firm, Vivendi, with 13,000 employees, agreed to the reduction to the thirty-five-hour workweek but increased its workforce by less than 1 percent (Croissandeau and Philippon 1999). In Germany, both Volkswagen and Daimler-Benz have struck agreements with the unions to reduce the workweek by one day, reducing wages by 10 percent and preserving existing jobs. All these plans have been moderately effective in reducing job loss through downsizing, but they have not been at all effective in creating new jobs.

The major benefit offered to workers by those who propose the shorter workweek is increased leisure. Yet even this conception is rooted in an anachronistic notion of the division between "wage work" and "leisure." Obviously, a four-day workweek can mean more recreation, rest, and relaxation, in which case any time not working can be considered leisure time. However, in the information society, a principal way that individuals would use time not "employed" in a job is to engage in enhancing their own education, in teaching (investing in) their children, or in earning additional income through home-based self-employment. Without a concerted effort to reintegrate the family into a network of learning and teaching that encompasses time spent both on and off the job, leisure time will erode further into an affirmation of the individualized worker, as disconnected from social networks in "relaxation" as in the workplace.[16]

The most positive aspect of job-sharing proposals is that they focus on increasing job security during a period of downsizing and worker separation from permanent jobs. They fit in well with an emphasis on in-firm training tied to profit-sharing incentives and have a direct connection between increased worker productivity and job security (Brown, Reich, and Stern 1993). In the short run, they may also forestall the tendency of firms to keep wages low even as they reduce the number of employees. In the longer run, however, part-time employment and contracting, more than job sharing, will have to increase sharply in Europe if large numbers of new jobs are to be created. The two-tier labor force that the job-sharing proposals would like to avoid is probably inevitable. From the standpoint of a learning society built around households that also need time flexibility to optimize their work and education strategies, the key is to focus attention on access to education for all citizens, whether they work in full-time jobs or not.[17]

Similar tendencies to hold on to the "traditions" of an earlier labor market exist in many other European countries and in Japan. Yet Switzerland, Austria, the Netherlands, Norway, Sweden, and, to some degree, Japan, have been more successful than France, Germany, or Italy in adjusting the "tradition" to the present global environment. The Dutch model is particularly interesting because the Netherlands have been able to achieve increasing employment in the 1980s and 1990s with rising productivity and at least slight wage increases. The Social Democratic coalition was able to do this through macroeconomic policy, incentives to reduce freeloading off government welfare, new financial instruments that stimulate expansion of domestic small business, and innovative agreements between labor and management built on trade union wage restraint and greater labor market flexibility (OECD 1998c).

The Dutch were able to extend the hours that businesses stay open, creating tens of thousands of new jobs. More important, by rewriting labor regulations so that part-time workers can retain full social security benefits and employers can hire temporary workers under certain conditions, employment has grown more rapidly than in other European countries. In European labor markets, unlike the Anglo-Saxon economies, an agreement among unions, business, and government is therefore crucial to increasing flexibility and employment.

The Fallacy of Technological Determinism

For the past two centuries, human "progress" has been intimately associated with technological change. For this reason, social scientists also look to technological change to explain the world they study. This is true across the ideological spectrum, from those who believe in the free market as the ultimate arbiter of all economic change and technology an important factor in production, to those who think that business and government cooperate to exploit workers and that technology is a crucial tool of that exploitation.

Technology is important, and the new information and communications technologies have had a tremendous impact on work. However, because technology is created by human minds, it has little meaning unless used by human workers and is employed in organizations run by people. These organizations, in turn, are situated in political and economic contexts that govern the conditions of work. Thus, when we talk about technology, we cannot forget about all those other human factors that affect its use and what it does to the lives of workers, employers, and citizens. In addition, these factors are themselves often in conflict. The inventors of the personal computer generally saw it as a tool of liberation, allowing individuals to communicate worldwide, get access to information not easily available otherwise, and have an impact politically. It can also be used, however, to control workers' time, just like the assembly line in Henry Ford's day.

Blaming technology for high unemployment or de-skilling or even falling wages for the less educated is simplistic and wrongheaded social science. It is technological determinism at its worst. Technology does indeed change work, but arguing that the greater diffusion of new technology is the source of the difficulties in France, Germany, and Italy (as well as Belgium and Spain or, for that matter, the United States and Holland) to simultaneously maintain employment and wage growth misses the point. The large variance in technological diffusion among these cases suggests that the problem is only partially related to information technology. The way governments have framed their macroeconomic, regulatory, and labor policies in response to the new global competition and the way firms organize work within those frameworks also play key roles in where countries end up on the job-creation and wage-increase spectrum.

Technology favors more educated workers over less educated workers, and it has also made possible the reorganization of production and innovation on a global scale, certainly influencing what workers do and how much they are paid. Yet technology is only a piece of the explanation for the reorganization of work in the new global economic environment. The reorganization of work has less to do with how many workers are employed than with how they are employed. The economic dilemma of the present historical period is not the end of jobs but rather the transformation of work. It is to that subject that I now turn.

Appendix

The two matrices in this appendix specify the typology I developed for analyzing the changing job structure in the United States in the past forty years (see figures 2A.1 and 2A.2).[18] Jobs are divided into three types: low-paying (Job I), middle-paying (Job II), and high-paying (Job III). This three-way division enables me to chart changes in the number of new jobs created as well as changes in the "quality" of jobs (as measured by the wages they command) by ethnic group and gender.

The division into job types I, II, and III is based on an analysis of average incomes in various industry and occupation categories. There is wide variation within categories, but in general what is defined here as a low-paying, middle-paying, or high-paying industry or occupation is characterized by low, medium, or high mean relative incomes, respectively.

Occupations are defined as regular census occupations. Industries are defined as regular census industrial classifications except for the division of manufacturing into three sub-categories—high tech manufacturing, which includes the three-digit industrial classifications (180, 181, 321,

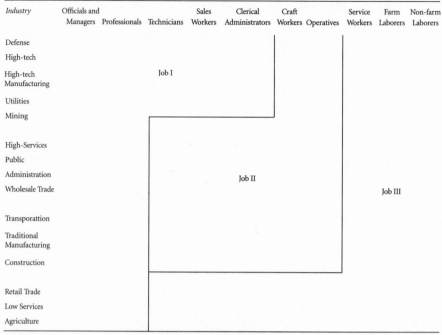

Figure 2A.1 Typology for Analyzing Job Structure (Men) *Source:* Author's compilation.

Occupation

Industry	Officials and Managers	Professionals	Technicians	Sales Workers	Clerical Administrators	Craft Workers	Operatives	Service Workers	Farm Laborers	Non-farm Laborers
Defense										
High-tech Manufacturing			Job I							
Communications										
Utilities										
Mining										
High-Services										
Public										
Administration				Job II						
Wholesale Trade								Job III		
Transporattion										
Traditional Manufacturing										
Construction										
Retail Trade										
Low Services										
Agriculture										

Figure 2A.2 Typology for Analyzing Job Structure (Women) *Source:* Author's compilation

322, 371, and 341), defense manufacturing (three-digit classifications 292, 352, and 362), and traditional manufacturing, which includes all other three-digit classifications (100 to 392)—and the division of services. The division of services is broken into two categories—high services (essentially banking, finance, insurance, and business services; three-digit categories 700 to 712, 721, 730, 742, 812 to 861, and 872 to 892) and low services (722, 731, 741, 750 to 802, and 862 to 871).

---

1. For example, the United States spends far more on information technology per worker than any other developed country (see table 2.6).
2. A puddler is a person who turns impure pig iron into steel by agitating a molten bath of iron to take out the impurities.
3. The end-of-jobs argument is also popular in Europe. See, for example, Aznar 1993.
4. These estimates exclude the Democratic Republic of Germany (East Germany), which became part of Germany in 1990. The estimates are based on the twelve countries that were members of the European Union in 1996. See OECD 1996a, appendix table D; OECD 1999, table 1.2. For the breakdown of the growth in private and public employment, see OECD 1994a.
5. An argument can be made that the growth of jobs should be estimated relative to population growth rather than in absolute terms. If a country has slow population growth, there might be a greater tendency to substitute capital for labor and slower growth of employment-intensive, people-oriented services, such as retail trade and real estate. An even better measure of such relative job growth is the ratio of employment to population for those age fifteen to sixty-four, reported annually by the OECD. Overall (men and women combined) ratios have declined slightly in Europe and risen in the United States and Japan. In the late 1990s (from 1995 to 1999), the ratios also rose slightly in Europe. That said, the absolute job growth shown in figure 2.1 is also a valid measure of the total capacity of an economy to produce jobs. This is particularly true given that the United States, unlike Japan, has allowed entry to significant numbers of immigrants at both the high and low ends of the educational spectrum. Europe also has considerable immigration, and if one includes Germany's absorption of the German Democratic Republic's labor force after 1990, the numbers get even larger, although nothing like those in the United States.
6. I shall have more to say about the Dutch model in the next chapter.
7. Studies measuring microelectronic use by industry have been done, but they are limited to a few countries. See OECD 1992.

8. The unemployment level *(UnN)* in 1995 is estimated as a function of spending on information technology per worker (TI) in 1994. The estimated equation is

$$UnN_{1995} = 12.72 - 0.0046 \ TI/worker_{1994}$$
$$(-1.40)$$

where the *t*-value is in parentheses below the coefficient for TI_{1994}.

9. For a further explanation of this phenomenon, see Brown, Reich, and Stern 1993.

10. See also, among other studies, Appelbaum and Schettkat 1990; Ozaki et al. 1992; Bushnell 1994; Wood 1989; Dean, Yoon, and Susman 1992; and Watanabe 1987).

11. High-paying jobs for men are defined as managerial and professional jobs in all industries plus technical, sales, and clerical jobs in high-paying industries. Middle-paying jobs include craft workers and operatives in all but retail trade, "low" services, and agriculture. Low-paying jobs are defined as all but professional and managerial jobs in retail trade, low services, and agriculture and service workers and laborers in all other industries. These are very approximate categories, but they give us a rough definition of job growth over time.

12. On the other hand, the President's Council of Economic Advisors reported in August 1996 that the growth of new jobs in the service sector between February 1994 and February 1996 was overwhelmingly in professional and managerial jobs and that 38 percent of all new job growth was in services. This suggests that at least in the latter part of the recovery phase, most new jobs were relatively high paying. Nevertheless, I found that between 1995 and 1998, middle-paying jobs increased rapidly relative to both higher- and lower-paying jobs. In part, this may result from the fact that I define technical, sales, clerical, craft, and operative jobs in construction as middle-paying jobs for males.

13. This notion has spawned the tradition that technological change increases skill requirements by eliminating low-end physical labor. The height of this tradition is reached in Bell's (1973) arguments that knowledge-based jobs will replace production work in the postindustrial economy. The counter tradition is that technology is used to de-skill work and gain control over the production process. Harry Braverman (1974), for example, argued that the shift from manufacturing production jobs to white-collar jobs did not mean that skill levels were rising, because the latter were also being de-skilled by new technology.

14. The main assumption of most job-sharing schemes is that the new technology is destroying jobs more quickly than new jobs can be produced, leading to a growing shortage of jobs and ever higher rates of unemployment. However, much of the massive literature on job sharing discusses it mainly in terms of circumventing the need for a new definition of a job for the convenience of in-

dividuals who wish to work part time. In that case, job sharing is not a way to save jobs, but only a way to convert full-time jobs into (voluntarily) part-time jobs. This practice is prevalent among professionals, particularly husbands and wives who wish to spend less time on the job and more the family. See Russell 1994.

15. Under the present law, the costs will be covered directly by an ecotax on the most polluting firms and a higher tax on profits beginning in 2001.

16. Perhaps no activity is more representative of this individualization than television watching. The average family in the United States has the television set on about fifty hours a week, and European families are slowly catching up. Although television can serve as a teaching device, and will soon be interactive, its main function is to provide noninteractive entertainment. Its numbing effect on children and adults has been documented in a number of studies (see, for example, Mander 1978).

17. Part of the problem in moving toward more imaginative solutions to job creation is the "insider" approach of some European labor unions. For example, Laura F., the commerce advisor to the Socialist mayor of a northern Italian city, told me how important it was to the city's small retail businesses to stay open on Sundays, when many tourists visit. One solution being considered was to hire young men and women willing to work part time with prorated benefits. These hours would not substitute for regular hours during the week. Businesses were almost universally willing to participate in this innovation, as it was sure to increase their profits, the employment of young workers, and the general attractiveness of the town as a tourist center. The commerce unions refused, mainly because it was unlikely that the young people hired to work on Sundays would become union members. Not getting anything out of the deal, the unions preferred to oppose any change.

18. An earlier version of this appendix appeared in the author's 1994 book, *Faded Dreams*. Reprinted with the permission of Cambridge University Press.

The Transformation of Work in the New Global Economy

Jobs are not going away, but work is undergoing profound change. Increased competition puts pressure on national governments to reduce protection and to make their industries more efficient. Businesses, in turn, transform themselves by looking for ways to increase productivity and reduce the cost of labor. The two key elements of the transformation are the flexibility of the work process and the networking of firms and individuals in firms.

By flexibility, I mean that work tasks and work time can be constantly adapted to changing products, processes, and markets. This makes workers increasingly autonomous in the work process. Firms demand higher skills, self-programming ability, individual responsibility, and a willingness to follow a flexible schedule and to work longer hours. Firms also reduce the ties that bind the firm to the worker. The goal is a "just-in-time" labor force that allows firms to increase the number of hours (and workers) when demand rises and to reduce hours when demand falls. In practice this means more temporary and part-time work, as well as more independent contracting to the self-employed. Some workers also seek weaker ties to the firm, preferring contract work and the freedom to contract with several different companies. Flexibility pushes workers to be "agile" in their work and in their movement from job to job.

By networking I refer to a new logic of the firm, where changing hierarchies and organizational forms are based on interactive connections between different layers and positions within the firm, between firms, and within the market. New information technologies allow for greater flexibility and networking; and globalization emphasizes interdependence, interaction, and constant adaptation to an ever changing environment. This environment affects workers in firms, creating a culture of individual networking across companies. Individual networking is a way both to learn about working conditions, projects, and innovations in other firms and to make strategic job moves in a flexible labor market. With e-mail and the internet, individual networking has no spatial or temporal limits. Employees of one firm, if they have the capacity and choose to do so, can access employees of other firms without ever leaving their workplace or home computer. In addition, just as the better networking firms are likely to flourish because of their better information and contacts, so will the better networking worker flourish in the flexible labor market.

Take Daniel Akre, a top-performing salesman in Silicon Valley who has worked for seven employers since graduating from college in 1987. "In all my interviews, the topic of 'job hopping' comes up," says Akre. "You have to explain to people that you are more diversified, wise, and agile than if you'd stayed at one job" (Ilana DeBare, "Keeping a Packed Bag at Work," *San Francisco Chronicle,* April 30, 1999). Akre represents a new breed of young professional: he is constantly on the lookout for a better job and is ready to jump firms if he thinks there is any chance his present employer might downsize him out of work. The company he works for is just as ready to cut back workers or hire people away from competitors.

This new logic of work and organization produce two main results: first, individuals or firms that are not able to operate in such flexible networks are gradually phased out or made marginal (unemployed or relegated to very low-wage work) by competition; and second, the flexibility of work induces the individualization of work tasks and the increasing differentiation of workers in relation to their employers, creating an extraordinary range of variation in working conditions.

Technology plays an important role in these changes. It shapes the way organizations restructure because it creates new kinds of networking possibilities and helps define the most economically efficient way to produce a given product or service, at least from the private firm's point of view. New information technologies facilitate the decentralization of work tasks and their coordination in an interactive network of communication in real time, be it between continents or between floors of the same building. Technology also contributes to increased competition because it compresses time and space. Thus, even if technology does not reduce overall employment, it does affect the transformation of work and the organization of production.

There are many parts to this transformation. The first is that firms increasingly view labor markets in global terms, and workers and nations also see the market as global, though to a much lesser degree. The second is that the nature of jobs in most of the developed countries is changing. The historical trend of salaried work and socialized production that was the dominant feature of the industrial era is reversing. Businesses want to create a flexible organization of work that is capable of rapid response to changes in demand. The proportion of "flexible" workers (part-time, temporary, self-employed, and contract workers) is increasing. The career job (full-time employment with a single firm until retirement) is gradually disappearing, and the duration of those that still exists is decreasing, especially for men in those countries in which permanent jobs (for men) are the mainstay of social policy. On the one hand, the emergence of lean production methods goes hand in hand with widespread business practices of subcontracting, outsourcing, moving facilities offshore, consulting, and, accordingly, downsizing and customizing. On the other hand, workers who are willing to work long hours and can get jobs that require them to do that can earn high incomes. Those (usually better-educated) workers who are able to network across firms can also move effectively to improve their access to higher earnings—in flexible labor markets, interfirm mobility and frequent job changes are rewarded rather than penalized.

Third, income profiles over work lives are becoming somewhat flatter, even for the highly educated: the average worker with any level of education does not move up the salary ladder the way he or, more rarely, she did in the past. Fourth, the wage labor force all over the world is rapidly becoming dominated by women, with enormous implications for the way work and families are organized. These trends, not the end of jobs, are what policy makers will need to understand and address politically in this century.

The New Global Economy

The rapid development of industrializing economies in Asia and Latin America, new information technologies, liberalization of trade, and global financial markets have contributed to the emergence of a truly global economy in the past ten years. A global economy is not merely a world economy that has existed since at least the sixteenth century (Braudel 1979). Neither is it an economy in which trade, investment, and resource exploitation take place worldwide. It is not even an economy in which the external sector is dominant. For example, neither the United States nor the bloc of Western European countries taken as a whole show foreign trade as a major part of their economic activity. A global economy is one whose strategic core activities—including innovation, finance, and corporate management—function on a planetary scale in real time (Carnoy et al. 1993). This "globality" became possible only recently because of the technological infrastructure provided by telecommunications, information systems, microelectronics machinery, and computer-based transportation. Today, unlike even a generation ago, capital, innovation, management, information, and core markets are globalized.

What Is Globalization?

Definitions aside, the meaning of globalization in the context of the way we view economies and societies is hotly disputed. Most of the discussion focuses on whether transnational institutions have replaced national economies and national states as the loci of world development. The argument against the globalization thesis is based on two major assertions (Amin 1998): the first is that so-called transnational[1] corporations are not really transnational but are, rather, multinational (Carnoy 1993). Transnational means that they transcend any national space. Multinational means that they have offices in many different countries but retain a high fraction of their assets in their home-base economy. They therefore depend heavily on those home-base nations' economic policies for their overall health. For example, IBM (International Business Machines), certainly the most transnational of major corporations, with a global innovation network and a highly internationalized management, floundered badly when its core U.S. business suffered in the recession of 1990 to 1992. Only through a total restructuring at home did IBM recover. Similarly, Japanese banks, also highly multinationalized and riding high globally in the 1980s, have fallen on hard times since the slowdown of the Japanese economy. These examples suggest that these global corporations are still situated nationally, in that their core activities still cannot transcend the economic health of their principal location.

The second thesis in the argument against globalization is that national economic regulation is still the main form of public economic intervention and control, and this is so because a high fraction of a nation's economic activities remain almost entirely domestic and distinctly unglob-alized (the health, construction, education, retail and wholesale, and res-taurant and bar industries, as well as many other service industries). If na-tional states choose not to exercise their power to regulate and redistribute, it is because they are subjected to domestic pressures generally orches-trated by national capital, not by transnationals.

These assertions, however, are not on target. I am convinced of that now, even though I have made some of them myself in the past. Besides the fact that multinationalization of firms has greatly increased—multinational firms now account for one-third of the world's economic output and two-thirds of world trade, with 32 percent of world trade composed of intra-firm trade, unreported in standard trade statistics (UNCTAD 1993)—the essence of globalization is contained not strictly in trade and investment figures nor in the percentage of a national economy that is national but in a new way of thinking about economic and social space and time. Firms, workers, students, and even children watching television or using the in-ternet at school are reconceptualizing their world, whether that world is defined as a market, a location for production, a place to work, a source of information, a place to vacation, or a source of environmental problems. The reconceptualization of space and time into what Manuel Castells has called the "space of flows" (Castells 1996, chapter 6) is partly the result of history (world wars that enlarged nations' geopolitical space, for example) and secular advances in ordinary technology, such as the speed of trans-portation. Yet it is also profoundly affected by new information and com-munication technologies that allow real-time interchange of knowledge between the most distant points on our globe. Information networks are also increasingly individualized, and this too has a profound effect on the way knowledge and information are transmitted and interpreted, and the way social life is organized. Workers, no matter where they are located, can network with fellow workers in various branches of the same firm and in other firms. An entrepreneur working at home can access masses of infor-mation about markets, products, prices, and contacts with other producers worldwide without relying on intermediaries. Students in schools can ex-change e-mail with students in a distant country instantaneously, bringing them together in real time and space. Individual consumers or political or-ganizers can reach out globally at extremely low (and falling, at that) cost to get or supply information pertinent to their activities. This both creates enormous possibilities for global interaction and puts a growing premium on the individual's ability to get and interpret information.

Globalization and National Economic Policies

Is the power of the nation-state diminished by globalization? The answer is both yes and no. Yes, because increasing global economic competition makes the nation-state focus on economic policies that improve global competitiveness at the expense of policies that stabilize the current configuration of the domestic economy or possibly social cohesion (Castells 1997). Yes, because the nation-state is compelled to make the national economy attractive for the mass of capital that moves globally in the "space of flows," and that may mean a shift of public spending and monetary policy from measures that favor workers and consumers to those that benefit financial interests. Globalization forces nation-states to focus more on acting as economic growth promoters for their national economies than as protectors of the national identity or a nationalist project. The "project" of the nation-state tends to become limited largely to enhancing increases in aggregate material gain measured nationally and much less the promotion of "equal treatment" among various ethnic groups living within national boundaries or among regions. Increasingly, the nation-state shifts power to local and regional governments and is less and less able to equalize the interests of various identities represented within its borders. It pushes the problems of ethnic conflict to the local level and increasingly limits its responsibility to developing the economic environment in which individuals can increase their material well-being and form more extensive social networks.

Richard Rosencrance, writing in *Foreign Affairs*, goes so far as to argue that the globalized nation-state will itself become "virtual." It no longer will focus on amassing production capacity but rather will invest in its people and determine overall economic strategy (Rosencrance 1996). The virtual nation-state is the site of production and encourages and stimulates investments from home and abroad that expand production activities. It also realizes, however, that for the national economy to prosper, its production does not have to take place at home; rather, it specializes in research and development, in design, in network, entertainment, and communication software, and in financial services. The role of the state is to negotiate for its own corporations' investments abroad and to attract foreign investment domestically. The state is a negotiating entity that uses its diplomatic and commercial skills to enhance payoffs to the nation's resources.

On the other hand, no, the power of the nation-state may not be diminished by globalization, because ultimately nation-states still influence the territorial and temporal space in which capital has to invest and in which most people acquire their capacity to operate globally.[2] Peter Evans's argument, and one that I have also made (Carnoy 1993), is that to maximize profits and protect their returns, especially from intellectual capital, globalized firms and globalized finance capital need efficient state apparatuses with well-developed civil societies that provide growing markets, stable political conditions, and steady public investment in human capital (Evans 1997). Research conducted in the 1980s and early 1990s shows that well-organized interventionist state bureaucracies in Asia's newly industrialized countries were an essential element in their rapid economic growth (see, for example, Amsden 1989; Evans 1995; World Bank 1993). Although the interventionist state's role has been irrevocably changed by the current crisis in Asia, international and local investment capital still require coherent state regulatory and other policies to restore confidence. Beyond the view that state bureaucracies are a necessary element in regulating and protecting firm assets, it is likely that societies with strong national identities and group cohesiveness provide the kind of stability under which financial risk can be accurately assessed, productivity can be raised with new team-based production innovations, and educational institutions work reasonably well.

The social costs of weak states may be much higher than supposed by those most committed to getting the state "off the people's back," in Ronald Reagan's famous phrase. Some analysts have called this underlying context for social and economic interaction "social capital" (Coleman 1988). Others have focused on "trust" (Fukuyama 1995). Even the World Bank, supposedly a global financial institution, has "rediscovered" the nation-state as important to social capital (World Bank 1997). A well-organized, efficient state apparatus regulating the "rules of the game" and implementing coherent economic and social policies attracts capital and high-skilled labor. Inefficient states drive them away.

Labor and Globalization

Is labor also globalized? It is increasingly so, but with the exception of the upper layers of professional labor, international migration is still relatively small. In 1993, despite global panic about floods of immigrants, only about 1.5 percent of the global labor force (80 million workers) worked outside their country—half of them, surprisingly, concentrated in sub-

Saharan Africa and the Middle East (Campbell 1994). Free movement of citizens within the European Union (EU) resulted in only 2 percent of its nationals working in another EU country in 1993. The proportion has been unchanged since the mid-1980s (*Newsweek,* special issue on jobs, June 4, 1993). In the early 1990s, immigrants as a proportion of the total population surpassed 5 percent only in Germany (about 7 percent). In France, the proportion was lower in 1992 than it had been in 1986. In the United Kingdom, it was only slightly higher than the 1986 level (*Newsweek* 1993). The United States has always been an immigrant society except for the forty years between the early 1920s and the early 1960s, and current trends are consistent with those of an earlier period of open immigration (Portes and Barach 1990).

However, recent rapid increases in immigration into Western Europe and Japan may signal a broad new wave of labor mobility and the beginning of distinct changes in the development of the host country's culture. In the past five years, a sharp rise in immigration into the EU—much of it illegal—from the Balkans and Eastern Europe, particularly to Austria, Germany, and Italy is changing significantly the number of immigrants living in these countries. In Japan, hundreds of thousands of new immigrants from the rest of Asia are also changing the complexion of Japanese society. The main concern with immigration to the United States, Western Europe, and now Japan is with the ethnic composition of the immigrants. Immigrants tend to be ethnically different from the core cultures of highly developed host countries. The higher birthrate among immigrants once settled in the host countries make the developed economies increasingly multicultural and multiethnic.

Although the "coloring" of predominantly white (or Japanese) societies does not necessarily imply a global labor market, increased multiculturalization of highly developed economies is one important feature of globalization. In the United States, for example, business is behind much of the political push for open immigration for both high- and low-skilled workers. Not surprisingly, information technology companies are among the most active lobbyists for increased immigration. They see a large supply of highly skilled engineers and computer programmers in India, China, and Europe who can fill their needs at lower wages than those demanded by U.S. high-end workers. United States (and Japanese) universities also now depend heavily on foreign science and engineering graduate students to do research on government-funded projects (Carnoy 1998). Foreign countries also have an interest in sending their students (and lower-skilled workers) to the United States, Europe, and Japan so that they can learn and bring back the latest technological skills and so that emigrant workers earning higher wages abroad can remit money back home.

Even if labor does not circulate globally to the same degree as do money and goods, the new dynamics of trade and investment, led by multinational corporations and transnational networks of firms, have increased the interdependence of labor markets (Bailey, Parisotto, and Renshaw 1993). Some economists claim that the impact of trade on employment and wages in the United States is very small (see, for example, Krugman and Lawrence 1994; see also Cohen 1994), but most believe that foreign trade has had a significant negative impact on the wages of less educated workers (Bluestone 1995). One estimate suggests that between 1960 and 1990, skilled workers in the North benefited from the process of globalization, both in employment and wages, but unskilled workers lost out in the competition from developing countries. Demand for unskilled labor in the North fell by 20 percent, and wages declined (Wood 1994).[3] Others have shown that the potential of mobility for firms in the global economy provides management with extra bargaining power in obtaining concessions from the labor force in the North (Shaiken 1993). Although indirect effects of globalization are not always visible, they do affect bargaining relations. They tend to reduce labor's share of economic surplus but simultaneously preserve jobs that cannot be easily exported, such as highly skilled jobs or those located in nontradable services.

Thus, even without a unified global labor market or a global labor force, global labor in the new economy is interdependent with other economic factors. Such interdependence is characterized by hierarchical segmentation of labor, not within countries but across borders. The new model of global production and management is tantamount to the simultaneous integration of work and disintegration of workers as a collective.

The Transformation of Work

To say that labor is being disaggregated, or separated, from the institutions and identities that formed around industrial work—such as promotion ladders, unions, and corporate loyalty—is to say that the very concept of a job is changing. In the years after World War II, industrial societies constructed the ideal of a full-time, secure job working thirty years for one company with ever-rising real wages. Pay in this job would be high enough that within American family households, only the man had to work. His wife could stay at home, raising the children and managing the household. The ideal of secure work and increasing consumption was matched by government policies that constructed social security (old-age pensions, unemployment insurance, and health insurance) largely around the ideal of a permanent job. This concept of secure, permanent work at rising wages for men and very little paid work for women is going by the boards, and the new information technology is only one cause of change.

The simplest description of the nature of this transformation is increased flexibility. Greater worldwide competition in the late 1960s and early 1970s put pressure on firms in developed countries to become more competitive, hence to reorganize work for higher productivity or lower costs of production (and often both). Firms that saw the handwriting on the wall began to reorganize work in such a way as to allow greater flexibility in responding to changes in demand for products. If they were multiproduct firms, they often tried to change the product mix. They also pushed for greater quality control, just-in-time deliveries of both input and output to lower inventories, flexible hours to meet production deadlines and to reduce labor costs during slow periods, and teams to promote multitasking. Japanese and European firms, with their paternalistic (in Japan) or highly regulated (in Europe) relations between employer and labor, had and continue to have a much greater incentive to raise productivity by training workers and developing new arrangements among their employees, partly because the downsizing option in these economies is much more limited. In some European countries—Germany, the Netherlands, Scandinavia, Austria, and Switzerland—the social contract that binds business to labor and the state is much less adversarial, allowing for accords that effectively tie wage increases to productivity gains (Flanagan 1983). Firms in those countries are much more likely to invest in worker training and to arbitrate national labor pacts because they have been able to realize large productivity gains in the past from such cooperative relationships. Yet even in these "neocorporatist" economies, competition is pushing firms and the state to demand worker concessions, including wage restraints and new kinds of labor contracts that allow for temporary and part-time work with reduced benefits and no employment guarantees. The Dutch model of economic growth stimulus and employment expansion has been based on precisely such concessions. Although part of the labor market operates under traditional "permanent employment" rules (under a wage restraint accord), most new employment is being created under nonstandard contracts (OECD 1998c). In the past fifteen years, Holland has had the most rapid growth of part-time and temporary employment in the OECD: in 1996, Dutch workers averaged fewer work hours annually (about 1,370) than workers in all other developed countries.[4] Other highly traditional welfare states such as Sweden have also moved in this direction, with considerable success (Edmund Andrews, "A New Swedish Prosperity Even with a Welfare State," *New York Times*, October 8, 1999).

Increased competition has driven many U.S. firms, with far fewer constraints on hiring and firing than their European counterparts, to reorganize work and develop employee incentive systems to increase productivity, adopting at least some elements of Japanese and European work systems. One important influence, at least in the auto industry, has been Japanese and European investment in U.S. production facilities, which has brought those work organizations directly to U.S. workers.[5]

On the cost side, even in the 1970s, many firms in the United States moved consciously to lower labor cost by hiring more immigrants and newly available married (or divorced) women. This option was much less acceptable socially (and legally) in Japan and Europe, at least until recently. Yet in Europe and the United States firms regularly retired older male production workers, often by closing entire plants. Similarly, firms everywhere in the developed countries began sending manufacturing offshore to lower-wage countries, where the hired part-time and temporary workers who were paid lower social benefits than workers at home and filled short-term labor needs. Globalization and the new information technology in the 1980s only accentuated these moves, in terms of both productivity enhancement and savings in labor cost.

The "High Road": Training Workers in More Flexible Work Processes

There is a spate of popular business books on the market today about the "best" U.S. companies and the business practices that make other countries, such as Japan, Germany, and Italy, produce such high-quality products. This growing literature makes it seem that the most effective way to increase flexibility is worker-centered, training-intensive, productivity-enhancing organizational innovations designed to make workers feel secure and part of a company team (see, for example, Peters and Waterman 1982; Pfeffer 1998; Johnson 1982; and Piore and Sabel 1984).

Worldwide, firms have adopted more flexible work organization. Beginning in the 1970s, Japanese work organization became the epitome of "best-practice" production. Quality-control circles, employee training, job rotation, work security, firm loyalty, and steady pay increases were all regarded as key elements in the success of Japanese firms, especially in manufacturing (Johnson 1982; Okimoto and Rohlen 1988). The quality and efficiency of German, Austrian, and Swiss production are also identified with a social pact between firms and unions that assures job security, job training, and rising wages in return for union commitment to raising productivity (Flanagan 1983). Michael Piore and Charles Sabel argue that the prototype of a "post-Fordist" model first appeared in certain regions of Italy, creating high-quality, flexible production centered on skilled workers in small- and medium-size firms with strong unions and relatively high wages.

In the United States, firms tend to provide little formal training for workers. Neither are relations between employers and workers as cooperative as those in Germany or Japan. It is telling, then, that researchers who surveyed U.S. firms to estimate how widespread productivity-enhancing organizational changes are and how deeply they penetrate companies have found that the proportion of firms introducing at least one employee-involvement practice is large and growing. Some firms have also begun to include a high fraction of employees in these practices.[6]

Paul Osterman at MIT asked almost seven hundred establishments nationwide whether four practices—self-managed teams, job rotation, total quality management, and quality control—enter into their work organization (Osterman 1994). His results suggest that about 40 percent use teams extensively, penetrating the workplace of more than 50 percent, "about one-third (14 percent) of those employ only this practice," and about 25 percent employ one of the other three practices extensively. However, only 10 percent of establishments extensively employ three of the practices simultaneously (Osterman 1994, 177). Osterman's data also suggest that a firm typically employs such practices because its management has worker-oriented values and follows a high-road strategy, emphasizing service, quality, and a variety of products rather than low cost. Even so, such high-road flexible work practices are not associated with merit promotions or greater job security in the firms that have adopted them.

Most analysts of business practices agree that despite apparent biases in the data collection in many of the surveys, "between one-quarter and one-third of U.S. firms have made significant changes in how workers are managed and about one-third of large firms have serious quality programs in place or have experienced significant gains from their quality programs" (Appelbaum and Batt 1994, 68). Yet some argue that the implementation of these practices represents not a single coherent strategy to build flexibility but rather a historical process that results in two very different models of work organization. The first is an "American version of lean production"; the second, an "American version of team production" (Appelbaum and Batt 1994, 7).

The two models evolved over the past thirty years. Firms introduced a series of employee-involvement practices, from sociotechnical improvements in the 1960s and early 1970s to quality circles in the late 1970s and early 1980s, total quality management in the middle to late 1980s, and networking in the flexible specialization model from the mid-1980s on. The various practices continue to operate side by side, even though some, such as quality circles, have been discredited in most U.S. applications. As these fads were adopted, the goal of efforts to implement change at the workplace shifted, "from the humanization of work in the 1960s, to job satisfaction and productivity in the 1970s, to quality and competitiveness in the 1980s" (Appelbaum and Batt 1994, 70).

Although many of the changes in the workplace are small, involve relatively few employees, do not change the work system in any fundamental way, and invest relatively little in training, a handful of firms, such as Xerox, Federal Express, Saturn, and Corning, show a "more serious commitment" to developing strategies for continuous improvement. Such firms are American versions of high-performance workplaces. Unlike the typical business trying employee-involvement practices, high-performance firms put a heavy emphasis on worker training, spending at least 5 percent and in some cases as much as 15 percent or more of payroll on self-directed, team-based systems.

More prevalent are firms that focus not on increasing productivity but on cutting costs by freezing wage rates, introducing two-tiered systems, or replacing base pay with pay for skill. For businesses worldwide, flexibility is as important for its ability to reduce labor costs and to increase or decrease the size of the labor force quickly and "painlessly" as for its capacity to raise labor productivity.[7] From the employer's point of view, bottom-line improvements under lean production and team production probably look alike. They differ, however, in "their mobilization of the work force and the relative weight they give to the strategic value of human resource and industrial relations practices," making the outcomes for employees very different (Appelbaum and Batt 1994, 7).[8] Lean production is a top-down strategy, using mainly managerial and technical expertise and centralized decision making. It focuses on lowering the wage bill without damaging productivity. Team production tends to decentralize discretionary decision making and develops structures of worker representation at different levels of the organization. It provides employees with greater autonomy, more employment security, and a greater guarantee of a share in any performance gains.

Workplace flexibility, thus, takes two major forms:

- the high road of improving productivity by developing high-performance workplaces based on worker training, worker participation, wage incentives, and job security. Both blue- and white-collar work are reorganized along new forms of a white-collar model in which workers pursue and are rewarded for achieving individual and collective performance goals and in which flexibility and fluidity are not viewed by workers as a threat; and
- the low road of reducing labor costs through outsourcing labor hires, fixed-term and part-time labor contracts, and pressuring government to reduce real minimum wages and the power of unions.

We can observe both types of practices spreading simultaneously not only among firms but also within firms, and this is beginning to be true now in Europe as well. The best-practice, high-performance U.S. firms committed to team production and a humanized labor environment also subcontract business services, employ temporary and part-time labor, downsize their labor force, and try to reduce wages and benefits paid in most of the firms' manufacturing and clerical jobs. We can also observe that most "lean production" firms, "low-roading" their way to flexibility by cutting their wage costs, have fairly stable core labor forces and pay relatively high wages and benefits to their core workers.

In Japan, because of the close relation between large firms and their suppliers, companies such as Toyota have been able, until the ongoing crisis of the 1990s, to maintain a stable core labor force by guaranteeing employment until retirement while outsourcing production to myriad suppliers who employ mostly part-time and temporary workers. In the current environment, however, even the tradition of the permanent core is being questioned.

European firms have also found ways around job permanency by hiring youth and women for short periods of time on temporary contracts and for longer periods in part-time jobs. This practice varies greatly from country to country, but some countries, such as the Netherlands, have essentially legalized such practice through a new labor accord in which the unions have agreed to hold down wage increases in return for employment guarantees in "core" jobs while allowing employment expansion to be carried out largely through part-time and temporary (that is, nonstandard) wage contracts. The Dutch model involves much more than increased hiring flexibility; it includes a new exchange rate policy, incentives to reduce freeloading off extremely generous government welfare, and measures facilitating small business expansion (OECD 1998c). The broad consensual agreement struck with the trade unions in the early 1980s, however, remains absolutely essential to job expansion in the Netherlands. It stimulates private business to invest in high-road flexibility but also allows them room for low-road flexibility, particularly the hiring of large numbers of youth and women on nonstandard contracts. The result has been increased private investment, economic growth, and employment as well as positive wage growth, but wage growth much closer to that in the United States than in Germany or France. The main difference between Dutch and American flexibility, however, is that Dutch workers who have part-time or temporary jobs are still protected under national health, disability, unemployment, and pension plans. Dutch working families also have access to subsidized day care.

The push for flexibility has affected both unskilled and skilled workers. Whereas most firms in the United States, for example, maintain a core "permanent" labor force, even in that core, subcontracting and consulting is a small but rapidly growing way to obtain professional and technical work. It is not only firms that benefit from flexibility. Many professionals add to their main job (full or part time) and to their income and bargaining power by consulting.

This highly dynamic work system interacts with labor institutions in each country. The greater the bargaining power of the labor unions, the greater the constraints to such flexibility, the less the impact on wages and benefits, and the greater the difficulty for newcomers in entering the labor force, and thus job creation is further constrained (Bielenski 1994). However, even the strongest labor unions have been unable to halt the slow but sure erosion of traditional forms of work based on full-time employment, clear occupational assignments, and a well-established career pattern over the life cycle. In the Netherlands, the economic crisis of the 1970s and early 1980s pushed the strong labor unions to reach an agreement with the government, promoting greater labor market flexibility in new jobs while preserving traditional contracts (and reduced working hours) in core jobs.

The social costs of flexibility can be high, especially the heightened level of anxiety it causes in individuals and families,[9] but recent research also emphasizes the potential transformative value of new work arrangements for social life, particularly for improved family relationships and greater gender equality in labor markets. Patricia Hewitt, for example, argues that growing diversity of working formulas and schedules offers the possibility of work sharing between those currently employed full time and those within the same household who are barely employed (Hewitt 1993).[10]

Why did this restructuring of the work process and of the relationship between capital and labor take place just as new information and communications technologies were coming onto the market? It probably occurred because of a confluence of historical circumstances, technological opportunities, and economic imperatives. To reverse the profit squeeze without triggering inflation, national governments and private firms have acted, since the early 1980s, to reduce labor costs, either by increasing productivity with relatively little employment creation (as in Europe) or by lowering the cost of creating new jobs (as in the United States). Japan, until recently, opted for maintaining full employment on the basis of enhancing productivity and competitiveness. Labor unions in most countries—the main opposition to a one-sided restructuring strategy—were weakened by their inability to represent new kinds of workers (women, youth, immigrants), to organize in new workplaces (private sector offices, electronics industries), and to be effective in the newly networked global enterprises.[11]

The historical redefinition of the relationship between management and labor, and thus of the work process, was made possible by new organizational forms facilitated by the use of powerful information technologies. The ability to simultaneously assemble and separate labor on specific projects and tasks anywhere and anytime laid the groundwork for the virtual enterprise as a functional entity. From then on, it was a matter of overcoming institutional resistance to this organizational logic. The extraordinary increase in flexibility and adaptability permitted by new technologies overcame the opposition of labor to the mobility of capital. It followed relentless pressure by business to make labor's contribution increasingly flexible. Productivity and profitability were enhanced, yet labor lost institutional protection and became increasingly dependent on individual bargaining conditions in a constantly changing labor market. Labor had become individualized. Society became differentiated, as it has for most of human history, differentiated between winners and losers in the endless process of unequal bargaining. This time, however, the rules about how to win became increasingly organized around knowledge that was itself broad enough to be flexible—general knowledge that forms the basis for constant relearning. Specific skills were not enough, because technological change constantly redefined appropriate skills.[12] Membership in corporations or even countries ceased to have its privileges, because stepped-up global competition kept redesigning the variable geometry of work and markets. Because of the revolution in information technologies, never was labor more central to the process of value making; but never, also, was the worker (regardless of his or her skills) more vulnerable to changes in work organization, because the worker had become a lean individual, farmed out to a flexible network whose whereabouts were unknown to the network itself.

Increasing Flexibility and the Decline of the Job

Thus, even with favorable interpretation of the U.S. data, and even with the characterizations of the Japanese, German, Dutch, and parts of the Italian economy as relatively high-road models, it turns out that many firms in the OECD countries (even in Japan) view increased flexibility in terms of both increased worker training and worker participation and a change in the nature of the labor contract. Firms change the relationship between worker and employer both by investing heavily in the retraining of permanently employed workers into new work organizations and by increasingly relying on temporary, part-time, and subcontracted labor for jobs that can be specifically defined both in terms of task and the time needed to do the job—jobs that have traditionally been defined by work rules that allowed workers to negotiate simultaneously wage rates and work speed and that protected more senior workers against layoffs. Such labor contracts are usually characterized as contingent.[13]

The main concern is that involuntary part-time or temporary work, and jobs in firms that are subcontracting for business services, are highly concentrated in what some economists call the secondary labor market. This part of the labor market is marked by dead-end jobs—jobs that do not lead to other, better-paying work and tend to be the first to go in economic downturns. They are also low-paying jobs, and workers are closely supervised. It is the secondary nature of the jobs that makes them consistent with a broader view of instability and contingency. In this view, it is not so much how long an involuntarily part-time worker is temporarily attached to a single firm or job that is relevant, but rather the fact that the worker is in a secondary, or inherently insecure, job, without training or promotion opportunities, and that this situation is involuntary. Even so, some contingent workers are clearly not in the secondary market. Engineers, computer programmers, highly skilled technicians, accountants, and other professionals may (or may not) choose to independently contract their services to a single firm or multiple firms rather than be a single firm's employee. Many professionals are also self-employed, providing services as corporations or partnerships.

Northwestern University professor Paul Hirsch argues that even managerial positions fall into this category. A manager's contract with the firm may last only as long as the project for which they are hired. Once the project is finished, they must move on (see Grossman 1998). Thus, even in large companies, managers may think of themselves as free agents, self-defined "self-employed" specialists who are not wed to any particular employer (Gould, Weiner, and Levin 1998).

Are these contracted or self-employed workers contingent in the same sense as secretaries or janitors working part time through a temp agency? In the bulk of contingent labor analysis, all such workers are lumped together, but there is good reason not to do so. Because a significant proportion of workers are voluntarily part time or self-employed or on temporary or nontraditional contracts, a more inclusive term for this kind of labor is nontraditional contract or, even better, part of what could be called flexible labor.

The major claims made by contingent labor analysts that job tenure is changing refer to the increase in involuntary part-time work in the 1980s;[14] the increase in temporary, contract, and consulting work (mainly the growth of business services) in the past seven years; and the recent trend toward downsizing even as the economy is expanding, a trend with a potentially large effect on older workers. The sum of these effects signify major changes in the relations between employer and employee and in the traditional full-time job at the heart of these relations. It makes work more contingent or perhaps, to be more accurate, more flexible than in the past.

The changes have four important elements:

1. The notion of time: flexible work means less employed time than a thirty-five- to forty-hour per week, full-year job
2. The notion of permanency: flexible work is based explicitly on a fixed-term contract with no commitment for future employment
3. The notion of location: although the vast majority of workers still work at business sites, increasing numbers of independent contractors work not on-site but in their homes
4. The notion of the social contract between employer and employee: the traditional contract is based on reciprocal rights, protections, and obligations, including, on the employer's part, social wages (health care benefits and unemployment insurance, for example), equal-opportunity protection, the guarantee of a certain degree of job security, advancement opportunities, and options for training and skill upgrading and, on the employee's part, loyalty, the assurance of product quality, and, if necessary, a commitment to work overtime as required to get the job done (U.S. Department of Labor 1988).

Flexible work in itself is by no means new. Certain industries, such as retail trade, construction, and agriculture, have long been marked by short-term, short-hour, and part-year conditions for employment. Flexible work now affects a much wider range of industries and occupations than in the past, however, and is no longer confined to certain groups, such as students, farmworkers, and women working for extra money to supplement the husband's family wage. A significant and increasing proportion of men and women seeking full-time, permanent work, it is argued, are forced to accept flexible work (U.S. Department of Labor 1988, 1).

The proportion of workers in nontraditional, full-time, permanent employment in most OECD countries has grown rapidly in the past fifteen years, reaching high levels by the mid-1990s (see figures 3.1, 3.2, 3.3, and 3.4). Although unemployment rates have declined in most European countries since the mid-1990s, the proportion of part-time and temporary workers continues to rise (see OECD 1999b, tables E and 1.9).[15] Data from the OECD indicate that in the United Kingdom, the country in which the

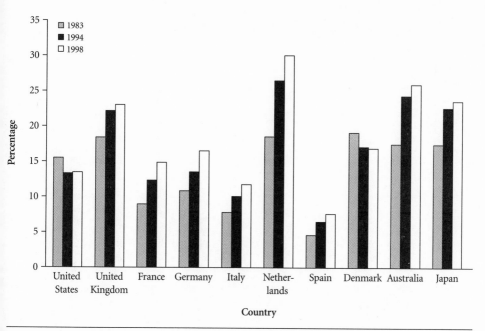

Figure 3.1 Share of Part-Time Workers in Employed Labor Force, by Country, Various Years (Percentage) *Source:* OECD 1996a, table E; OECD 1996b, table E.

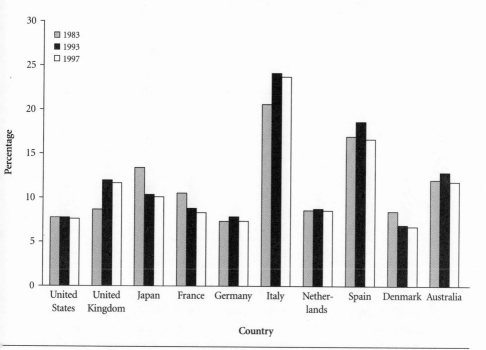

Figure 3.2 Share of Self-Employed Workers in Employed Labor Force, by Country, Various Years (Percentage) *Source:* OECD 1993a; OECD 1995; OECD 1998b.
Note: 1997 figures approximated from data in OECD 1998b.

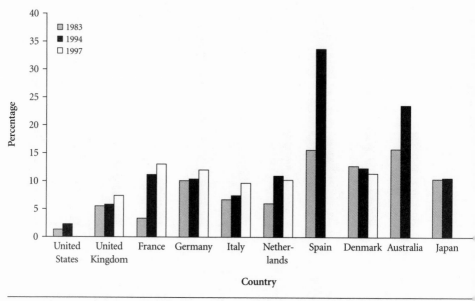

Figure 3.3 Share of Temporary Workers in Employed Labor Force, by Country, Various Years (Percentage) *Source:* OECD 1996a, table 1.6; OECD 1999b, table 1.9

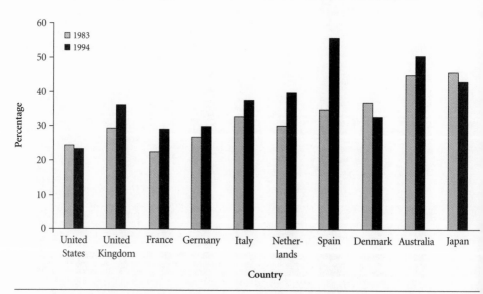

Figure 3.4 Share of Non-Standard Forms of Employment in Labor Force, by Country, 1983 and 1994 (Percentage) *Source:* Tables 3.1, 3.2, 3.3. *Note:* Sum of part-time and temporary workers adjusted for overlap between the two categories.

Industrial Revolution spearheaded the worldwide historical practice of salaried employment and standardization of labor, 36 percent of workers in 1994 were not employed on a permanent, full-time basis. The bulk of the labor force are part-timers (85 percent women), accounting for 23 percent of employed workers.[16] The broad category of flexible work takes different forms (self-employment, part time, temporary work), depending on countries' fiscal and labor regulations. In France, nonstandard employment represented 30 percent of the labor force in 1994, spread fairly evenly across the three categories. About 40 percent of Dutch and Japanese workers were employed this way in the 1990s, mostly part time. Both countries have relatively low unemployment (6.5 percent in Holland and 3.5 percent in Japan in 1995). The nonstandard employment champions are Spain and Australia, though for different reasons. Australia has a huge percentage of part-time workers, many of them temporary. Spain has seen a steep growth in the number of temporary workers, few of whom are part-time workers. The Spanish phenomenon is partly the result of a rigid, traditional labor market for both men and women that allows flexibility mainly through temp contracting. In Australia flexibility is achieved through hiring mainly women part-time workers.

In the United States in 1993, self-employment accounted for 7.7 percent of the nonagricultural workforce, part-time work for 17.5 percent, and contract labor, or temporary work, for about 2 percent, adding up to about 27 percent of the labor force. This is at the low end compared with other OECD countries and reflects the high degree of flexibility that U.S. employers have in the regular employment contract (Hammonds, Kelly, and Thurston 1994, 85). Temporary work is increasing rapidly in the U.S. economy, based on its tendency to outsource labor, which is facilitated by online transactions, not just in manufacturing but increasingly in services as well. In a 1994 survey of America's 392 fastest growing firms, 68 percent were subcontracting payroll services, 48 percent tax compliance services, and 46 percent administration of claim benefits (Jonathan Marshall, "Contracting Out Catching On: Firms Find It's More Efficient to Farm Out Jobs," *San Francisco Chronicle*, August 22, 1994). There is also evidence that in California, which should be seen as pushing the envelope in terms of new organizations of work, the proportion of labor with nonstandard contracts in 1999 was about double the 27 percent estimated for the United States as a whole in 1993. A survey of California workers shows that less than half were in full-time, regular, wage contract jobs (Health and Policy Studies 1999). These numbers suggest that in a highly mobile economy dominated by high technology, business services, and entertainment—in other words, the economy of the future—the majority of workers will not have full-time, permanent, traditionally salaried jobs.

The Shift to Self-Employment

Higher levels of education in the information age do not just provide more trainable employees for the information age workplace. One of the most profound transformations of the information age workplace is its increased opportunities for self-employment, especially for people with concrete, high-level service skills. Self-employment (in agriculture, crafts, and commerce) has been a dominant feature of the work system for most of human history. As late as the 1950s in continental Europe and Japan, a high fraction of the labor force was self-employed, mainly in agriculture and small-scale commerce. Relatively stable, employed, full-time work has characterized the labor process for only the past one hundred years or so. A gradual return to self-employment could be a natural outcome of greater work flexibility, the shift to a service economy, the availability of low-cost information technology, and increasing levels of education and knowledge in the labor force. The possibilities for workers to gain skills working as employees should also enhance their ability to move out of employment into self-employment. Nevertheless, these trends are not yet apparent in the developed economies (figure 3.2).

According to *Business Week,* the growth of new small businesses in the United States is providing increasing opportunities for self-employment at higher average wages per hour than that provided by traditional employment. In addition, capital invested by the self-employed in their own businesses can pay high returns compared with most other investments (Michael Mandel, "Business Rolls the Dice," *Business Week,* October 17, 1994, 89). Scholarly analyses of self-employment, however, show that self-employed women earn, on average, about 25 percent less on an hourly basis, and that only a small group of highly educated white men (*Business Week* readers) do better (Kalleberg et al. 1997). Nevertheless, the perception that self-employment can provide reasonable income and independence is an important one in a world in which control of time has increasing value.

The difference between the growing self-employment opportunities of the future and those of the past lies in their knowledge intensity. High-technology services are organized around information rather than commodities. Furthermore, information technology makes it possible for small businesses to avail themselves of relatively inexpensive accounting and marketing software, to locate themselves in the home, to operate on a part-time basis, and to be family-centered as part of a mixture of family wage employment activities, self-employment activities, and child development activities. Because it is knowledge intensive, the new self-employment may occupy an increasing proportion of formerly employed workers who have acquired knowledge and skills as employees and develop their own businesses based on that experience.

The shift to self-employment makes sense from another standpoint. Education seems to contribute most to higher productivity for the self-employed individuals who have direct control over the application of their knowledge to the production of goods and services. For example, the only empirical studies that show a positive relation between education and productivity are studies of self-employed farmers (Schultz 1975; Welch 1970). The economist Theodore Schultz attributes that relation to the ability of more educated farmers to adjust to economic disequilibrium. They tended to adopt innovations more rapidly, apply those innovations more effectively, and adjust more quickly to price changes in their products by changing product mix. Furthermore, the effect of education on productivity became noticeable only for farmers who had college-level education.

Over and above any risk they take in terms of their earnings, self-employed workers incur a much higher cost in paying for standard benefits than do those who are employed by others. In Europe and the United States, the self-employed pay high health care premiums and have to bear the full cost of pension plans. Group health care discounts are generally not available to individuals in the United States. Again, the job-centered approach to benefits penalizes those who do not have traditional full-time jobs.

Increased Flexibility and Job Tenure

Increases in labor flexibility tend to reduce the average length of time people hold a particular job. This changes the meaning of a job, especially in those countries in which a job has come to represent long-term employment in a particular type of work. The ideal of permanent, single-employer work evolved in the nineteenth and early twentieth centuries as a re-action to the booms and busts of free market industrial economies, in which workers had been cast loose from self-employment in agriculture or crafts. Control over work time, working conditions, and wages have been the main issues for workers' associations since early in the past century. Workers at that time still had to contend with the temporary nature of most work, however. When large, anonymous corporations emerged as the major form of business organization, these companies developed "inter-nal" labor markets and the concept of long-term employment with the same firm, independent of the person running it. The combination of workers' organizations pushing for greater employment stability and em-ployers whose interests now lay in having a stable "core" labor force from which workers could be selected for promotion produced a level of job permanence unknown in the past. In the United States, these arrangements were governed primarily by state-sanctioned and state-adjudicated con-tracts between union and employer. In Japan, the arrangements were im-bedded in a social contract under which large corporations, the state, and unions assumed joint responsibility for improving Japanese society. In Eu-rope, governments sanctioned the arrangements with legislation that made it increasingly difficult to fire individual workers without due process and employer penalties.

Each of these systems of governing job turnover has its particular features. In Japan, it creates highly dualized labor markets. In the large-company tier, job permanence in a paternalistic environment is taken for granted as a cultural norm. Only 40 percent of Japanese workers have jobs in that tier, however, and even the large-company tier is now beginning to change, offering workers pension alternatives that no longer assume a per-manent job (Stephanie Strom, "Japan's New 'Temp' Workers," *New York Times*, June 17, 1998). Most women and many men work in a much more flexible second tier of smaller companies, in which job permanence is not considered part of the labor contract. Many of these firms subcontract to the corporate giants. Japan has a high fraction of part-time and temporary jobs in a labor market popularly associated with lifetime employment be-cause only part (mostly males) of their workforce have permanent jobs.

Continental European labor markets are governed by extensive national legislation that emerged from historical accords between employers and relatively powerful labor unions. Thus almost all businesses, whether large or small, are affected, and almost all labor is protected against easy dis-missal.

Work in the United States has had the least permanence, both because workers are spatially mobile relative to European and Japanese workers and because most workers were never covered by the union contracts that governed turnover. In 1982, Robert Hall wrote, "Though the U.S. labor market is justly notorious for high turnover and consequent high unemployment, it also provides stable, near-lifetime employment to an important fraction of the labor force" (Hall 1982, 716). Using 1979 Current Population Survey (CPS) supplemental data on job tenure as of 1978, he estimated that about 29 percent of whites and 26 percent of blacks would hold one job for more than twenty years during their work careers, although the typical worker in 1978 held a job that had lasted or would last eight years. He also estimated a significant difference between men and women: 37 percent of men but only 15 percent of women would hold one job lasting twenty years. By their mid-forties, though, both the typical male worker and the typical female worker had held about nine different jobs. Longer periods spent out of the labor force by women almost exactly offset the shorter duration of the jobs they held (Hall 1982, 723).

The new global competition has impacted job turnover in many of these labor markets. Hall's conclusions about job stability for older male workers using 1979 data suggest that despite the influx of women and youth during the expansion of the 1970s, job stability after the age of thirty was as much a feature of the U.S. labor market as high job mobility. That argument set the stage for the subsequent debate among economists about increasing job turnover and decreasing job tenure in U.S. labor markets. Although much of the debate revolves around biases in the estimates from cross-sectional data at different points in time and from evident misreporting by workers on job changes, the general conclusion seems to be that a significant proportion of white men and probably both black and white women with higher levels of education end up in jobs with long tenure, and that this feature of the labor market did not change perceptibly through the 1980s and into the early 1990s. In other words, the U.S. labor market has always been marked by high turnover and many job changes— the average male American worker held nine jobs in his career—as well as about one-fourth of workers in highly stable jobs. Average tenure is low (mean 6.8 years, 28 percent of employees with less than one year of job tenure) and seems not to have changed much since the 1970s (table 3.1).[17] Recent research using longitudinal data suggests that even in the United States, men's job tenure is falling among the young, among blacks, and, since 1990, among older workers. At the same time, job stability probably fell substantially for workers without a college education and for black workers (Marcotte 1995). There is also evidence that in the recession of the early 1990s, older white-collar workers—a group that traditionally has been characterized by high job stability—may have also been affected by declining job stability, particularly those with less job tenure (Farber 1993).

Japan, the newcomer into the high-income club of G-7 countries, profited in the 1980s from globalization, achieving high growth rates and moving an increased proportion of workers into long-term, secure jobs. Average job tenure—or the average number of years a worker stays in the same job—was already high in Japan in 1979, at 8.9 years, compared with other OECD countries. Even so, average tenure kept rising through the 1980s, surpassing that in Germany and France by 1991 (see table 3.1). This means that more Japanese workers were getting access to long-term jobs. Japan was exceptional among major OECD countries in that both men and women in all age groups had generally increasing tenure (OECD 1993a, chart 4.2). Yet the recent (and long) recession has forced large Japanese corporations to question whether they can sustain job permanence for their employees (Strom, "Japan's New 'Temp' Workers"). Although unemployment has increased little during this long and increasingly severe recession in what seemed to be unassailable Japanese growth, this may be the case because many part-time working women and young men simply fade out of the labor market, and others who lose full-time jobs move into part-time work.

The opposite trend is taking place in the European economies with traditionally long job tenure, such as France, Germany, and Spain, largely driven by higher unemployment rates and the growth (especially in Spain) of nonstandard labor contracts (for an analysis of the relation between job tenure and unemployment, see ILO 1996, figure 2.2). In the mid-1980s, these three countries had high average job tenure (higher than Japan's) of 10.7 to 11.2 years. By the mid-1990s, tenure had fallen in all three for both men and women, most consistently among the young (table 3.1; OECD 1993a, charts 4.2 and 4.3; OECD 1997a, tables 5.5 and 5.7). The percentage of workers with tenure of less than one year rose, particularly in Spain, where temporary work shot up in the early 1990s. Retention rates charted over five-year periods (comparing 1990 to 1995 with 1980 to 1985) show that they fell sharply in France and Spain, (and Finland) overall and in Germany among those workers more than forty-five years of age (OECD

Table 3.1 Tenure of Workers, by Country, Various Years

Country	1979 Tenure Less than One Year (%)	1979 Average Tenure (Years)	1985 Tenure Less than One Year (%)	1985 Average Tenure (Years)	1991 Tenure Less than One Year (%)	1991 Average Tenure (Years)	1995 Tenure Less than One Year (%)	1995 Average Tenure (Years)
Australia	22.3	6.5	22.9	6.6	21.4	6.8	25.2[a]	6.4[a]
Canada	26.4	7.3	26.6[b]	7.6[b]	23.5	7.8	22.7	7.9
France	—	—	13.1[b]	10.7[b]	15.7	10.1	14.4	10.4
Germany	—	—	8.5[c]	11.1[c]	12.8[d]	10.4[d]	9.8[e]	10.8[e]
Italy	—	—	—	—	—	—	8.5	11.6
Japan	10.6	8.9	9.4	10.3	9.8[d]	10.9[d]	7.6	11.3
Netherlands	—	—	11.7	8.9	24.0[d]	7.0[d]	13.1	9.6[e]
Spain	—	—	15.2[f]	11.2[f]	23.9[g]	9.8[g]	24.8	9.1
United Kingdom	—	—	18.0[b]	8.3[b]	18.6	7.9	18.6	8.3
United States	28.2[h]	6.4	28.9[i]	6.7[i]	28.8	6.7	26.0[a]	7.4[a]

Source: OECD 1993a, table 4.2; OECD 1997a, tables 5.5 and 5.7.

[a]1996.
[b]1984.
[c]1986.
[d]1990.
[e]1994.
[f]1987.
[g]1992.
[h]1978.
[i]1983

1997a, table 5.8). Already high unemployment rates increased, and the accords between union, employer, and government that dominate their labor markets have come under assault. Business is pushing for legislation that would allow the hiring of new workers under less stringent controls and the hiring of younger workers at lower minimum wages. Some companies, such as Daimler-Benz, have told the powerful German metalworkers' union that they have to reduce working hours at their German plants or move production abroad. Although the population as a whole is generally opposed to such changes, in practice, job tenure is decreasing anyway.

Workers in other European countries characterized by already lower average job tenure also suffered declines in full-time work. I have already discussed how Great Britain sharply increased nontraditional work contracts from 1985 to 1993 and how the Netherlands worked out a new national accord with its labor union confederations that keeps real wages rising very slowly and allows for a major expansion of part-time, often temporary, work. These moves were reflected in a fall in job tenure in Great Britain, down to 7.9 years in 1991; and in the Netherlands, a very sharp drop of almost two years from the previous interval (1985 to 1990) to seven years of average tenure, putting that country's labor force at almost the same average tenure as those in the United States and Australia, among the most fluid labor markets in the OECD. Job tenure rose again in both countries in the early 1990s, although other data from Eurostat give lower numbers than those reported here. Dutch and English men still have longer average tenure than American men. Dutch women, on the other hand, now have the shortest tenure in the OECD (OECD 1993a, chart 4.3).

Wage Decline and Increasing Wage Inequality

So far, I have discussed firms' increasing flexibility mainly in institutional terms—that is, in terms of employers' (and employees') search for flexibility through alternative employment arrangements. The more traditional (at least in neoclassical economists' terms) form of labor market flexibility, however, is the flexibility of labor price. Employers seek to reduce both the fixed cost (social benefits) and variable cost (wages) of labor in order to lower total labor cost. From the employer's standpoint, a major objective of alternative employment arrangements is to lower social benefits and turnover cost. Wages are less under the control of employers, but to the extent that they can introduce technological change that saves on labor, move production abroad, and use their political power to reduce union influence, keep minimum wages low, or keep immigration flowing, employers will do so.

If anything, this form of increased flexibility has had a greater effect on workers in the most flexible national labor markets, such as those in the United States, Australia, and New Zealand, than alternative employment arrangements. In the United States, for example, three clearly defined trends mark the period from the mid-1970s to the mid-1990s. First, the real wages of much of the workforce, especially those without college education and especially men, have steadily and sharply declined (Carnoy 1994; Bernstein et al. 1999). Second, the distribution of earnings has become more unequal, with inequality increasing roughly in line with the distribution of formal education across gender, race, industries, and occupations. Third, the earnings gap between the higher educated and those with no more than a high school education increased substantially (figure 3.5; OECD 1996a, chart 3.3; Bluestone 1995).

The other Anglo-Saxon economies—those of Australia, Canada, New

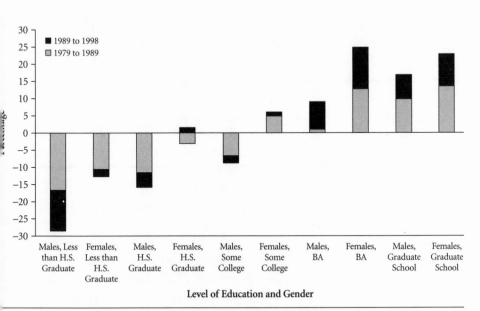

Figure 3.5 Real Wage Growth, United States, by Level of Education and Gender, 1979 to 1989 and 1989 to 1998 (Percentage) *Source:* Estimated from data provided by Jared Bernstein, Economic Policy Institute, Washington, D.C. See Bernstein et al. 1999.

Zealand, and the United Kingdom—did not conform completely to the U.S. model in the past two decades, but their labor markets behaved much more like that of the United States than did Japanese, continental European, and Scandinavian markets. Australia had positive but very low real wage growth, rather constant earnings inequality, and higher wage growth for lower-educated men (OECD 1997a, chart 4.2a). Canada saw positive overall wage growth, increased earnings inequality (OECD 1996a), and somewhat higher growth of earnings for higher-educated men. Wages increased more for higher-educated than for lower-educated workers in the United Kingdom from 1985 to 1995, and earnings inequality increased sharply, second only to the rise in earnings inequality in the United States and Canada. Both changes were consistent with the U.S. experience—not surprising, given the similarity of Margaret Thatcher's and Ronald Reagan's policies in the 1980s. Unlike the slow rise in overall wages and the sharp fall in U.S. wages for less educated workers, however, British wages rose rapidly for all workers in this period (OECD 1996a, table 3.1 and chart 3.3).

The model does not at all fit non–Anglo-Saxon economies. Workers in other continental European countries and Japan got substantial real wage increases from 1985 to 1995, with the highest in Germany and Japan (in addition to the United Kingdom), but the earnings gap between higher- and lower-educated workers fell or remained stable (OECD 1997a, chart 4.2a). In contrast with the experience of the United States, the United Kingdom, and Canada, earnings distribution has changed little over the past twenty years in continental Europe and in Japan (figure 3.6).

This suggests that less flexibility in labor markets such as Germany's may mean rising wages and productivity and less earnings inequality among those who have work, but also high levels of unemployment, whereas high levels of flexibility like that seen in the United States labor market may mean low or negative wage growth and high earnings inequality. It also suggests that labor markets can be made more flexible with relatively low levels of unemployment, large wage increases, and large increases in earnings inequality, like in the United Kingdom; or with relatively low yet positive wage increases and little or no increase in earnings inequality, like in the Netherlands; or with relatively high increases in wages and small increases in earnings inequality, like in Japan (for earnings dispersion data over time, see OECD 1996a). All these combinations exist in the real world, and all are associated with countries that have participated strenuously in the adjustment to a new global economy in the information age.

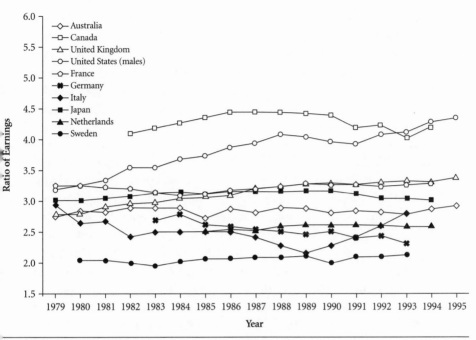

Figure 3.6 Trends in Earnings Dispersion, by Country, 1979 to 1995 (Ratio of Ninth to First Decile of Earnings) *Source:* OECD 1996a, table 3.1.

The variety of changes in wage structures and earnings distribution among economies that are all facing the same globalization process and whose firms are all adjusting to the same world market conditions puts into perspective attempts by U.S. economists to explain why wages for the less educated have declined so sharply in the past twenty-five years and why income distribution has become more unequal. The discussion in the United States reflects the broader discussion of changes in wage structure and income distribution incorporated in OECD and European documents and even discussions of the "Asian miracle" (World Bank 1997). It focuses on two major causes of these changes: technological change and political change.

The Technological Argument

Is high technology use associated with higher wages? As in the relation between technological change and the demand for skills, the evidence on the link between the use of new technology and workers' earnings is mixed.

Traditionally, the research on the effects of technology on earnings uses indirect measures of technological change (such as total factor productivity growth, spending on and employment in research and development [R&D], or the residual in the wage equation) and of skills (such as the level of educational attainment, experience [usually a function of age], or relative wages). This research on skill complementarity in the United States suggests that industries that are more technology intensive (higher R&D spending and employment) are marked by the presence of workers with higher education and by higher returns to education (Bartel and Lichtenberg 1987; Griliches 1969; Allen 1993; Berndt, Morrison, and Rosenblum 1992; Mincer 1991). There is no evidence, however, that this relation "accelerated" in the 1980s with the increased use of information and communications technology. Steven Allen's 1993 study estimates that technological change, as measured by the share of R&D scientists and engineers in total employment, accounts for about one-half the increase in returns to schooling in the 1980s for workers in manufacturing, but only 7 percent for the entire labor force. He also concludes that the rate of technological change was greater in the 1980s than in the 1970s. The rising change in the relation between wages and technology is concentrated in college graduates and is unrelated to the wages of other groups, indicating that the effect of more R&D spending on wages is limited to a substantial, but still minority, portion of the labor force—those with higher levels of schooling.

The most direct evidence on the relation between technology and wages is provided by economist Alan Krueger. He shows that individuals in the U.S. labor force who use computers earn 10 to 15 percent higher wages than workers who do not (Krueger 1991). Educational groups whose relative wages rose in the late 1980s were those working in jobs in which computerization grew the most. He concludes that investment in computers can explain one-third to one-half of the increase in the payoff to schooling observed from 1984 to 1989. A more recent study by John DiNardo and Jorn-Steffen Pischke, using similar data on German workers, shows that computer usage increased markedly between 1979 and 1991 and that, like Krueger's U.S. workers, German workers using computers enjoy wage premiums relative to workers who do not (DiNardo and Pischke 1996). DiNardo and Pischke also show, however, that German workers using low-tech items such as pencils, telephones, and calculators enjoy wage premiums almost as high as those of computer users. These results raise serious issues about what the Krueger results on wage premiums really measure.

Other research claims that technology, as measured by investment in computers and the share of scientists and engineers in employment, had no greater, and perhaps a lesser, effect on wage inequality in the 1980s than it did in the 1970s (Mishel and Bernstein 1994). Using Current Population Survey (CPS) data from the early 1970s, 1979, and 1989, Lawrence Mishel and Jared Bernstein suggest that the estimated impact of the technology-related trends on the growth of the gross wage differential (comparing the ninth and first deciles) was substantially lower in the 1980s as a result of the strong deceleration of technology's effect on the bottom of the wage distribution. Increased investment in computers apparently contributed to wage equalization in the bottom half of the distribution. They also argue that the growth of within-group wage inequality was not driven by technological change. "Our findings suggest that technology has a continuing transformative effect on the wage and employment structure, as suggested by the skill-complementarity literature. Nevertheless, we find that technology's impact on labor market outcomes was no greater, and perhaps less, in the 1980s than in the 1970s. This implies that technological change associated with new investment, R&D activity and computerization was not the predominant factor driving the growth of wage inequality in the 1980s" (Mishel and Bernstein 1994, 37).

In a broad review of the evidence on the argument that information technology is responsible for the decline in the relative wages of less educated Americans, David Howell and Susan Weiler also conclude that the evidence "does not offer much support to the conventional view that wage restructuring of the 1980s was the result of technology-induced shifts in the demand for skills. Indeed we suggest that the wage restructuring of the 1980s was largely independent of skill restructuring" (Howell and Weiler 1998, 362).

The Political Argument

Have institutional changes and declining incomes for less educated workers reduced wages even as skills have increased? The political argument departs from the skill-mix argument and focuses on changes in institutional relations, or "wage norms." In this explanation, employers "choose high or low starting wages and a particular wage-tenure profile for strategic reasons" (Weiler 1998, 358). Richard Freeman (1993) makes a similar argument that in slack labor markets firms have leeway to strike innovative wage contracts and affect wage outcomes in other ways. A key factor in the way firms set wages is employers' bargaining power (Howell and Wolff 1991). Historically, this asset has been significantly influenced by political and ideological conditions and government actions in favor of labor or employers. What changed in the United States in the 1980s to influence the "discretion" that firms had in setting wages?

According to one analysis, two major shifts occurred in the 1980s that changed the institutional context in which wages were negotiated (Howell and Weiler 1996). First, the United States turned away politically from the New Deal, with its corporatist overtones, and toward the private market. Part of this shift resulted from voters' perception of the declining power of the state to influence markets in an increasingly global economy (Castells 1997). Another part came, however, from a major effort by corporations to raise the share of private profits in the gross national product (Bowles, Gordon, and Weiskopf 1983; Carnoy, Shearer, and Rumberger 1983). The election of Ronald Reagan and the implementation of strong antiunion policies, including the replacement of striking air traffic controllers in 1981, set a tone for bargaining that put employers in the driver's seat. Another expression of the change in political climate was the failure of legislators to approve any increase in the nominal minimum wage from 1981 through 1988, reducing the real minimum wage by 30 percent, back to 1950 levels. Combined with federal policies that allowed near-record levels of legal and illegal immigration, much of it of low-skilled workers, and severe anti-inflation policies that produced high levels of unemployment in the early 1980s, declining minimum wages put increasing pressure on the pay of lower-skilled workers.

Second, the 1980s were marked by increased competitive pressure in goods markets to lower costs, particularly labor costs, and the decline in communication and transportation costs allowed firms to locate production more cheaply in lower-cost labor markets. Just as important, however, the financial sector placed increased pressure on producers in the 1980s to increase profit margins. Big institutional stockholders, such as the large pension and mutual funds, grew tremendously in the 1980s and decreased the average period of share holding from seven years in 1960 to two years in the 1980s. The growth of pension funds and the aging of the U.S. population made more Americans identify with the value of their asset holdings, worry about the inflationary consequences of higher wages, and side with the financial sector in its drive for higher profit margins.

These competitive pressures and the pressure to increase profit margins produced an overwhelming emphasis on cutting labor costs and a downward shift in wage norms (Howell and Weiler 1996; Kochan, Katz, and McKersie 1986). Employers became more confrontational and took actions in labor disputes that might not have been politically acceptable in the past. By the mid-1980s, they also began to substitute temporary labor and part-time workers for permanent, full-time employees, effectively lowering average wages for similarly skilled workers—who often had more education—doing the same job.

The institutional argument is supported by two kinds of studies. The first shows that earnings inequality did not rise as much, especially at the low end of the earnings distribution, in countries such as Canada, France, and Germany that were exposed to similar changes in the relative demand for low-skilled workers (Freeman and Needels 1991; Freeman and Katz 1995). These studies conclude that rising minimum wages and the maintenance of more balanced bargaining power between employers and labor were crucial in keeping the wages of low-skilled workers from falling significantly in those countries.[18] The second measures the effect of the decline in unionization and the minimum wage on the increased inequality in wages in the United States in the 1980s (Card 1996; DiNardo, Fortin, and Lemieux 1996; Freeman 1993; Fortin and Lemieux 1996).

For example, in their 1996 paper, Nicole Fortin and Thomas Lemieux simulate the effect of changes in the minimum wage and in the rate of unionization by contrasting the actual wage distribution from CPS data with the counterfactual distribution that would have prevailed if the real value of the minimum wage had remained constant and by putting more weight on union workers than on nonunion workers in 1988 to simulate what would happen if unionization rates were switched back to their 1979 levels. They conclude that

> in the case of men, de-unionization and the decline in the minimum wage both played an important role in the rise in wage inequality. De-unionization contributed to the "disappearance" of the middle of the distribution while the fall in the minimum wage played a key role in the collapse of the bottom of the distribution. By contrast, de-unionization had little impact on the female wage distribution while the decline in the minimum wage reshaped dramatically the lower end of the distribution. . . . Labor market institutions played an even more dramatic role in

changes in the distribution of wages among the whole workforce (men and women together). We find that de-unionization and the erosion of the real value of the minimum wage account for 50 to 70 percent of the rise in wage inequality between 1979 and 1988. (Fortin and Lemiuex 1996, 1–2)

Both types of studies provide strong evidence that institutional settings and resulting government policies and firm behavior can affect not only income distribution but also the wages of certain groups of workers. These influences can be more powerful than the influence of technology; that is, they can fundamentally shape firms' wage strategies in the process of technological change. They can also shape organizational change associated with the introduction of high technology. Organizational change, in turn, is intimately linked with wage strategies, the development of "flexible" forms of production, and the constructing of meanings of competitiveness and profitability. Increased labor market flexibility therefore does not necessarily mean increased income inequality. Neither does more information technology mean lower wages for less educated workers. Although flexibility and computers have been intimately connected with declining wages for less skilled workers and higher wages for higher-skilled workers, countries such as the Netherlands have been able to achieve relatively low rates of unemployment by increasing labor market flexibility without increasing wage inequality. The U.S. and British labor market models are not the only game in town. Although many economists have tried to blame technological change (because of its differential effect on the demand for high- and low-skilled labor) for the increase in U.S. earnings inequality, enough evidence exists to show that at least part of the increase came from the government's minimum wage policy in the 1980s. This is borne out by the fact that in the late 1990s, marked by tight labor markets and increasing real minimum wages, earnings distribution in the United States tended to become somewhat more equal, reversing the trend of the previous twenty years. This, despite the continuing adoption of new technology.

The confusing link between flexibility, technology, and inequality has miscast the positive role of increased labor market flexibility and information technology in a political context that emphasizes greater earnings and wage equality. New technology and labor market flexibility are essential to new organizations of work that make firms competitive. The fact that in the U.S. political context, firms increased flexibility while reducing wages for less educated workers does not mean that firms in other political contexts, given the opportunity, would not be able to achieve greater flexibility without increasing wage inequality. The U.S. experience from 1992 to 1998—marked by rising real minimum wages, some restoration of balance to bargaining between unions and employers (Rothstein 1997), and a slight decline in income inequality from 1996 to 1998 but also continued moves toward greater labor market flexibility and increased use of information technology—suggests that an alternative exists.

Flattening Lifetime Income

Most analyses of changing labor markets focus on wage movements for workers with different levels of education. These changes by level of education are important because they affect a society's overall wage and income distribution. Business efforts to become more competitive also impact earnings in different age groups, however, and this occurs even in those countries in which governments pursue policies that keep wage distribution across education groups relatively stable. Much of the almost universal decline in labor force participation by older men during the past generation was based on worker preferences for earlier retirement. At least some came from the phasing out of OECD manufacturing in the face of competition from new entrants in the global market, such as newly industrialized countries in Asia and Latin America. Declining participation meant a more rapid and earlier downturn of average income for men. If a typical male worker expects that he will have to retire (leave the labor force) at age fifty-eight rather than at sixty-two, his expected income after age fifty-eight declines accordingly.

Labor turnover studies of the 1980s and 1990s suggest a new phase of this process. Even when workers face earlier retirement, they most generally assume that the company they work for at the age of forty-five will be the one they retire from. They also assume that between their mid-forties and their late fifties, their wages will rise to reflect their increased seniority and greater responsibility. In much of Europe, labor laws make this a reasonable assumption for workers whose industries or firms are not threatened with shutdowns or severe declines in sales. In the United States, however, and in the OECD's other more flexible labor markets, downsizing is becoming a regular part of work life. Older workers are especially vulnerable when firms "rationalize" their labor forces. Downsizing is largely a euphemism for reducing the number of "obsolete," higher-priced older employees, usually in their middle to late forties and early fifties, and replacing them with younger, more recently educated, and lower-wage workers.[19] Unlike their younger counterparts, older workers who have to find new jobs suffer longer periods of unemployment and sharp wage declines once reemployed. The costs of job loss for such older workers in terms of lost income are high. The Princeton economist Henry Farber estimates that the average real wage loss for a worker displaced from a full-time job and reemployed in a full-time job was about 10 percent in the early 1990s (Farber 1993). Along with the incomes of workers younger than thirty-five years of age, the incomes of middle-aged males declined in the United States from the mid-1970s to the mid-1990s. Not only did the wages of young age cohorts decrease, but the period of the average male worker's "prime" working life, defined by upward wage mobility, became shorter. This was apparently true for college as well as high school graduates, which means that even well-educated (highly skilled) workers are now subject to this broader meaning of job insecurity: as they reach middle age, workers experience not only shorter job tenure but also flattening or even declining incomes. Nevertheless, beginning in the mid-1990s, income flattening appears to have reversed, at least for prime-working-age workers, due mainly to the long economic expansion of the 1990s and the resulting tight labor market. Median earnings of young college graduates are now increasing, although they remain below salaries of thirty years ago.

These trends are reflected in the changing pattern of incomes for males with high school or college education from different age cohorts. One way to show these changes is to estimate mean incomes for those men who were twenty-five to thirty-four years of age (average twenty-nine years) in 1949, 1959, and 1969, and then in 1979 as they reached higher ages. The cohort that was twenty-nine in 1949 experienced a steep rise in real income that continued until they were forty-nine years old (in 1969) and dropped off when they moved into their fifties. The same holds true for the group who turned twenty-nine in 1959, but the drop-off in their fifties was steeper. My generation, the cohort that turned twenty-nine in 1969, had the highest starting point for their income profile but had a much flatter profile in their thirties and forties than the preceding two cohorts. This trend continued for the cohort that turned twenty-nine in 1979. As they reached the prime of their working lives in the 1980s, the profile of age and income for male high school graduates became nearly flat, and the profile for male college graduates continued to flatten relative to earlier groups (figures 3.7 and 3.8). However, in the 1990s, the trend reversed. Median earnings of male college graduates increased in the 1990s, although a thirty-nine-year-old in 1999 still earns less than in 1969 or 1979. Compared with workers in the 1980s, male high school- and college-educated workers are also earning more as they grow older. The question we cannot answer yet is whether the steeper earnings curves for men in their thirties in the 1990s will continue to be steeper as they reach their forties and fifties. Our guess is that they will not be as steep as in the 1960s because labor markets value older male workers less than in the past. The slope of the earnings curve for thirty-nine- to forty-nine-year-olds in 1989 to 1999 suggests this pattern.

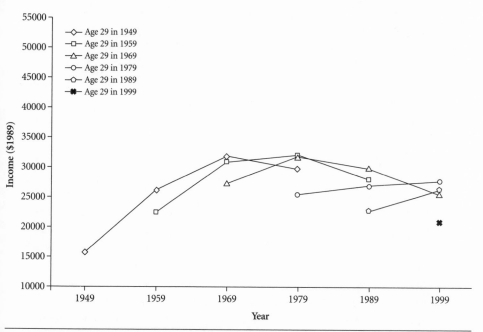

Figure 3.7. Longitudinal Age-Income Profiles, Male High School Graduates, United States, 1949 to 1999 *Sources:* Estimates from U.S. Department of Commerce, Bureau of the Census 1981a, 1981b, 1984, 1993, 1999.

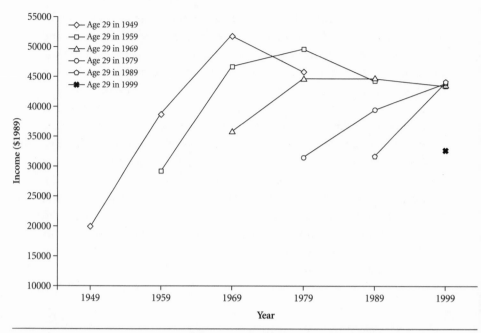

Figure 3.8 Longitudinal Age-Income Profiles, Male College Graduates, United States, 1949 to 1999 *Sources:* Estimates from U.S. Department of Commerce, Bureau of the Census 1981a, 1981b, 1984, 1993, 1999.

The Feminization of Labor Markets

Another big change in OECD labor markets in the 1970s and 1980s was the rapid increase in the presence of working married women. Part of this increase was the result of the expansion of the services industry, traditionally more feminized than manufacturing or construction. Another factor, one that gained momentum in the 1980s, especially in labor markets marked by greater flexibility, was women's move into professional and managerial jobs traditionally reserved for men (Carnoy and Gong 1996).

Married women enter the labor market more easily in more flexible markets for two main reasons. Many women opt for part-time work and flexible hours because, for better or worse, in OECD societies women are responsible for (unpaid) family-based activities. Historically, traditional full-time career jobs and job protection have been allocated to men. In the past, women got such jobs in a residual way, usually only in sectors associated with "women's work"—in schools and health care, white-collar service jobs, and certain blue-collar jobs (in the clothing industry, for example). In sectors in which relatively secure jobs are still generally held by men, (male) employers are less likely to hire women, except for jobs that are part time or temporary or both. If the only jobs available (owing either to legislation or to cultural norms) are full-time, permanent jobs, married women are less likely to be able to take them, and male employers are also less likely to consider women for them.

Between the early 1970s and the late 1990s, women entered the labor markets of most OECD countries in large numbers. This entry was characterized by five different patterns. The first can be called the rigid, traditional model. In Italy and Spain, for example, the ratio of employment to population remained relatively low for women, and the percentage of women working part time was low in 1973 in Italy and remained low at the end of the 1990s in both Italy and Spain (tables 3.2 and 3.3). Labor market rigidities kept women in traditional women's jobs, and almost all women worked in jobs that were called full time.[20] The second pattern, one of intermediate or low job growth, is one in which the proportion of women in the labor market did not increase rapidly, but the proportion of women working reached a high level and the proportion in part-time jobs reached an intermediate level. France and Germany are examples of this second pattern. The ratio of employment to population for women age twenty-

Table 3.2 Ratio of Employment to Population, Women, by Country, Various Years

Country	1979	1983	1990	1994	1995	1998
Australia	48.8	49.5	63.0	62.7	65.2	65.6
Denmark	—	76.8	80.3	75.2	75.9	77.7
France	59.5	61.9	65.1	66.6	67.5	68.0
Germany	53.3	53.7	59.6	65.8	66.3	67.6
Italy	36.2	38.8	43.5	43.1	47.0	48.6
Japan	55.2	58.1	62.9	63.4	63.2	64.0
Netherlands	33.0	38.0	51.6	59.8	61.3	67.1
Spain	28.9	29.4	37.2	38.9	40.2	44.8
United Kingdom	—	60.2[a]	68.6	69.3	69.5	71.7
United States	59.0	62.0	70.6	71.5	72.2	73.6

Source: OECD 1992, table H, 276; OECD 1996a, table B, 189; OECD 1999, table C, 234–36.
Note: Data are for women age twenty-five to fifty-four.
[a]1984.

Table 3.3 Part-Time Employment as Share of Total Employment, Women, Various Years
(Percentage)

Country	1973	1983	1990	1995	1998
Australia (A)[a]	28.2	41.8	44.1[b]	45.4	—
Australia (B)[a]	—	—	38.5[b]	40.2	40.7
Denmark	—	34.5	29.3	25.4	25.4
France (A)	12.9	17.6	19.6	22.3	—
France (B)	—	20.1	—	28.9	—
France (C)	—	—	21.7	24.3	25.0
Germany	24.4	—	29.8	29.1	32.4
Italy	14.0	16.4 ·	18.2	21.1	22.7
Japan[a,c,d]	—	29.5	33.2	34.7	39.0
Netherlands	—	44.7	52.5	54.7	54.8
Spain	—	—	11.5	15.9	16.6
United Kingdom	39.1	40.1	39.5	40.7	41.2
United States[c]	—	22.9	20.0	20.3	19.1

Source: OECD 1997a, table F, 178; OECD 1998a, table E, 240. Australia (A) and France (A): OECD
1997. France (B): OECD 1996a. Australia (B) and France (C): OECD 1997, table E.

Note: Part-time employment is defined as working less than thirty hours a week.

[a]Data refer to actual hours worked.

[b]1991

[c]Employees.

[d]Less than thirty-five hours a week.

five to fifty-four was about 60 percent in France and 53 percent in Germany in 1979 and rose to about 68 percent in both countries by 1998. Yet
the proportion of women working part time (less than thirty hours a
week) increased in France from 13 percent in 1973 to 25 or about 30 percent in 1998, depending on the data set; and in Germany, the proportion of
women who said they worked part time rose from 24 percent in 1973 to 32
percent in 1998. In countries with more flexible labor markets and moderate job growth, such as the United Kingdom and Australia, the ratio of employment to population for women increased rapidly in this period, but
the proportion taking part-time jobs was high and, in Australia, also rose
substantially. In countries, such as the United States, with flexible labor
markets and rapid job growth, the proportion of women of the same age
cohort in the labor market increased very rapidly (from 59 percent in 1979
to 73 percent in 1996), but the proportion working less than thirty hours a
week essentially remained constant at a relatively low 20 percent.

We see yet another pattern in the Netherlands, and this may presage the future in continental Europe. Like Italy, the Netherlands had relatively low female participation rates in 1979 (about 35 percent). Women's ratio of employment to population in Italy increased rapidly in the next nineteen years (from 36 percent to almost 49 percent), but the proportion of women working less than thirty hours a week stayed low, at about 23 percent. The Netherlands' ratio of employment to population rose from 33 percent in 1979 to 67 percent in 1998, and a major portion of these women entered the labor force in part-time work. In 1998, 55 percent of women in the Netherlands worked less than thirty hours a week, up from 45 percent in 1983.[21] The Dutch pattern represents an attempt to preserve a core "rigid, traditional" labor market while expanding job growth through part-time work.

Overall job growth and increased numbers of part-timers are not the only reasons for increasing women's participation. The Scandinavian countries provide state-supported child care as well as flexible labor hours and early on incorporated married women into many full-time jobs that had part-time characteristics. Flexible labor markets plus social services meant to support family flexibility allowed an increased proportion of women to enter the labor market—the higher the rate of growth of jobs, the lower the increase in the proportion of women entering part-time jobs and the higher the increase in the proportion of women taking full-time jobs. Even under those conditions, Finland's and Sweden's sharp slowdowns in economic growth in the late 1980s had a major negative effect on labor force participation by both men and women. Yet flexibility in the form of available part-time and temporary jobs contributes significantly to expanded women's labor market participation. So also does U.S.-style wage and hiring flexibility, with the added feature that in that pattern women are more likely to be absorbed into full-time jobs, and children are more likely to find themselves in low-quality child care or home alone (Fuller et al. 1997).

There is a flip side to this coin. Women have characteristically taken jobs when single, abandoned those jobs when they started a family, and tried to reenter the labor market when their children were all in school. Most find that they cannot get the same type of job and face lower pay than when they left work in their twenties. One popular response to this situation in the United States is to go back of school (usually postsecondary) to acquire a higher degree. This requires a flexible education system that allows adults to attend school. A large fraction of the new students in U.S. universities in the 1970s and 1980s were women, many above thirty years of age. Women have acquired an unusual degree of flexibility in moving on and out of the labor market and in acquiring the knowledge needed for social mobility.

Flexible Labor Markets: The Future Is Now

Labor markets have changed in the past thirty years. Flexible labor markets have permitted rapid expansion of jobs and the incorporation of vast numbers of new or returning workers (particularly married women), many of them in lower-wage jobs and many of them (again mainly women) in part-time work or in other forms of nontraditional labor contract. The result has been new jobs and women's incorporation into labor markets but not necessarily higher average real wages, especially for men. In many countries, new labor arrangements have meant higher labor turnover for men and more unequal wage distribution for both men and women. Although both doomsayers and free market optimists have blamed technology for the falling real wages of less educated workers, at least some of the evidence suggests that technology may be only one of the villains in that aspect of labor market change. The wage distribution in any society is undoubtedly affected by the apparent bias of new technology for more highly skilled labor. A more or less equal distribution, however, could also result from government policies regarding the minimum wage and from the power of unions in wage bargaining.

Increased labor market flexibility also has social implications. With flexibility, workers are individualized—separated from the social institutions that grew up around guaranteed, stable, long-term jobs. These institutions included the internal labor market in the firm itself (Cappelli 1997), the neighborhoods that developed around firms and industries, and labor unions. When firms are constantly reorganizing in a competitive environment, work tends to be stripped of its social meaning, such as its contribution to the culture of an organization or identification with the overall project of a firm, even in firms that invest in the teamwork of high-road flexibility. The firm itself is in constant flux.

This is particularly true for the increasing percentage of workers on nonstandard work contracts in OECD countries. Such workers are considered "task specific" rather than identified with the organization. They are individualized in part by the firm's conscious policy of separating them from the "work group." The job of the nonstandard, task-specific worker is to do rather than to be. At the same time that nontraditional contract workers are separated from the firm, they are also separated from the traditional networks of workers' associations and job-based benefit organizations. In today's economies, workers are pushed to operate in labor markets as individuals, disconnected from any single firm, from their neighbors, and from any labor organizations. Successful workers build individualized portfolios that can be marketed for a wide range of jobs and construct individualized information networks to do the marketing.

Because of its social impact, a flexible work environment needs an appropriate institutional support system. Traditional points of stability for workers have been the nuclear family and the neighborhood community. As I show in the following two chapters, however, the nuclear family and traditional community are also in the process of profound change. With that change they do not, on their own, have the capacity to reintegrate flexible workers. This is especially true because their traditional structures and roles are further stressed by flexible work. New institutions are needed, and indeed, some are already on the way.

---

1. For an early definition of transnationals, see Barnet and Muller 1974.
2. A major problem in jumping on the end-of-the-nation-state bandwagon is how to separate objective reality (for example, increased global financial flows, increased global trade within and between multinational companies, declining public employment) from an ideological position pushed by these same financial interests, multinational companies, the United States, and international organizations seeking to increase their power on the basis of a global economic order. According to Peter Evans, "The effect of a global ideological consensus (sometimes aptly labeled the 'Washington consensus') on individual states goes well beyond the constraints imposed by any structural logic of the international economy. . . . The economic logic of globalization does not in itself dictate eclipse [of the state]. While globalization does make it harder for states to exercise economic initiative, it also increases both the potential returns from effective state action and the costs of incompetence. Only when viewed through the particular prism of our current global ideological order does globalization logically entail movement toward statelessness. This global ideological order grows, in turn, as much out of the prejudices and ideologies of dominant global actors as out of any logic of interests" (Evans 1997, 72, 73–74).

3. The argument that demand for unskilled workers fell during this period and that this was the cause of wage declines for unskilled work is challenged by a number of economists. See, for example, Howell and Weiler 1998.

4. The proportion of men and women working less than twenty hours a week rose more rapidly in the Netherlands than in all other countries as well. See OECD 1998a, charts 5.1 and 5.2; see also OECD 1997a, appendix table F.

5. A well-documented case is the joint venture between Toyota and General Motors (GM) in Fremont, California, in which Japanese management took over a conflictive, low-productivity GM plant, employed the same unionized autoworkers, and transformed the operation into the most productive GM plant in the United States. See Brown and Reich 1989.

6. For national-level surveys, see U.S. GAO 1987; Lawler, Mohrman, and Ledford 1992; Osterman 1994. For nonrepresentative surveys, see Development Dimensions International 1990; Grant Thornton Accountants and Management Consultants 1991; Little 1992. The information in the surveys comes almost universally from managers and consultants, not from employees directly involved in the changes. The estimated degree of reorganization is therefore probably biased upward.

7. In another version of this analysis, Charles Derber argues that business is transforming itself in "two fundamentally contradictory directions." One is toward "cooperative capitalism," which uses the ideas of worker-centered cooperative work arrangements that emphasize security and training. The second moves toward "contingent capitalism," which emphasizes measures that reduce labor cost, including downsizing, moving operations offshore, wage reductions, and generally eliminating job security and training. See Derber 1994, 15.

8. Eileen Appelbaum and Rosemary Batt support these conclusions elsewhere with surveys of workers who are involved in innovations in three occupational groups (network craft workers, semiskilled office workers, and semiskilled machine operators) in two industries, telecommunications and apparel. They find that network craft workers benefit the most from innovations through greater autonomy and self-satisfaction, but they also have greater workloads (Batt and Appelbaum 1995).

9. For social problems associated with part-time work, see Warme, Lundy, and Lundy 1992.

10. Hewitt's interesting study is pointedly cited by Freeman and Soete 1994.

11. For an assessment of the decline of traditional unionism under new technological conditions, see Carnoy, Pollack, and Wong 1993.

12. For an empirically grounded elaboration on this theme, see Carnoy and Fluitman 1994.

13. Audrey Freedman of the Conference Board of New York is given credit for

originating the term in 1985 (Polivka and Nardonne 1989). Her definition, however, did not have the negative meaning that it has come to have in the 1990s. "Three years ago . . . I pointed out that a company can offer relatively stable employment to its core workforce only if that regular workforce can be augmented by many kinds of 'contingent' employment arrangements. This seems to have been the first time the phrase 'contingent employment' was used. It is a term that connotes conditionality. I described these conditional and transitory employment relations as initiated by a need for labor—usually, because a company has an increased demand for a particular service or product or technology, at a particular place, at a specific time" (U.S. Congress 1988, 35).

14. Chris Tilly finds that "until about 1970, the part-time growth trend was driven by expanding voluntary part-time employment, as women and young people desiring part-time hours streamed into the workforce. But since that time, the rate of voluntary part-time employment has stagnated, and the growing rate of involuntary part-time work has propelled the upward trend. Of the 3.3 percent increase in the rate of part-time employment between 1969 and 1993, 3 percent is accounted for by the growth in involuntary part-time work" (Tilly 1996, 14–15). An OECD survey of fifteen OECD countries indicates that 19 percent of workers were involuntarily employed part time (OECD 1999b, table 1.14). This figure varies from a high of 41 percent in France to 3 percent in the Czech Republic and 6 percent in Holland.

15. In Japan, where the unemployment rate is rising, the proportion of part-time workers (measured as those working less than thirty-five hours a week) rose from 20 percent in 1995 to 24 percent in 1998.

16. I was careful not to double count temporary workers who were also part-time workers.

17. A recent Field Poll of California workers confirms that job tenure is low (22 percent of employees with less than 1 year in the present job and 45 percent with less than 2 years, and only 21 percent with tenure of more than 10 years). Median amount of time on the job is 3 years, compared with the national average of 3.8 years, mainly owing to California's younger labor force. The much lower median U.S. job tenure (3.8 years), compared with the mean (6.7 years), better reflects how long most people have been in a job. See Ilana DeBare, "Poll Finds Mobile State Workforce," *San Francisco Chronicle,* April 30, 1999.

18. Other economists (See Robert Samuelson 1996, for example) claim that "shadow" income inequality is much higher in France and Germany if unemployment rates are taken into account. In other words, the earnings of low-skilled workers would fall if those employed would "share" the existing set of jobs with the unemployed.

19. One writer claims that the main reason for downsizing is to boost a company's

stock price: the stock market apparently values moves to lower the size of a company's labor force, on the assumption that most firms are overstaffed, keeping potential profits lower than possible (Downs 1995). Yet, Alan Downs also shows that these same companies usually hire large numbers of workers within a year of downsizing, because the original firings actually have a significant negative effect on productivity. The new workers, in turn, need to relearn all the skills and company culture that older workers already possessed. So the net effect seems to be replacement of older with younger workers.

20. Yet many so-called full-time jobs, such as teaching, are defined in Italy by only twenty to twenty-four hours a week at the job. In other countries, the same profession defines full-time work as thirty to thirty-six hours at the school site, making it more consistent with international definitions of full-time employment.

21. The percentage of Dutch men working part time also increased rapidly, from 5.6 percent in 1983 to 11 percent in 1996.

4

The New Family and Flexible Work

In the mid-1970s, my colleague, Henry Levin, and I interviewed hundreds of workers in Silicon Valley. We were trying to understand how the new high-tech workplaces might differ from more traditional industries. Quite accidentally, we learned about another, even more important phenomenon: a major change taking place in the relation between family and workplace.

One striking difference between the electronics industry and other manufacturing at that time was the number of women on the computer assembly lines and in the "clean rooms," the atmospherically controlled areas where computer chips are made. Following the invention of the printed circuit in the 1960s, women, because they commanded lower wages, had replaced high-skilled solderers on the electronics line. They pushed components into boards all day long. We wondered how women viewed this repetitive, often stressful work. Surprisingly, they seemed to love it. "I'm my own person here," one woman told us. Another said, "It gives me a paycheck independent of the old man's. I don't have to wait for him to decide how much I can have." A group of women on their lunch break laughingly recounted their even more repetitive home lives. "At least here, we have a social life," said one. "I have friends, conversation, other adults." Another woman commented, "Ever spend your whole day around kids? Then the only adult in your life expects you to take care of him, too?"

These conversations with semiskilled women workers made it clear to us that by 1975, at least in America, the family was hardly the idealized, romanticized institution of women's magazines, political rhetoric, or Sunday sermons. For factory workers, repetitive work was hard but could still be a rewarding respite from home life. Besides, it paid, and a paycheck meant power—purchasing power over consumer goods, independence from those who used to provide the household's only paycheck, and a sense of self-worth that housework and care of the family did not provide. In that sense, the conversations were hopeful.

There was, however, a darker side to what these women were saying. In the developed countries, the post–World War II family, for all its lack of equality between men and women, had been one of the foundations of a remarkable economic expansion and an even more remarkable educational expansion. By setting a standard of two parents, stable in their relationship, responsible for raising children and investing in their education, the postwar family had been successful in achieving some lofty goals. If this standard were collapsing, what would replace it?

Since we conducted these interviews, a lot more has changed. Global competition and the new work environment described in the previous chapter brought droves of married women into full-time work for reasons other than social life or a limited degree of financial independence. As the job tenure of working men became more uncertain and, in some countries such as the United States, as their real wages fell, wives and mothers took jobs to keep family consumption even or growing. For most women, combining work and family shifted from being a choice to a norm. For men, having a family also changed. It no longer meant coming home to a peaceful environment in which a housekeeper wife had taken care of domestic matters. This neat division of labor between men and women, which reached its height in the post–World War II welfare state, became increasingly rare. Couples today are more likely to raise children in the interstices of their common wage-working lives than in gender-divided social roles. Whether or not they want to, men who father children are much more likely now than in the past to be involved in domestic workplace stresses on a day-to-day basis, and women who become mothers are more likely to have to work full time as well as to assume most of the caretaking role for the family. To some extent families have always been sites of struggles over money; now, gender roles and time are added to the conflict. Many men and women are delaying or reconsidering family life altogether for just this reason.

The family and work are both as old as humankind. Work has always sustained the family. Families have been crucial to meeting the affective needs of both men and women and supporting the transition toward new forms of work. Ideally, the nurturing effects of family life are critical for psychological support, social stability, economic security, and creative socialization of young people entering the workforce. During major economic transitions, the ability of the family to adapt in producing new kinds of knowledge and skills needed in the new workplace is crucial to its success. Even the "ideal" family of legend and literature, however, was constructed on a foundation of highly unequal relations between men and women. Families were often (if not usually) held together by economic necessity rather than by love and affection. In every historical epoch, many, if not most, families were conflictive and provided little affective sustenance to its members. Physical and sexual abuse were commonplace.

The family "worked" to reproduce generation after generation of men and women who were able to "function" in human society. It worked also to produce new kinds of knowledge and to support men and women as they adjusted to changes in workplaces. Yet it did so as a highly imperfect institution, more often dysfunctional than the idealized stereotype invoked by religionists and politicians. Moreover, it did so at an enormous cost, largely borne by women, who were required to bear the responsibility for raising children as well as contributing to the family's economic viability.

Eventually women would rebel against their assigned role, a role that, for all the rhetoric extolling family life, was considered of low status by a male-dominated society. In that society, money and material gain reigned. By the time the current workplace transformation began in the 1970s, the latest round of this rebellion was in full swing. This is where Levin and I stepped in to conduct our interviews in Silicon Valley.

In the mid-1960s, the divorce rate began to rise dramatically. By 1975, one in three marriages in Santa Clara County, California, and in most of the rest of the United States was ending in divorce. Married women were coming to work in Santa Clara County's electronics industry in 1975, but not because their nuclear families particularly needed the money. Emerging from the family and going to work was a movement for identity: wage work gave these women a new self-definition. The income earned and their wage-earner status made them more powerful in their families and simultaneously allowed them to hedge against the possibility of going it alone, in the event their marriages failed. Working also redefined them socially. It gave them access to a life outside the claustrophobic confines of their culturally assigned family workplace, access to the same interactions so valued by men.

Independently of the advent of new technology or increased business competition, the women's movement fought for and began to win a profound transformation of gender relations both in the family and in the workplace. All this happened just before workplace organization and business practices began to change. However, like work transformations in the past, this one is putting great stress on families. In the United States, work transformation steadily eroded the wages of most men. By the 1980s, families in Silicon Valley and much of the rest of the United States could not move up the consumption ladder on one wage, or even a wage and a half. Single women who were heads of their households struggled to maintain themselves by working full time but earning only 60 to 80 percent of a man's pay for comparable work. Wives worked full time to help their families get ahead as their husbands' real wages stagnated or declined. In many parts of Europe, men's wages did not fall, but unemployment rates rose to record levels. As never before, these new stresses have come at a time when the family is going through some great changes on its own.

Unraveling the meaning of this combined process—the restructuring of both work and the family—for the 800 million men and women in the postindustrial countries is not easy. Many things are happening at once.

- The family is going through profound change. Women worldwide are demanding and winning new "rights," such as equal access to wage work (if not to equal wages) and a transformation of traditional relationships within the family. In all the developed countries, it appears that women today are much less willing to devote their lives to raising children than were women a generation ago, although family changes vary greatly among the developed countries. Southern Europe and Japan have much lower divorce rates and lower rates of women's participation in the labor force than northern Europe, the United States, Canada, Australia, and New Zealand. In southern Europe and Japan, fewer married women with children work, and women and men tend to stay within more traditional family structures. Are these differences part and parcel of durable cultural differences among societies, or are they temporary? Is there a relentless transformation in gender relations, whatever the current differences, that will reach into all developed societies to transform the family?
- Labor markets are also being transformed, and these changes also vary across countries. The variation seems to be related to changes (or lack of change) in the structure of the family. Are changes in the family be-

ing spread and hastened by the new transformations of the workplace? This raises the question whether the present moves by business to make labor markets more flexible are entwined with, or even dependent on, new, much more "flexible" families.

- The transformation in labor markets places new demands on families. To do well in flexible labor markets, workers need to have extensive information networks. Workers with more and better education are better able to adjust to change, have more access to information, and have larger networks and more choices. These demands of the flexible labor market favor highly educated parents, and affect both the parents themselves and their children. The networks needed for parents to be effective in flexible labor markets require more sophisticated decision making and organization than in the past. Families without the capacity to make informed decisions or the resources to act on them are still forced to be flexible, but in a much less sustainable fashion. Some countries have publicly subsidized systems of support for working parents that make it easier to work and simultaneously maintain a healthy family. I call this subsidized family the "public family." Other societies in this group rely heavily on the rapidly changing private family to raise children. Yet that does not seem to inhibit parents from working long hours anyway. Are new institutions required to support "new" families in a rapidly changing work environment? Will workplaces take on new functions to support the "new" family? Without new organizations aimed at helping families acquire these skills, can families be successful in the new environment?

With the sea change in work and families, the postindustrial society faces a brand new dilemma. Today's workplace demands well-informed, highly organized, stable families that can support workers and their children in a flexible work environment. The new work environment is marked by greater job instability. This means that family members are changing their work situations more often than in the past (and may suffer more frequent layoff periods), and job changes may mean acquiring new skills, hence more education. Future workplaces are likely to be even more flexible than those of today, so whatever pressure adults feel about their own need for more education is compounded by the educational needs of their children. All this adds up to a world in which family involvement in children's education is more important and complex than in the past.

It also adds up to enormous stress on the family. Anticipating these stresses, many young people have second thoughts about forming families, and those families that do form are likely to be more unstable. What results is a serious social contradiction: the new workplace requires even more investment in knowledge than in the past, and families are crucial to such knowledge formation, especially for children but also for adults. The new workplace, however, contributes to greater instability in the child-centered nuclear family, degrading the very institution crucial to further economic development.

One solution to this dilemma may be to maintain more traditional industrial-era job markets, in which one parent (traditionally, the man of the household) can earn a wage high enough to sustain a family, and labor markets are rigidly organized to protect those with jobs. The experience in countries such as Spain and Italy, however, where formal labor markets are still rigid, suggests that this solution does not work. For one thing, market rigidity is difficult to maintain in the face of global competition. Rigid labor markets organized around male workers also tend to ignore the struggle that women have waged for new identities, putting them under pressure on a second front. In addition, although empirical studies show little if any link between the degree of labor market rigidity and overall unemployment rates, rigidity may have unintended and highly undesirable consequences: labor market rigidity seems to contribute to higher youth unemployment and would therefore contribute to delayed marriage and lower fertility rates (OECD 1999b, chapter 2). Rigidity may also lower fertility rates even further because in male-run rigid markets, maternity leave apparently increases the risk for working women of permanent job loss. Thus, although labor market rigidity may still make life more peaceful at home by easing pressure on family time, it tends to reduce new family formation and increase tension because women are forced to maintain unsatisfactory, traditional roles.

Changes in the way women define their identity and the increased demands placed on the family by flexible production pose serious potential problems for the economies of developed countries that will have to be faced down the road. As labor markets in these countries inevitably become more flexible, incorporating more married women into wage-earning jobs and asking men to be more flexible in their schedules and often more dedicated to work, the adjustments in the way private structures, family, and the government support families will condition future labor productivity and political stability. Ironically, the societies with the least flexible labor markets today might be best positioned to move to greater flexibility in the future if they are able to maintain the private and public family support structures they have in place now. The societies with the most flexible markets today may be least well positioned to sustain flexibility unless they make drastic changes in family support systems.

Even more than in the past, the family in a flexible work system is a central hub of productive and reproductive activity. Because of the new demands placed on the traditional family by flexible labor markets, and because the traditional family as a social form is disappearing so quickly in developed countries, the family may have to be redefined, often with the help of the community and the state. Before thinking about the kind of help needed, we need to get a clear picture of how families are changing in various OECD countries. This is the task I take on in this chapter.

Work and Family: A Brief History

For millennia, the two central human activities of reproduction and production were unified under reproduction. Family members worked almost wholly to reproduce and maintain themselves. They organized themselves into families and clans to achieve that aim. Even today, in poor agricultural countries, most people engage in subsistence farming. Their work essentially involves providing shelter and raising enough food to feed their families. How that largely reproductive work became divided into different activities based on gender is a crucial part of the story of work and the family. It has important implications for what we are witnessing today all over the world as women undo thousands of years of being defined by certain work and family roles.

When work became more connected with employment and wages, work and family became separate activities, defined mainly by gender. By the nineteenth century, men in the industrializing countries had won the battle for the "family wage," defined as sufficient pay for a man to sustain a family without the necessity of his wife's working for pay. It was many years before average pay was high enough to make the family wage a meaningful reality, but by the turn of the twentieth century, only about 10 percent of women in the United States and Europe were in the labor force. The other 90 percent worked at and around the home. Because men worked long hours producing goods in factories or selling them, and then spent additional hours with other males in leisure activities, they were not home much. Reproduction was now formally separated from production, and reproductive work from productive work. The separation was based almost entirely on a gender-based division of labor.

Informally, however, the institution of the family was still crucial to work because it allowed employers to count on men to work where and when needed and to count on women to raise the next crop of male wage workers and female home workers. Much of the literature about nineteenth-century life expresses concern as to whether men could be made responsible enough to allow women to maintain their families.[1] The tension between exploiting men at the workplace and keeping children above the line of abject poverty and moral degradation is a central theme of the Industrial Revolution. That said, it should be added that families also provided psychological sustenance to both men and women in what was often a harsh world. Even when work was physically difficult and there was little time for leisure, there was always the love of the children. Children were increasingly valued in and of themselves rather than as sources of income and wages or protection against destitution in old age (Aries 1962).

Michael Young and Peter Willmott (1973) characterize the family as passing historically through three stages: Stage one defined the family as a "production unit,"[2] in which all members worked in the home, farm, or small-scale home factory, doing home work, market work, and raising children. Men and women were totally dependent on one another, and the home was the center of all activity, including income-generating activity. In stage two, this home-centered family broke down, with disastrous consequences for women. Both men and women (and children) were employed outside the home, but when there were young children in the home, women could not work, and men controlled income. There was little incentive for men to limit the number of their children because they could still keep control of income, and children could go to work at a young age for additional family wages. Women suffered the most, and children almost as much. In *Angela's Ashes*, Frank McCourt writes of a much later time, in the 1930s, when the vestiges of this life still hung on for poorer families:

When Dad's job goes into the third week he does not bring home the wages. On Friday night we wait for him and Mam gives us bread and tea. The darkness comes down and the lights come on along Classon Avenue.

Other men with jobs are home already and having eggs for dinner because you can't have meat on Friday. . . . She sits at the kitchen table talking to herself. What am I going to do? Till it's late and Dad rolls up the
stairs singing Roddy McCorley. He pushes in the door and calls for us,
Where are my troops? Mam says, Leave those boys alone. They're gone to
bed half hungry because you have to fill your belly with whiskey.
(McCourt 1996, 25)

This stage began to change with an important, and little discussed, phase
of women's efforts to gain control over their bodies and their time. At the
end of the nineteenth century, middle-class women began to understand
their fertility cycles and simply refused their husbands sex during periods
of greatest fertility. The practice spread slowly, and this form of contracep-
tion, combined with the use of condoms, child labor laws, and compulsory
schooling, which made it increasingly costly to have children, reduced family size even before World War I. Families became smaller, emulating a
trend in the increasingly well-off middle class. Women's liberation movements at the end of the nineteenth century also won women the right to
leave men who abused them.

The smaller family of the late nineteenth and early twentieth centuries
gradually led to married women's returning to the workforce after the
twenty years or so that it took to raise all the children to the working age of
fourteen. Although the percentage of married women active in the wage
labor market was small in the 1920s, it rose until the Great Depression. The
other factor that changed the family was technology—electric refrigera-
tors, stoves, washing machines, and home tools that revolutionized home
work and actually made it more interesting for men to come home and do
things around the house. Fewer children and higher wages made the home
more pleasant. Families had money to spend on goods they did not actually need to sustain themselves. The family increasingly became a center
of activity for men as well as women, with men and women forming a consumption partnership around the home and the family. Young and
Willmott see the family as crucial to the expansion of the domestic economy in the industrial stage of development, and increased consumption of
consumer durables as its main new function. Thus, rather than just reproducing sources of cheap labor for industrial expansion (as at stage two)—
at the expense mainly of women, who were responsible for that reproduction, while men led essentially separate lives—in stage three, which devel-

oped to its height after World War I, men and women were partners in consumption. Many thought that because this modern family unit was freed from the need to work collectively, it could focus more on spiritual, noneconomic needs and concerns and would become a more democratic union among life companions (Calhoun 1919, cited in Ehrenreich 1983, 4). This stage reached its highest point in the 1950s and 1960s and gives us the model for the "traditional family" extolled today by neoconservatives in almost every country.

Young and Willmott miss two important points about the stage three family. First, it was not only a consumption family but an investment family, investing in its children so that they could earn more than their parents and move up the consumption ladder. This investment role became increasingly important in the post–World War II period, spreading from upper-middle-class families down to the working class. Although welfare state support for families began originally in the 1930s in order to maintain consumption, this role became subordinated to maintaining and enhancing the family's investment role in producing sources of ever more productive labor for the more flexible, competitive economy.

By the 1980s, with flexible production and the increasing importance of education in determining access to high-paying jobs, the investment role became even more important. As both parents worked longer hours, even when the children were young, parents were likely to consume all kinds of services that had been available only to higher-income families in the past, and, in the best of cases, such services have large investment components that enhance the health and learning of children. In Europe and now Japan, child care, preschool, and especially health care are provided by the state and subsidized precisely because of the state's concern with the family's investment role. Families themselves—particularly mothers—want more of these publicly provided services both because they need a break from child rearing and because they believe that children learn better in such collective environments.

The second point that Young and Willmott could not foresee in the early 1970s was that even as it reached its apex, the stage three family was already in the process of transformation. The consumption partnership formed in part because the trend of smaller families and higher incomes was already dissolving as they wrote. Women wanted broader options, including participation in the social world defined by work, and greater decision-making power over the larger shape of family life, including the division of family labor. Women's increased access to jobs offered them possibilities to gain some economic independence from men. As divorce rates increased, women were even more compelled to work for wages in order to protect themselves financially in the event of a family breakup and its consequent loss of income.

The Transformation of the Family

The transformation we observe in the traditional family of developed countries is inherently, as the feminist literature defines it, a crisis of patriarchy—a weakening of the family unit based on the economic and moral control of an adult male.[3] A decade ago, economists Samuel Bowles and Herbert Gintis saw the phenomenon as a struggle by women for democracy in the authoritarian family "site" (Bowles and Gintis 1985). Feminist writer Barbara Ehrenreich has made a case, also more than a decade ago, that the transformation was a result not only of women's revolt against men's domination but of the "collapse of the breadwinner ethic," a revolt by men against the expectation that they would distribute their higher incomes to women and children through the family wage system. In Ehrenreich's words, "Men still have the incentives to work and even to succeed at dreary and manifestly useless jobs, but not necessarily to work for others" (Ehrenreich 1983, 12).

Sociologist Arlie Hochschild, in her detailed look at the conflict between work and family in a large American corporation, characterizes this transformation as the increasingly complex relation between what men and women feel about raising a family and their need to seek satisfaction from work outside the home. As women fight for a different range of choices and much more control over how the family is defined, and men cope with this reality, family life takes on a very different meaning for both men and women. "In this new model of family and work life," she writes, "a tired parent flees a world of unresolved quarrels and unwashed laundry for the reliable orderliness, harmony, and managed cheer of work" (Hochschild 1996, 44).

The ever increasing entry of women into the labor force in most OECD countries and the formation of the two-wage-earner family has a tremendous impact on individual families. So does the increased ability and willingness of men and women to undo marriages (see Cherlin 1981). The family loses the stability provided by having the activities of one member—usually, the woman—centered in the home, accepting a single source of wage earnings that is not hers. Two separate individual projects and two separate working schedules make the compatibility of the individual work projects and the family project more difficult in the longer run. Women's rising wage contribution to family income increases their bargaining power in the family and undermines the political structure of the traditional patriarchal family.

No surprise, then, that the interaction of social forces producing these changes is having a measurable impact on what we call the family. The measurable impact is only the tip of the iceberg, however. It hardly touches the psychological and social effects, expressed in Hochschild's interviews; but it does reveal a process of change moving across countries.

Data for the developed countries show three significant changes:

- Marriages were much more likely to dissolve in 1990 than in 1960. True, divorced people often remarry (and redivorce). The fact that marriages are more likely to be "temporary" arrangements, however, and that more marriages are recombinations of previously married people redefines the meaning of the family.
- The increased difficulty in making marriage work, the increased participation of women in professional life, the apparently decreased willingness of men to enter into marriage, and now, in the 1990s, the greater insecurity surrounding work have all delayed marriage and child rearing, have increased the prevalence of partnerships without marriage, and have greatly reduced women's fertility rates. Birthrates have fallen below population reproduction levels in most of Europe and Japan.
- Later marriage and reduced rates of marriage and child rearing, in combination with more divorce, more single parenting, and an aging population, have meant that in 1990, a smaller percentage of the population lived in a nuclear family household headed by a married couple than in 1960.

Just as interesting as these trends is the way they vary across countries. At one end of the spectrum among major OECD countries, Italian and Spanish families are much more likely to conform to the traditional pattern of a nuclear family, but they now have very few children. At the other end of the spectrum, the structures of United States and Scandinavian families have changed the most, with high divorce rates and proportionately much fewer nuclear families. Birthrates in the 1980s and 1990s were much higher in the United States and Scandinavia than in Italy and Spain, however. The Swedish rate dropped in the mid-1990s but still remains above the low levels in southern Europe. Other countries are spread out in between. In the United Kingdom, the birthrate is nearer to that of the United States and Scandinavia, whereas France, Germany, and particularly Japan have lower birthrates, closer to those of Italy and Spain.

There is also variation among different groups within countries. For example, in the United States, immigrant families from Mexico and Asia tend to be more traditional: they have more children, lower divorce rates, and are more likely to live in extended families. In Europe, immigrants, mainly from North Africa, also live in more traditional families than people who have grown up in Europe.

Even so, younger women in the countries at the more traditional end of the spectrum, such as Spain or Italy, or from immigrant groups behave toward family life in ways similar to nonimmigrant women in the United States. They delay marriage and pregnancy, they want to work rather than stay home, and if, after having children, they can get a job, they arrange for day care (often with the mother's parents) rather than spend all their time taking care of children themselves. The sharp drop in fertility to extraordinarily low levels in Italy and Spain is another sign that traditional family life is changing radically and that women's (and, to some extent, men's) conceptions of family life are being transformed everywhere in the developed world. This implies that many of the differences in numbers among countries may reflect the behavior of older women who, unlike older non-immigrant American women, tend not to divorce even if unhappy in marriage. The differences may also reflect certain economic factors, such as children staying home to much higher ages than in the United States because they cannot get jobs. Nuclear families are a larger proportion of families in such situations, partly because high unemployment among youth prevents young people from moving out and living alone.

Divorce increased in all OECD countries beginning in the mid-1960s and the early 1970s. In some countries, divorce and even multiple divorces in individuals' lives became commonplace. There were, and continue to be, major differences between countries. The United States and Scandinavia had divorce rates in the mid-1960s that were already higher than 1990 rates in Italy or Spain. In 1965, Denmark, for example, registered fifteen divorces for every hundred marriages; the rate in the United States was even higher, at about twenty divorces per hundred marriages. Rates in the United Kingdom, France, and West Germany were lower, at about ten divorces per hundred marriages, and Italy, Spain, Japan, and Portugal all saw fewer than five divorces for every hundred marriages.

No matter where they started out in the 1960s, divorce rates increased in every one of these societies. Increases began earlier in some countries than in others, however, and rose much faster in some than others. Figures 4.1 and 4.2 illustrate the trends. Crude divorce rates, as measured by divorces per one hundred marriages, began rising first in the United States, then in Scandinavia, the United Kingdom, and Germany in the late 1960s, reaching the highest European levels in Denmark and Sweden. By the mid-1980s, more than one in every two marriages in the United States ended in divorce, and in Denmark and Sweden, almost one in every two. Rates in other countries, such as the United Kingdom, also rose very rapidly, reaching Danish and Swedish levels in 1985 from a much lower starting point. By 1995, the divorce rates in France and Germany had risen to more than

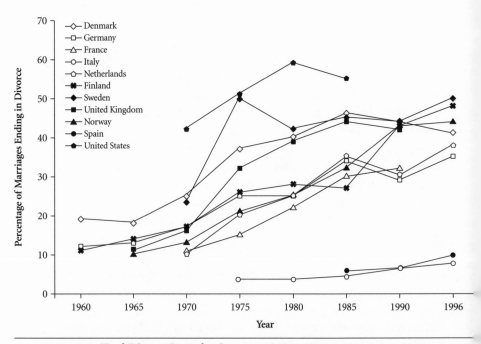

Figure 4.1 Total Divorce Rates, by Country, 1960 to 1996 *Source:* Eurostat 1999, table F-20. United States: Bruce, Lloyd, and Leonard 1995.

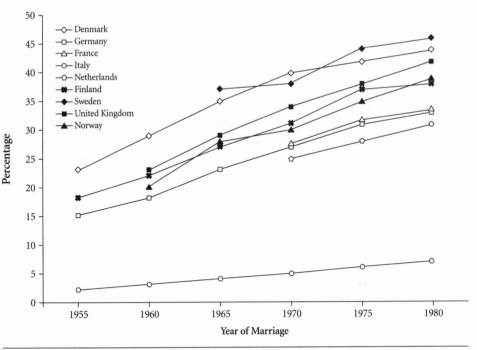

Figure 4.2 Share of Marriages Ending in Divorce, by Year of Marriage, 1955 to 1980 (Percentage) *Source:* Eurostat 1999, table F-22.

30 percent. Despite changes in divorce laws in Italy and Spain, divorce rates there also rose, although slowly, and they remained relatively low even in the 1990s.

Divorce rate increases were driven by two main factors, the first of which was economic. The average family income in most of these countries had reached high levels by the 1960s, and in other countries, farther south, by the 1970s and 1980s. Although women often pay a high price for divorce, in that they usually carry the financial and emotional responsibilities for raising the children, high-income societies provide much greater possibilities for women to absorb the cost of separation. In higher-income economies women are much more likely to find wage employment and to obtain government help in the form of welfare and child care or other family support, in addition to whatever they can collect from their former husbands.

The second factor was women's changing conception of themselves and their rights within their families. Whether because of an increased sense that women could leave unhappy marriages or, as Ehrenreich argues, because of men's unwillingness to tolerate women's demands for greater rights, the rate at which marriages dissolved shot up in the 1970s and 1980s in countries in which divorce was legal. It lost much of its social stigma, no matter how traumatic it continued to be at a personal level. In places in which divorce was illegal, such as in the Catholic countries of southern Europe, women organized massive movements to change the law.

The overall cultural view of the family and its place in society does, however, shape how women and men interpret their marriages, their relationships with their children, and the institution of marriage. This is especially true for older men and women in the more traditional societies. Even when divorce laws changed, the older generation of women and men who grew up and married before the 1970s in places such as Italy, Spain, and Japan is apparently more likely to stay with their traditional roles in ways women and men in the United States or Scandinavia, for example, are not.

Is this changing in the traditional countries? Is the process of transformation in gender relations bound to incorporate men and women everywhere into a view of marriage that is close to the American or Swedish model? A careful look at the data suggests such change as a likely scenario. Although there is some indication that the divorce rates have stabilized in some European countries (those with moderate to high divorce rates) and in the United States, they have neither declined nor stabilized in southern Europe. Italian and Spanish rates continued to rise into the 1990s. Although divorce rates there remained at relatively very low levels, rates of legal separation appeared to increase rapidly after 1985. In Spain, for example, whereas the divorce rate rose from 9 to 13 percent from 1985 to 1991, the separation rate increased from 12 to 19 percent. Divorce and separation now characterize well over a third of all Spanish marriages (Alberdi 1994).

Fewer Marriages, Later Marriages, Smaller Families

Increased divorce rates are only one aspect of the decline of intact traditional nuclear families. People have to get married to form traditional families. Some would argue that a couple living together with their children is a sufficient condition for calling them a family. In societies that still consider formal marriage as an indicator of commitment between adults, however, such arrangements usually imply less commitment to permanent cohabitation and to the couple's children.

The rates of first marriages in the population declined steadily in all OECD countries between 1960 and 1985 and have risen only slightly since. Among European Union countries marriage rates fell most in Denmark, France, England, and the Netherlands, with French rates dropping to the lowest levels. Rates also fell in countries such as Italy and Spain, especially after 1975 (Alberdi 1994, figure 2.1). In France, first-marriage rates in the population of adult men and women in 1990 were about one-half what they were in the early 1960s; in Denmark and Italy, they were about 60 percent of the earlier rates. These are enormous drops in one generation and reflect, among other things, a much greater reluctance on the part of individuals to commit themselves to marriage at any age.

The average age of first marriage is also rising, albeit slowly, and much more in the richer northern European countries than in the south, where the rate generally started out higher than in the north and declined until ten years ago. In Germany and France, for example, men married at an average age of twenty-seven in 1960, and women at twenty-four. After declining by one year in Germany and two years in France, average age at first marriage increased, beginning in the mid-1970s, to more than twenty-eight years for men and twenty-six years for women by 1990. Italian and Spanish men and women also marry relatively late—twenty-eight years of age for men and twenty-five for women—though this has declined slightly since 1960. American and British young people marry about a year younger than their continental counterparts. Again, the age curve is U-shaped between 1960 and 1990, falling until 1970 and then rising.

The higher age at first marriage in lower-income OECD countries in 1960 was partly the result of economics: married couples prefer to live apart from their parents, and affording a separate place to live is more difficult in lower-income countries. So couples wait longer to marry. The recent rise in marriage age in most OECD countries, however, is related more to women's new role in labor markets and, in Europe, to the difficulty for young people in getting any job at all. By the late 1970s, many more single women were entering work careers that prompted them to delay having children, hence to delay marriage. In the United States, the fastest growing group among women are those who have their first child between thirty and thirty-five years of age. The average American woman still marries before the age of twenty-five and has her first child in her early twenties; but this group is declining proportionately, whereas the cohort of women who have their first children after the age of twenty-five is increasing proportionately. Besides women's move into careers, the difficulty in getting a job in some European countries makes young people further postpone marriage and childbearing.

There is an important caveat to the connection between age of first marriage and childbearing. In some countries, such as Denmark, Sweden, Norway, France, and Great Britain, the proportion of births recorded to unwed mothers has increased phenomenally since the 1960s. As late as 1975, the figure in France, Great Britain, and Norway was only 8 percent. By the 1990s, it had climbed to almost a third of all births. In Denmark and Sweden, the proportion of births to unwed mothers was already somewhat higher than in the rest of Europe in the 1960s. By 1990, almost half of Danish and more than half of Swedish births were out of wedlock. Nearly all OECD countries showed an increase in such births during this period, but even by 1990, the rate in most remained below 10 percent.

Why more out-of-wedlock births? One reason is that couples living together decide not to marry yet have a child together (and eventually get married). Another is that a woman who is not married or even living with a partner may want to have a child. Teenage girls are more likely to have children without getting married in societies that are losing the tradition of "forcing" the father of the child to marry the young woman. In Denmark, France, and Sweden, having a child out of wedlock does not prevent the mother or the couple from receiving full family benefits, including a child subsidy, continued schooling, and high-quality, publicly subsidized child care. This has almost certainly contributed to the boom in extramarital births. Even so, most couples with children, even in freewheeling Scandinavia, get married eventually (or separate). In the United States family benefits are much more limited, but until recently, unwed mothers could qualify for welfare payments without working, and many urban U.S. high schools now provide day care for teenage mothers, whether married or not. Despite protests from many conservative groups who claim that any government program that implicitly sanctions out-of-wedlock parenting should be stopped, the numbers of children born to unwed mothers are just too large to be explained away by the easy access to government assistance.

Yet delaying marriage still tends to reduce family size. Families today (whether or not the couple is married, and whether or not the mother lives alone with her children) have far fewer children than families in the past. In many countries, the decline in the average number of children born to women between the ages of fifteen and forty-four has been spectacular (see table 4.1). This has been as true for Mediterranean countries as for those in northern Europe, the United States, or Japan. For example, the average fertility rate in 1960 in West Germany was about 2.4; in France, 2.7; in Great Britain, 2.7; in Italy, 2.4; in Spain, 2.9; and in Sweden, 2.2. By 1997, many of these had fallen to 1.5 or below, and all saw substantial declines. By the mid-1990s, the fertility rate in Spain and Italy had fallen to 1.2, the lowest in Western Europe. In northern Italy, fertility rates are now hovering around 1.0 birth per woman. In Japan, fertility rates have also fallen, to an average of 1.4 births per woman. There is real concern in all these countries about population size and the demographic shift to much older populations because of these low birthrates. The Swedish rate in 1990 reflects increases in all the Scandinavian countries in the late 1980s, largely the result of government subsidies designed specifically to promote larger families. When these were cut in the mid-1990s by government austerity policies and employment rates among youth rose, fertility fell again.[4] The United States rate reflects the baby boomer generation coming into childbearing age and the fact that many of the new immigrants continue to have large families.[5] For Japan and most European countries, immigration encounters strong political opposition, suggesting that the population in the European Union may well fall substantially in the next twenty years.

Fewer first marriages, later first marriages, and fewer children per family

Table 4.1 Projected Fertility Rates, by Country, Various Years

Country	1960	1970	1980	1990	1997
Denmark	2.4	2.0	1.6	1.7	1.8
France	2.7	2.5	2.0	1.8	1.7
Germany	2.4	2.0	1.6	1.5	1.4
Italy	2.4	2.4	1.6	1.3	1.2
Japan	—	—	1.8	1.5	1.4
Netherlands	3.1	2.6	1.6	1.6	1.5
Spain	2.9	2.9	2.2	1.3	1.2
Sweden	2.2	1.9	1.7	2.1	1.5
United Kingdom	2.7	2.4	1.9	1.8	1.7
United States	3.6	2.5	1.8	2.1	2.1

Source: Eurostat 1997a, 66, annex 1; Eurostat 1997b, 70; Eurostat 1999, table E-9.

Note: Total fertility is defined as the number of children a woman age fifteen to forty-four would be expected to have in her lifetime, given the fertility rate in that year.

mean that the task of raising children occupies men and women in the prime of their lives far less than in the past. Even if women do not work while their children are growing up, they now spend an average of fourteen years preoccupied with young and preteen children. Men, in turn, even when they are the sole source of family income and stay married for life, have less costly families than in the past, and families that divert them less from other activities. Family life with children is a much less central adult activity in our societies than it was thirty years ago. We may think and talk about the ideal of family life—husband, wife, and children living together, with both parents focused on raising the children—as much as in the past, but our reality is quite different. We are gradually relegating the upbringing of children to a secondary role in our lives.

The Changing Family Structure

The decline in fertility combines with greater longevity to reduce the proportion of the population living in nuclear families (married couple with children). This still varies considerably even among the highly developed and globalized economies of the OECD. The reasons for the variation are several. Most important, the social and cultural milieu in which family decisions are made differs from country to country. This is especially true regarding women's and men's views of marriage and divorce, living in an "extended family" (with or near the couple's parents), and whether a married woman with children should work. Although this milieu has changed drastically in all OECD countries in the past thirty years, differences still exist. Furthermore, economic conditions vary. Unemployment rates are much higher in some parts of Europe. Youths have an especially hard time getting a job, so many remain unmarried and continue to live with their parents. Finally, social policies concerning public child care and family payments differ from country to country.

Family structure in all the postindustrial countries is marked by certain changes consistent primarily with the flight of younger men and women from the traditional nuclear family (including the rapid disappearance of the extended family) and by the consequent individualization and isolation of adults. It varies, however, because not all societies have reached the same stage in the willingness of couples to break up marriages, and not all societies have reached the same degree of isolation of young adults from their parents. Societies also vary in their capacity to employ young people, in their labor market policies, and in their family policies, all of which affect family structure.

In northwestern Europe and in the United States, divorce rates are high and participation of married women in the labor force has risen substantially since the early 1960s. Contrary to the United States, northwestern European countries nearly all provide a network of supportive state and community institutions to families, such as long postpartum family leaves, accessible high-quality day care, good public schools and after-school care for primary-school children, and good local public transportation. These countries are also characterized by a relatively high percentage of people still living in small cities and towns. All this provides a "public family" that is able to socially integrate children as an extension of a transformed "private family."

In southern Europe and Japan, average divorce rates are relatively low but rising, participation of married women in the labor force tends to be lower than in northern Europe and the United States, public day care and other family support is much more readily available than in the United States but less so than in the most "public family" countries such as Scandinavia, and the traditional role of grandparents in family life is much greater than in the rest of the OECD. Youth unemployment rates are also much higher in countries such as Spain and Italy. This affects marriage rates, living arrangements, and fertility.

To illustrate this variation, in figures 4.3 and 4.4 I estimate the share of families in five countries that are living in traditional nuclear families, extended families, and other forms of family structure in the 1990s and in about 1980. At one end of the spectrum are Denmark and the United States, which have gone through big changes in the past generation and in which only a small minority of adults live in a traditional nuclear or extended family. At the other end of the spectrum are Spain and Japan, which are also going through changes but still remain fairly traditional.

In 1970, more than 40 percent of U.S. households were composed of married couples with children. By 1995, this percentage had fallen to one-quarter. More than half (54 percent) of all Americans in 1995 still lived in a nuclear family, meaning a married couple with or without children, but that was down from 70 percent in 1970 and 75 percent in 1960 (U.S. Bureau of the Census 1992, 1996). One-fourth of Americans were living as singles in 1995, up from 13 percent in 1960 and 17 percent in 1970.

Further down the spectrum, about one-half of all Danes in 1997 lived in

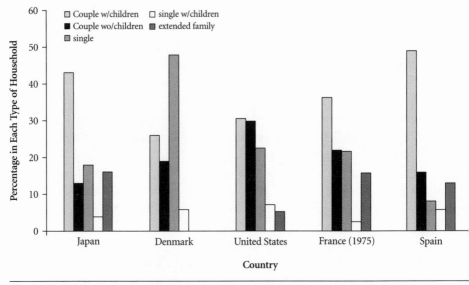

Figure 4.3 Family Structure, by Country, 1975 to 1980 *Sources:* Denmark: Danmarks Statistik, Socialforskningsinstitutet 1992, table 4.4. France: INSEE 1996, 298. Japan: Ministry of Social Welfare 1997. Spain: Alberdi 1994, chapter 2. United States: Castells 1997, figures 4.12a and 4.12b.

single-person families, and 45 percent lived within a nuclear family. Only 22 percent of Danes, whether married or not, had children under the age of eighteen in the household, and only 14 percent were married with children. Even if we add unmarried couples with children, the figure is only 18 percent. Excluding adult children (above the age of eighteen) living at home underestimates the total number of married and unmarried nuclear families by as much as 8 percentage points, but this still means that the "traditional" nuclear family of a married couple with children of any age represents a maximum of about one in five families in Denmark.

At the other end of the spectrum, the composition of Spanish households has also changed, but much less so than in the United States or Denmark. The dominant living arrangement in Spain, as in the United States, is the nuclear family. In 1970, almost 70 percent of Spaniards lived within a married-couple family, with or without children, and in 1991, the figure had dropped only slightly, to 65 percent. Of this proportion, about one-fourth in 1991 were married without children. This means that somewhat less than one-half (48 percent) of all Spanish households consisted of mar-

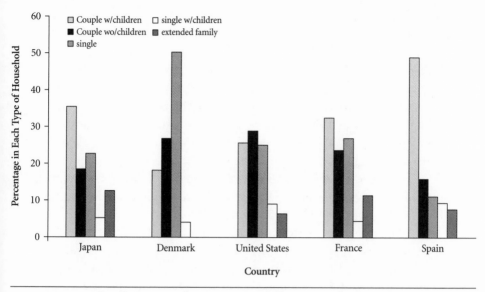

Figure 4.4 Family Structure, by Country, Mid-1990s *Source:* Denmark: Danmarks Statistik, Socialforskningsinstitutet 1997, table 75. Other countries: see figure 4.3.

ried couples with children, almost double the U.S. proportion. This was down from about 53 percent in 1970 (Alberdi 1994, 149-55).

One reason for the slow decline in the category of married couple with children is high youth unemployment. Because young people cannot get jobs, they continue to live with their families well into their twenties and even early thirties. In the 1990s, the average age at which a Spanish child left his or her parents' household was about twenty-eight. The family is assisted in this arrangement by "indirect" government assistance. Many Spanish (and European) men in their late fifties are already generously pensioned and can continue to support a family. Publicly provided medical care is also available through the family to all members in the household, regardless of age. Beyond these incentives for children to stay at home, in Spain (and Italy and even France), it is culturally acceptable for children in their twenties to live with parents, well beyond the age at which parents need to care for them. Although many Spanish parents may live in households with children, a high proportion of them have little parental child-rearing responsibilities beyond helping their children financially.

If we adjust for the fact that in about one-third of Spanish nuclear families all the children are above eighteen years of age, and if, instead, we count only families with minor children, only 32 percent of Spanish families could be called nuclear, not much more than in the United States. The family categories that have grown most rapidly are the same as those in the United States: individuals living alone and households headed by single parents. Single-parent households in Spain increased from 6 percent of all households in 1981 (there was no measure of this category in 1970) to almost 10 percent in 1991, a figure that is even higher than in the United States. Between 1970 and 1991, the number of individuals living alone increased from 7 to 11 percent of all households, still far lower than the 25 percent in the United States. These last two figures can also be accounted for, at least in part, by the tendency of adult children in Spain to continue to live in the households of their parents.

Thus, the direction of change in Spanish households is the same as in the United States, but the household structures remain far different. In Spain, the married couple with children remains the dominant form of family life, in part for economic reasons. At the same time, we see the structural changes occurring in Spain that have so transformed American families: older people tending to live alone rather than in extended families, more unmarried people living alone, more households headed by single parents, and more married couples living together but without children.

The family trends in France are similar to those in the United States and Spain but fall somewhere between the two. Even in 1968, only 36 percent of French families could be considered nuclear families. By 1990, this figure had dropped to 33 percent, a slow decline. One reason that a higher percentage of French families are nuclear families rather than couples living without children is that their children, like those of Spain, tend to stay in the family until a much later age than adult children in the United States. At least part of the slower French decline in nuclear families can be explained by rising unemployment rates and the increased probability that older children in France live at home.[6]

The data also show that no matter how much the French family shares this commonality with Spain, many fewer French than Spaniards live in nuclear families, and more French than Spaniards live as couples without children. The proportion of couples without children in France rose from 1968 to 1990, from 21 to 24 percent of family units or families, about twice the Spanish proportion. More men and women live alone in France than in Spain, at a level similar to that in the United States. The percentage of those living alone in France also rose from 1968 to 1990, from 20 to 27 percent of families (INSEE 1996, 298). The share of extended (complex) French families declined from almost 20 percent to 12 percent, about the same as the level and decline in Spain, and that of single-parent families increased from a low 2.9 percent of all families in 1968 to a still low 4.5 in 1990. This suggests that the changes in family structure happening elsewhere are also happening in France, and they are fairly close to the changes in the United States, though they are not quite as rapid or as acute. There is no denying, however, that a much smaller proportion of French women than American (or Spanish) women raise their children alone. Thus, growing divorce rates and increasing out-of-wedlock births in France make for a disintegrating traditional family, but excellent public day-care and preschool systems, combined with long postpartum family leaves and long paid vacations, greatly cushion the decline of the traditional family.

Like the Spanish, the Japanese are heading toward fewer traditional family arrangements, but much more slowly than the United States or even Spain. The main change in Japan (as in Spain) has to do with the number of children in the typical Japanese family, not with radical shifts in lifestyle or even high divorce rates. As everywhere else in the OECD, increasing life spans and smaller families have meant more couples without children. In 1975, only 12 percent of Japanese couples had no unmarried children living with them. Twenty years later, this figure had increased to 18 percent. The proportion of married couples with and without children, however, remained constant, at almost 36 percent. The prevalence of the extended family as a living arrangement declined, and the proportion of single-person households increased to 23 percent, still only one-half the Danish figure. As in France and Denmark, the proportion of households headed by single parents is only 5 percent, half that in the United States (see, for example, Saboulin and Thave 1993).

In sum, the traditional family is on the decline in all these countries, yet significant differences remain. These differences are related to national culture, labor markets, and public policies regarding family support. The changes in family structure also affect what happens in labor markets. The persistence of more traditional families in Spain and Italy, for instance, allows for high rates of youth unemployment to be absorbed by families willing to continue supporting their children at home even in adulthood. The persistence of traditional, rigid labor markets supported by traditional family structures has, in turn, unintended effects on future families. Today's low fertility rates in southern Europe and Japan means fewer children and fewer nuclear families in the future.

Who Is Having Children?

Except in a few places such as Sweden in the late 1980s and early 1990s, where fertility rates rose as an effect of postponed childbearing among older women and hefty monetary subsidies for each child, and the United States, with an increase in the female population of childbearing age and a large immigrant population, women in OECD countries are averaging far fewer children than those of a generation ago. One of the many reasons for the drop in fertility rates is that women's average education is much higher now than ever before, and better-educated women are more likely to engage in career work and to postpone marriage and childbearing. Because they start having children when they are older, they end up having fewer children than less educated women who marry younger.

This is the dominant pattern in countries for which information on fertility rates by women's level of education is available. The U.S. data (see table 4.2) show that the fertility rate in 1994 for those women with no more than a high school education is much higher than for women with at least some college education. Women who have completed college have somewhat more children than those who have only some college, implying that the influence of higher incomes on fertility rates may kick in at this upper end.[7] The data for Great Britain (table 4.3), which represent the expected

Table 4.2 Total Fertility Rate by Race or Ethnicity and Level of Woman's Education, United States, 1994

Level of Education	Non-Hispanic White	Non-Hispanic Black	Hispanic	Total
0 to 8 years	1.9	4.5	4.1	3.2
9 to 11 years	1.9	2.4	3.4	2.3
12 years	2.4	3.6	3.8	2.7
13 to 15 years	1.3	1.7	1.6	1.4
16 years or more	1.7	1.6	2.0	1.7
Total	1.8	2.3	3.0	2.0

Source: Matthews and Ventura 1997, 4.

Note: Data are number of births per woman in the population, age fifteen to forty-four.

Table 4.3 Mean Number of Expected Children, by Age of Woman and Highest Level of Education, United Kingdom, 1990

Level of Education	Age 20 to 24	Age 25 to 29	Age 30 to 34	Age 35 to 39	Age 40 to 44
None	2.12	2.44	2.40	2.41	2.32
Other	2.30	2.21	2.16	2.07	2.04
GCE 'O' Level	2.20	2.10	2.06	1.95	2.07
GCE 'A' Level	2.21	2.09	1.98	1.93	1.84
Total	2.21	2.18	2.14	2.12	2.12

Source: Office of Population Census and Surveys, table 10.14.

rather than the actual number of children, suggest the same pattern. In the immediate post–World War II years, when income would be expected to have a major effect on childbearing, women with less education had fewer children than those with more. However, beginning with women born in the 1950s, the expected fertility rates among less educated women are higher than for those with more schooling. The differences are smaller than in the United States and are, among younger women, probably over-estimates of the number of children they will have, given that the actual fertility rates in Britain are closer to 1.8 than 2.2. Fertility rates for Norway also confirm that higher-educated women have fewer children than the less educated and that this pattern is becoming more prevalent among younger women.[8]

Greater levels of fertility among less educated, lower-income families affects societies, especially in the current global environment. It means that most children may be growing up in families that cannot adequately prepare them for the ever higher educational requirements needed to succeed in labor markets. This is not to say that higher-educated men and women make better parents than those with less education. Being a parent in the global economy, however, requires much more information than was needed in the past, and the stakes in children's educational success are much higher. On average, less educated parents are increasingly at a disadvantage in supplying what it takes for young children to be prepared to do well in school.

This potential problem is accentuated by three other factors. The first is that in some OECD countries, income distribution has grown much more unequal in the past generation, with the real incomes of less educated families stagnating or even declining. (This trend is documented in chapter 3.) The second is that in some countries, a high fraction of females heading households are poor not only because they command lower salaries as women, but also because they have low levels of schooling. The third factor is that in some countries, public investment in the early care and education of children is low. Under these three conditions, the ability of the children of less educated families to escape poverty is the exception rather than the rule.

The comparison of the condition of children in Great Britain and the United States is interesting because in both countries over the past twenty-five years, income distribution became much more unequal, divorce rates and the proportion of single mothers rose rapidly, and the fertility rate was higher among the less educated. Yet the proportion of children living in poverty or near-poverty in the mid-1980s was lower in Britain than in the United States (27 percent versus 37 percent), and the proportion living in extreme poverty was much lower in Britain (figure 4.5). Two factors ac-

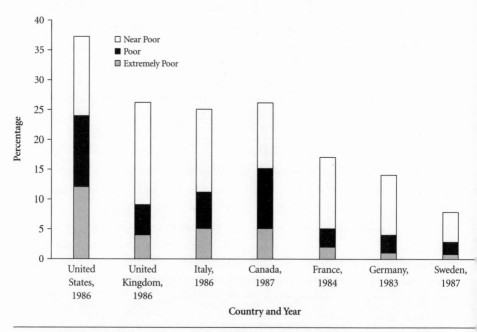

Figure 4.5 Children Growing Up in Poverty or Near Poverty, by Country, Mid-1980s (Percentage) *Source:* Data supplied to author by Lee Rainwater from Luxembourg Income Study. See Atkinson, Rainwater, and Smeeding 1995.

count for this difference: wages paid to less educated workers in Britain rose in real terms but fell in the United States, and the British government's family support for the very poor was much greater than U.S. support.

Both the British and U.S. situations pale when compared with the services provided to support children of less educated families in continental Europe, especially in France, Germany, Benelux, Austria, northern Italy, and Scandinavia. In France, only 17 percent of children lived in poverty in the mid-1980s, and in Sweden, about 8 percent. This does not even account for the high-quality child care and preschooling available free to low-income families in France and Sweden. Thus, in these societies, low-income families are not denied access to child care and preschools that are on a par with the same services paid for by better-educated, high-income families.

Because less educated parents tend to have larger families, the provision of free educational and health services to low-income (less educated) families reflects a distinct approach to dealing with children in those families. The "traditional" extended family model relies on older family members to take care of children when married women work and is also good at absorbing high youth unemployment by allowing children to stay at home well into adulthood. With globalization, the traditional option seems to result in the fewest number of children, even in low-income families. Yet because the family is still the entity responsible for raising children, differences in access to information and networks extant among social groups are likely to be reproduced from one generation to the next. The U.S. family is no longer traditional, and thanks to a dynamic economy, fertility rates are relatively high. Families that do have young children are likely to raise them "privately" but with decreasing emphasis on family time. Children are also much more likely to leave their parents' homes earlier, usually in their late teens, to live alone or with other young people. In this model, informational and networking inequalities are accentuated by high fertility rates among the least educated parents, increased stress in all families, and low availability of alternative support systems for the "private" family.

In contrast, the "public family" approach in many continental European countries provides long maternity and paternity leaves and high-quality government-subsidized child care so that women or men can spend uninterrupted time with very young children and can then enroll their children in developmentally oriented child-care and early education programs when the parents return to work. To the degree that the public family can partially offset unequal information and networking, future inequalities may be reduced. This approach may be crucial to helping low-income families adjust to flexible labor markets and to reducing the "distance" between the children of less and more educated parents in an information society.

Changing Work and the Changing Family: An Ecocultural Global Phenomenon?

The changing family is part of a changing structure of work and a changing labor market. With more intense global competition and a more globalized worldview, time takes on greater importance. A more flexible work structure is one that better utilizes an individual's time in performance of a greater number of tasks. A more flexible work structure also affects family life in positive and negative ways. Today's young woman wants a life that includes wage work and professional accomplishment. For most, staying home and tending to children is not enough. Labor market flexibility has the positive effect of allowing men and women greater possibilities for combining their competing desires to work and to raise children. On the negative side, because flexible work is acutely time sensitive, it puts increased pressure on workers to be available for work as they are needed. It also makes workers more concerned about their total commitment to their work, which necessarily relegates family life to a much lower priority.

On the positive side, flexible labor markets in countries such as the United States, Great Britain, Scandinavia, and, to some degree, Japan allow a high percentage of men and women from fifteen to fifty-four to find jobs. Where flexibility includes relatively easy exit from and reentry into the job market, couples have the greatest choice about having children, especially regarding questions of when and how many. From this standpoint, labor market flexibility has a positive effect on fertility rates. The situations in Italy and Spain, in which formal labor markets are highly rigid, provide a good contrast. There, unemployment among youth (from fifteen to twenty-four years of age) is above 35 percent, the ratio of employment to population for young women is only about 20 percent (compared with 55 percent in the United States, 59 percent in the United Kingdom, and 44 percent in Japan), and exit from and reentry into employment is difficult at any age for both men and women. High unemployment among youth delays marriage and family formation, and once a Spaniard or Italian gets a job, he or she is likely to keep it at all costs, even if the wage allows only a very small family or none at all. Labor market rigidity restricts family choices in Italy and Spain, even though other aspects of their societies, such as close ties with grandparents willing to help with child rearing, favor larger families. Greater labor market flexibility could have a positive effect on family size.

Flexibility also has a major downside for family life, however. In his famous time and motion studies, Frederick Taylor was able to extract more output from each worker by breaking down a single task into parts; the worker could thereby be made to speed up, producing more in a given amount of time (Taylor 1911). An efficient assembly line requires that each worker do one repetitive task as quickly as humanly possible during the eight hours on the line. Today, the production problem is different. Each employee has to do many different things, often at different times. The question is how to organize the company's workforce to accomplish these complex tasks most effectively and at the lowest cost. Usually, this means having workers move from task to task and varying the number of working hours, depending on the company's needs that day or that week. From the company's standpoint, the best employees are those that can do many different things on constantly changing schedules. Because many workers are not willing to fit into such schedules, companies are hiring more temporary workers for specific tasks to be done in specific time periods, downsizing part-time workers, and eliminating certain divisions and/or expanding others. Many larger companies, like the one in which Arlie Hochschild conducted her interviews for *Time Bind,* simply want more time on demand from their workforce and favor those employees who are regularly willing to sacrifice other activities, including time with family, to the company's needs. Hochschild concludes that "while the mass media so often point to global competition as the major business story of the age, it is easy to miss the fact that corporate America's fiercest struggle has been with its local rival—the family" (Hochschild 1996, 203-4).

The family in today's flexible production environment has to struggle with its employers for time, but even if couples did not have this conflict, those that Hochschild interviewed seem to prefer spending time in the workplace to spending it in the family. This is a product of many forces, but high among them has to be the value that Americans have always placed on material gain as the sovereign, or even sole, measure of status and success. It is telling that in the late 1970s and 1980s, as the average wages of American men fell, average family income rose, mainly because the proportion of wives and mothers working full time increased significantly (Bluestone and Rose 1997). Barry Bluestone and Stephen Rose have shown that between 1973 and 1988 the average working family purchased an 18.5 percent increase in real earnings with a 16.3 percent increase in hours worked. The average family earnings, in the absence of such increase in hours worked, increased only 1.8 percent. Another way to look at this phenomenon is that of the more than 13 million women in the United States who entered the labor market—that is, as "new" workers—between 1979 and 1993, 73 percent went to work full time.[9] The U.S. average real wage (corrected for changes in the cost of living) fell (for men and women combined) 9.7 percent between 1975 and 1995, and the median income for all males with income fell 8.2 percent. Median real income for families, however, rose 9.2 percent during the same period. This suggests that married women, working at lower average wages than men, more than made up the difference in family income by working more hours, on average, than in 1975.

The trends in family life have been similar in other developed countries. The relationships that families have been able to develop between work time and family time, however, appear to be different from the American arrangement, in part because some European governments have been willing to subsidize public families by granting long maternity leaves, among other things; in part because labor markets in countries such as Italy and Spain are particularly rigid; and in part because tastes for the mix between work, child rearing, and adult leisure activities differ from country to country (Hofferth 1989; U.S. GAO 1994).

This last point is worth exploring. Continental European families are likely to be smaller, and workers less willing to work long hours, than their American counterparts. Thus, continental Europeans seem to be choosing both fewer average hours of work (see table 4.4) and a lower lifetime commitment to child rearing. The average number of hours worked each year in European countries and even Japan have declined significantly since the 1970s, but hours in Australia, New Zealand (not shown), and the United States have not. The United States is unique in having increased the average number of hours worked each year.

Families in Europe and Japan are also likely to be having fewer children than those in the United States or the United Kingdom. At the extreme, younger women in the Mediterranean countries and Japan have "solved"

Table 4.4 Average Annual Hours Worked per Person in Employment and Self-Employment, by Country, Various Years

Country	1973	1979	1983	1990	1994	1996	1998
Australia	—	1,904	1,852	1,869	1,879	1,867	1,861
France	1,904	1,813	1,711	1,668	1,635	1,645	1,634[a]
Germany	—	—	—	—	1,602	1,576	1,580
West Germany[b]	1,868	1,764	1,724	1,610	1,580	1,557	1,562
Italy[c]	1,842	1,748	1,724	1,694	1,682	—	—
Japan	2,201	2,126	2,095	2,031	1,898	1,919[a]	1,879[c]
Netherlands[c]	1,724	1,591	1,530	1,433	1,388	1,374	1,365[a]
Spain	—	2,022	1,912	1,824	1,815	1,810	1,821
United Kingdom	1,929	1,821	1,719	1,773	1,728	1,738	1,737
United States	1,924	1,905	1,882	1,943	1,945	1,951	1,957

Source: OECD 1997a, table G; OECD 1999b, table F.

[a]1997.

[b]West Germany series is shown for continuity with period before early 1990s.

[c]Data are for dependent employment only.

the conflict between work and their caregiving roles by avoiding having children altogether. The marriage average age is high, and families have become very small. It is true that once couples join together and have children, they are more likely to make the traditional family decision that the wife will focus on child rearing and the husband will provide for the family's financial support. In countries like Japan that have some labor market flexibility and low unemployment and in which the traditional family is still the norm, women are more likely to accept their subordinated status as caregivers and not work when their children are young. Most women in Japan, for example, still work before they marry and have children and afterward work as part-timers without career perspectives (see Kamo 1990; Nomura et al. 1995). Japanese women have apparently been taking temporary part-time jobs to get their children into high-quality government-supported day-care centers (day care is not available for nonworking Japanese mothers)(Nicholas Kristof, "Yokohama Journal: Japan Invests in a Growth Stock: Good Day Care," *New York Times,* February 1, 1995). In Italy and Spain, on the other hand, women who do get work tend to keep their full-time jobs even when they have children at home (Gruppo Onda 1991). This is made somewhat easier by a standard thirty-six-hour work-week in Italy and the possibility for some women of a workday lasting from 8 A.M. to 2 P.M., allowing them to be home before their children return from school.

France represents an interesting alternative because French family structure is not all that different from that of the United States and is not nearly as traditional as that of Italy or Spain. French women in the prime of their working and child-rearing lives are about as likely as American women to be employed (68 percent versus 73 percent in the mid-1990s) and are much more likely to be employed than Italian or Spanish (or Japanese) women. The labor force participation rates for French men are lower than those for American men (74 percent versus 85 percent), and exactly the same as the rates for men in Italy and Spain. The result is that about the same percentage of the labor force in France and the United States are women (46 percent). Are the choices French men and women make about family and work different from those being made by Americans, and if so, why?

One real possibility is that because fewer jobs are available in France than in the United States, French men and women may not have been able to work as much as they have wanted. The French labor force has grown much more slowly than the U.S. labor force in the past twenty years. The main economies of continental Europe did not generate many new jobs during this period (see chapter 2 of this volume). With slow employment growth, the French economy was simply not incorporating many new workers in the 1980s and 1990s, although many of those who did find jobs were women. This has pushed the French to retire earlier than Americans and has kept French young people out of the labor force longer.

The shortage of jobs may also be affecting other work choices that impact the family life of couples with children.

- Of the 2 million additional women who entered the French labor force between 1979 and 1993 (a 21 percent increase in the number of working women), only 32 percent went into full-time jobs. Compare this with the 73 percent of American women who took full-time jobs when they entered the labor force in this same period.
- The average annual hours worked per person in employment in France fell from 1,813 hours in 1979 to 1,668 in 1990, but rose in the United States, from 1,905 to 1,943 (table 4.4). The probability of participation in the labor force may have increased for French women,

but because they took more part-time work, there was, overall, a re-duction in the average amount of hours French workers worked.

At the same time, these may be choices that French families would make even if more work were available. The interaction between work contexts, shaped in part by politics, and individual choices regarding family life is so pervasive that it is impossible to say for sure whether such different values exist. The French might be choosing to work less than Americans. If such a choice is being made, it is mainly at a social, not merely an individual, level. There is much greater political pressure in France to maintain the family wage (a wage, earned by males, large enough to maintain a family). Male wages have risen in France and fallen in the United States, which has made the choice of whether to work harder (or to work longer hours) less pressing for French families than for U.S. families. Average male earnings in France rose about 7 percent (OECD 1997a, table 1.5), and French family income rose about 10.3 percent (INSEE 1996), compared with a decline of 7 percent in the earnings of American males working full time but an in-crease of about 3 percent in mean real family income, from 1984 to 1994 (*Economic Report of the President* 1999, table B-33). Thus, the French fam-ily increased its real consumption power more than the average American family, but the increase in French family income required a smaller in-crease in the number of hours worked than for families in the United States.

The French government has also been under political pressure to main-tain its widely available, subsidized, high-quality day-care system (Marlise Simons, "Child Care Sacred as France Cuts Back on Welfare State," *New York Times*, December 31, 1997). This allows even women who do not work to be relatively free from child-care activities for at least part of the day and clearly makes it easier for families in which both parents work to place their children in high-quality care situations. Economists have ar-gued that such subsidized day care needlessly pushes women to transfer child-care responsibilities to the public sector at taxpayer expense (Rosen 1996). In the French case, however, it may actually promote greater child-care responsibility because it releases women for part of the day from ac-tivities they prefer to do part time without forcing them into full-time work to cover the expense of child care. Given that French women (and men) are averse to full-time child care but not necessarily to part-time child care, the combination of high-quality, subsidized child care, part-time work for one adult of the nuclear family, and full-time work for the other—both jobs at rising real wages to allow for increased family consumption without resorting to increasing amounts of time worked—may be a more positive way to sustain the family in the current transition than the American "solution" to globalized competition.

Thus, beyond the hindrance of the shortage of jobs, French women (and men) may also be making different choices from those of American women (and men) regarding work and family. Although young women everywhere increasingly prefer to spend part of their time in the world of work instead of being locked full time into a child-care function, this comparison between the United States and France suggests that different advanced industrial societies may provide different social and economic contexts for women's choosing between work and family. In addition, it suggests that women themselves might make different choices in these different societies. Choices may vary at both the individual level and in a collective political sense because of different values about the balance between increased material consumption and family life.

Work is becoming more flexible across the OECD, as indicated by the increased proportion of workers in part-time, self-employed, and temporary work, the decline of job tenure in more traditional labor market economies, and the increasing emphasis on multitasking and team work in many workplaces (see chapter 3, this volume). For more and more workers in the OECD, the secure lifetime job is a thing of the past. Family structures may also vary across the OECD countries. Ironically, countries such as Italy and Spain, with more traditional family structures and highly "inflexible" labor markets, seem to be penalizing family life as much as or more than countries with highly flexible labor markets. Rigid labor markets severely reduce fertility rates. In addition, although economies with flexible labor markets can penalize family life if work becomes the all-consuming focus that flexibility demands, labor market flexibility might favor family life under the right conditions. These conditions include a "public family" structure that supports the desires of both men and women to forge identities that include both work and family.

Flexible Workplaces and the New Family

The other side of this story is that relying on traditional family structures to sustain flexible production is risky. Far from losing its fundamental importance to work, the family will be even more crucial as the economy shifts to flexible, knowledge-based production. Not only is an ever increasing proportion of jobs in the OECD organized around "knowledge" rather than physical skills, but today's younger workers are likely to need to acquire new kinds of knowledge at different points in their working lives as they move through different kinds of jobs.

The family in a flexible work system is a central hub of productive and reproductive activity. When it is potentially "strong" (with two highly educated adults at its core) it serves as a risk hedge against periods of unemployment and as a source of child development support for its offspring, of investment capital for adult and child education and job training, of networking for job searches and upward mobility, and of personal security. and growth. Networked into larger information and communication systems, the family can also become a production unit.

Yet low birthrates can threaten population reproduction and future economic growth. Divorce rates throughout the OECD, even in more traditional societies, will almost certainly increase and then stay as high as those in the United States or Scandinavia. Increased stress on families, even on those with traditional supports, as they try both to raise children and to satisfy the need of both women and men for status and social interaction as wage earners in remunerated work, could have a serious negative effect on adult productivity and the well-being of children. The combined effect of flexible production, with its demands for individualized, work-focused activities, women's fight for greater equality in the family and labor market, and the increased importance of the family as an investment unit now shapes the emergence of the next stage of family life. The family could and should be the social institution that tempers the stress induced by the processes of disaggregation of labor and individualization of social and economic life. For the family to be able to play its fundamental role of sustaining work, it has to be redefined and strengthened under the new cultural and technological conditions of our societies.

The U.S. model is appealing to employers and many politicians in Europe because its potential for job creation and low unemployment stand in stark contrast to Europe's frustrating struggle to create jobs and reduce unemployment. American-style flexible markets, however, have a downside that makes them understandably unappealing to the average European and Japanese: flexibility not only expands job growth, but it is characterized in the highly deregulated economy of the United States by stagnant or falling wages for a significant percentage of workers. Most workers have to pay much more attention to keeping their jobs because of the continuing threat that they might lose them. Flexibility also tends to increase the number of hours family members work. In lower-skill jobs, American-style flexible markets encourage people to work more in order to earn more rather than lobby for a higher wage for the hours they do work. In high-skill jobs, high pay is the norm, but only for those who are willing to commit themselves to a supercharged work schedule, meeting crucial deadlines at all costs and outcompeting other workers in the do-or-die global economy. In some of these higher-skill occupations, the financial incentives are great: workers who make the right moves may earn a lot in a few years. Thus the long hours have a potentially high payoff. All this promotes higher profits, economic growth, and higher average family income but at the cost of job security, more intensified family work schedules, and increased individual stress and isolation.

Europeans and Japanese may admire the vitality of the current U.S. "job machine," but consider the American system of work and family relations too socially costly. They read about high levels of open poverty, deteriorating living conditions, lack of child care, stressful dual workdays, long commuting hours, downgraded schools, social violence, and a high fraction of the young male black and Latino populations in prison. Americans tend to live either in cities that are no longer very safe for children and adolescents or in suburbs, with their own risks for young people, as indicated by the increasingly frequent and shocking killings in suburban schools. According to a 1994 national survey, child care in America is of such poor quality that children's development is at risk (Fuller et al. 1997). All political parties and leaders invoke a strengthened family as a solution to the nation's social ills, but social legislation supporting the family lags behind that of all other industrialized countries. Most children in the United States not only live in families broken by divorce (Susan Chira, "Struggling to Find Stability When Divorce Is a Pattern," *New York Times,* March 19, 1995), but more than a third also live in or near the poverty line. In some ethnic minorities the crisis of the family is very deep, playing a major role in perpetuating the underclass status of a significant segment of the minority population (Wilson 1987). About one-half of all African American children are conceived out of wedlock, and many do not know their fathers (Jaynes and Williams 1990). Not only do less educated mothers in the United States have more children than higher-educated mothers, just as in other OECD countries, but they are likely to raise their children in relatively worse economic conditions, with less access to child development and early educational services than in most of the rest of the OECD.

The third issue for Europeans concerned with the American model of flexible work is that it puts ever increasing emphasis on work and earnings themselves as the be-all and end-all of human existence. This is not a completely new phenomenon in America. Yet with increased competition in the globalized economy and the rapidly rising capacity to use "world time" to enhance productivity, the very best workers are now those who never sleep, never consume, never have children, and never spend time socializing outside of work. As Hochschild argues, it is in the employer's interest to make the workplace more socially congenial for workers because they will then be willing to spend more time there. It is also in the employer's interest to make workers believe that if they do not spend more time there, the employer will find someone else who will.

The socially congenial work organization is hardly alien to the Japanese or to many Europeans. Japanese workers are especially known to put company loyalty above almost all else, and Japanese companies to demand such loyalty in return for guaranteed employment. Indeed, many of the methods used by American and European companies to build company spirit and dedication were imported directly from Japan. In Japan, company loyalty means long hours of work. In 1979, the average employed Japanese worked about two hundred hours more a year than the average U.S. worker, and even today, after several years of recession, the average workweek in Japan is only slightly fewer hours than in the United States. However, these long hours are largely restricted to male workers. Married Japanese women with children are likely not to work ouside of the home or to work part time. The relative intactness of traditional family relations in Japan still provides for male loyalty to the company and female loyalty to the family. Fewer Japanese families may have children today than a generation ago, but those who do still tend to divide their work responsibilities along gender lines.

Europeans may not have Japanese-style company loyalty, but a high fraction of European men work under guarantees similar to those given the Japanese. Furthermore, Europeans do not have to work as many hours. Although the OECD data on hours worked are not strictly comparable, employed French, German, Italian, and British workers have consistently worked many hours less than the average American worker, even in the mid-1980s, before today's employment problems. With four to six weeks of paid vacation, full-time French, German, and Italian employees work up to a month less than their American counterparts. They also retire earlier and get better pensions, without having to worry about 401(b)s, 401(k)s, or personal savings plans. Thus, many Europeans have carved out a work system that is secure, relatively high paying, and replete with benefits in time that give both men and women the luxury of a comfortable family life, should they choose one. In more traditional societies, such as those of Spain and southern Italy, a strong family structure is probably responsible for greatly attenuating the worst effects of high unemployment and the shrinkage of the welfare state (Leal 1993). Spanish and Mezzogiorno (as the area from Rome south is known) societies have remained socially calm in the face of unemployment rates of 20 to 25 percent in the 1990s (with only about 60 percent of the unemployed in Spain, for example, receiving insurance). The large majority of unemployed are women and youth who continue to live with their husbands and parents, supported by them and by the social security system. All family members are entitled to social security payments by virtue of their relationship to just one salaried worker in the family. Young people, on average, reside at home until their late twenties, most often under conditions of total individual freedom (Zaldivar and Castells 1992).

Thus, despite the promise of more much-wanted jobs, most Europeans and Japanese are not anxious to work in American-style flexible labor markets, even though to some extent they already are. In most of Europe, this is not because of fear that more women will work nor that relations between men and women will change: a high fraction of European women already work for wages or salaries, and gender relations have changed in most countries without the introduction of American hiring and firing flexibility.[10] Nor is resistance to the possible introduction of more part-time and temporary work the reason. Back in the late 1970s, the Scandinavian countries, as well as others, including Great Britain and Japan, had part-time job rates that were as high as or higher than those of the United States. Nor, in Japan, is it a problem of being wedded to more work. Japanese men are heavily committed to their jobs yet seem to want to keep their wives at home. However, in Europe, increasing the number of hours that full employment requires could be a serious political problem.

None of these reasons is grounds for major resistance to a U.S. version of flexible markets. Rather, the common ground is that Europeans and Japanese see U.S. flexibility as a combined assault on their rising wage rates, on social incorporation through the social benefits of work, and on the relationships they have established between family, work, and leisure—a relationship that puts constraints on employers in Europe from demanding intensive, year-long work schedules from their workers and in Japan from drawing married women into career, full-time work.

Resistance to American-style flexibility does not mean that Japanese and European work organization is not changing. Nor does it mean that Japanese and European workers will be able to preserve the balance between work and family that to one degree or another is already in flux. Nor does it mean that the present U.S. work system is socially desirable or even sustainable. Where, then, will Europe, Japan, and the United States end up as they remodel their societies for the new global economy?

Some Policy Implications

The answer to this question lies, at least partly, in the shift to more knowledge-intensive work for all. The developed countries are quickly becoming knowledge societies in which communicative, cooperative, and cognitive skills rather than raw materials, human strength, and machines form the basis for the production of wealth. Because knowledge is more important in work, and because women's identities are increasingly associated with income-earning capacity, family formation (including the age at marriage, the number of children, and the timing of the children) is increasingly determined by the pattern of knowledge acquisition, such as the length of professional development and career formation. The quality of family life will increasingly be gauged by learning opportunities for adults and the capacity of the adults in the family to provide learning opportunities for their children. The intense emphasis on learning as a factor in life decisions has already occurred in upper-middle-income groups (more highly educated men and women), whose women are choosing to establish careers (to pursue higher levels of education and to take jobs with high levels of learning opportunities) before having children. The availability in Europe and Japan of subsidized child development centers that care for youngsters of all ages—and, in the United States, the lack of such centers—shapes the sustainability of marriages and the number and timing of children, especially for professional couples. Such learning-driven behavior as a dominant shaper of family formation, now limited to better-educated young people (who are necessarily more fully sensitized to the implications of flexible labor markets), will move into the rest of the population, just as reduction of fertility rates among the middle class moved into the working class at the beginning of the twentieth century.

With knowledge and information playing such potentially important roles in flexible work, family formation, and family relations, support systems consistent with improving both individual productivity and family life should be increasingly organized around enhancing access by both children and adults to high-quality learning opportunities. The integration of households into learning networks is the linchpin of a flexible, knowledge-based work system. Government family policies are fundamental to this integration, because the state, whether local or national, is the only institution that has both the material resources to support the household's investments in its members and the political motivation to do so. Such policies need to enhance the family's capacity to invest in learning without interfering in the privacy of its decisions. The state can do this by helping the family acquire education for its children even as parents are on flexible work schedules; giving parents new opportunities to further their own education and training; guaranteeing family health care even when family members are unemployed or studying; providing widely available training on child care and child development to youth, prospective parents, and parents, using fiscal policies to reward families that invest in education; and strictly enforcing laws that ensure that parents, whether they are divorced or married, living together or not, contribute financially to the support of their children.

The acquisition of knowledge depends heavily on early childhood development, and early childhood takes place in families. Not only are most parents uneducated about child development, but in the free market Anglo-American model, collective society pays little attention to the crucial early years of a child's learning. Again, this is an attitude left over from preindustrial and industrial society, when how much knowledge children acquired in school was far less important to their work lives.

Those OECD countries that have been especially conscious of children's welfare when both parents or a single parent work, or even as a respite for women who do not work, provide all-day, high-quality subsidized day care. In Scandinavia and France, day care is the centerpiece of family policy, and is beginning to be so in Japan. In all these countries, day care is organized by the state around well-trained, certified teachers who specialize in early childhood development.

With individuals in families facing more intense pressures in their work lives yet still having children, governments need to take the issue of child development even more seriously. Child development centers are the key to meeting the household's need for parents' job flexibility and children's early enriched learning. They are expensive, and as in the case of higher education, parents who can afford to pay should. In France, parents do contribute on the basis of ability to pay, and in the United States, where publicly supported child-care centers are the exception, financial responsibility for high-quality childhood development is borne almost entirely by the families themselves. This means that low-income parents are denied access to high-quality care with an enriched development focus. Thus, from such early care on, knowledge development in a market model is highly unequal—precisely the opposite of what a flexible, knowledge-based society needs for sustained development.

The state (again, because it is the only institution that has the resource mobilization power to do so) also has to insure high-quality health care for all children, even before they are born, and has to invest in the education of parents regarding the responsibilities and skills of parenthood. Because most early childhood education takes place in families, even where the state subsidizes child development centers, parents are children's main teachers; yet most parents are hardly prepared for that role. Secondary schools and universities need to require parenting courses and need to emphasize child development responsibilities of parents. If anything, an educational focus of this kind will convince many young people to delay parenting until they can fulfill their children's learning needs.

Beyond early childhood development, governments need to make schools into community learning centers, where parents can leave their children in a learning environment during parents' working or education hours and during school vacation periods when parents do not have vacation time. The community learning center should also be a place where parents and seniors can engage in learning activities—some related to their children's education and some to adult activities, including community-run business courses for the self-employed. (I discuss this in more detail in the next chapter, in which I deal with the changing nature of community in the new, individualized, disaggregated labor society.)

Currently, parents in Europe and the United States are induced to have more children through family income entitlements, tax deductions for dependents, and welfare for mothers with dependent children. In the knowledge economy, fiscal inducements should be tied to investment in education and training, not simply to having children. The Clinton administration's proposed middle-class tax cut, which provides tax deductions for the costs of children's college education and for adult training, are a step in this direction. A similar deduction should be allowed for children's preschool and parents' education toward a degree. The part of the middle-class tax cut that gives an additional tax credit of five hundred dollars just for having a child, with no restrictions on how that money is used, is a step in the wrong direction.

This focus on state support for families through investment tax credits for education and training and the direct provision of high-quality early childhood development also means that the state needs to reconceive the way it views and delivers education. Local existing educational institutions—from primary and secondary schools to community colleges and universities—are the logical sites around which the state can build all-day, all-year, cradle-to-grave learning networks for households to hook into, whether parents have jobs or are self-employed. Yet these institutions have to evolve to meet varying needs in various communities. The demand for both full-day children's education and adult education, for example, may be far greater in low-income areas than high-income communities. Government allocation of resources for education should be responsive to such unequal needs as part of equalizing opportunities and social protection, particularly in light of the fact that less educated families have more children but a weaker capacity to provide them with the information and networks needed to be productive in a flexible, knowledge-intensive economy.

Which model is more likely to be able to respond to this integrative challenge? The U.S. version has the distinct advantage of a highly flexible educational system that allows young people and adults to leave and reenter, change majors, and retrain for new careers at just about any age. Americans also have a high propensity to form voluntary associations responsive to new demands in the society. These are taking on many of the organizational responsibilities for new learning systems, even though they usually have to rely on state funding, particularly in low-income communities. Flexible education and voluntary, private local organizing is consistent with labor market flexibility, lifelong education, and responses to the need for knowledge formation in a rapidly changing economy. American women have been especially inclined to use this flexibility to shape their reentry into the labor force after raising young children or divorcing. The greatest growth in college enrollment in the 1970s and 1980s came from women thirty or more years of age returning to school to train for better jobs. Flexibility has also allowed for modular add-ons to basic public education, such as private after-school tutorial programs.

The U.S. model has major drawbacks, however, in meeting knowledge needs for a flexible economy. Americans and America's political leadership seem unwilling to confront the public crises of the family and related child poverty. One way to deal with these crises is to invest heavily in early, high-quality, publicly funded education for low-income children. Child development centers, so central to Europe's "public-family" approach to poverty, are virtually absent in the United States. Beyond early childhood education, the schools of the future will probably have to serve as dawn-to-late-evening community knowledge centers. I discuss this concept in greater detail in the next chapter, but I want to mention here that under the actual U.S. model, families unable to pay privately for "extra" educational services privately are at a tremendous disadvantage. For that to change, the larger community has to be willing to publicly pay for new forms of knowledge provision. In the current environment, this may not be easy to achieve politically.

Europe and Japan have much more rigid educational systems than the United States. Adult education is not readily available in France, Italy, and Germany, and it is unusual for young people to leave the educational system and reenter later. Even changing majors in university can be difficult. Women seeking to redefine themselves are hardly well served by an educational system that is youth-centered and highly linear. This makes educational responses to the crisis in the traditional family more difficult. It is hard to imagine the present French or Italian educational system, or even the local state-run German system, for example, being sensitive and responsive to changing wage-earner family needs. Although voluntary associations in continental European countries (where the state is expected to "take care of things") are rarer than in the United Kingdom or the United States, they do exist, but they are not taken as seriously by public officials. I recently interviewed a parents' council at a Bergamo, Italy, primary school. Their major complaint was that the school would not change its timetable to eliminate half-day Saturdays to accommodate family needs, even when the parents' council presented a well-thought-out plan to teachers and the administration. No reason was given. This is typical of these systems, and it reflects the rigidity and arrogance of teachers' unions and centralized bureaucracies, whatever their advantages in student achievement might be.[11]

However, despite growing disillusionment with the nation-state at many levels, continental Europeans (and the educationally more flexible Scandinavians) are much more willing than Americans (or the British or Australians) to acknowledge the role of the public sector in equalizing opportunity and providing important services. Japan relies less on government agencies than on corporate organizations for lifelong support systems, but the Japanese, like the continental Europeans and Scandinavians, have a relatively homogeneous society and a sense of collective responsibility for each other. Voters in all these countries support public funding for child-care centers and early childhood education. Continental Europe, Scandinavia, and Japan provide generally high-quality subsidized programs for young children, and these, together with other family support programs, have contributed to a significant reduction in child poverty in the past three decades.

Can this sense of collective responsibility and willingness to organize and spend substantial public funds on early childhood education be extended to developing lifelong, flexible systems that provide education in response to changing family needs? Or is it more likely that Americans and American political leadership will extend their current advantage in flexible education by taking responsibility for high-quality, publicly funded early education and other forms of family education and networking support systems?

This is a fundamental issue for the viability of these societies in our high-speed future. Obviously, the capacity of an economic system to innovate and organize the production of goods and services is crucial in a competitive global system. Social cohesion is also crucial, however, and the family as the main institution of social cohesion needs help in an age of flexible production and changed gender roles. The capacity and willingness of a society to provide this help, especially in the form of support for learning and learning networks for families that have limited capacity to provide them privately, will be major elements in sustaining innovation and work systems over the long haul.

---

1. This problem did not end in the nineteenth century. See, for example, Frank McCourt's *Angela's Ashes* (1996). In today's environment, the issue has translated itself into difficulties in collecting child support payments.
2. I have characterized early family production as inseparable from reproduction; Young and Willmott characterize the family as totally devoted to production. The two characterizations show the difficulty in separating production and reproduction in subsistence culture. At some point, however, family subsistence production also becomes a source of accumulation, with the product of family work much greater than that required just to fill the family's basic needs. This is the flip side of the coin, making the family a production unit.

3. For early works that conceptualized the crisis, see, for example, Millett 1970; Mitchell 1971.

4. The rise in Swedish fertility rates in the late 1980s and early 1990s also resulted from a "bubble" caused by women in their thirties who had delayed childbearing in the previous decade and the tendency of younger women to have more children because of increased subsidies and better economic conditions.

5. With fertility rates among whites in rapid decline, continued high fertility and immigration of non-Europeans is dramatically affecting the composition of the young population in states such as California, even while the percentage of adult white voters remains high. There is less concern about family issues when the groups having children are less "like" the voting population. See Maharidge 1996.

6. In 1982, 45 percent of French people age twenty to twenty-four lived at home with their parents, and 30 percent lived as a couple; in 1995, 54 percent lived with their parents, and 19 percent as a couple. See INSEE 1996, 326.

7. The higher birthrates for these highly educated women are also affected by the current pattern of high rates of first birth for older, college-educated women who postponed childbearing until their thirties. The high fertility rates for those women with low levels of schooling are heavily influenced by the much higher proportion of higher-fertility Hispanic women with lower levels of schooling and the slightly higher proportion of black women with only high school education or less. See Matthews and Ventura 1997.

8. The Norwegian study shows that fertility rates for women with only the minimum compulsory education (seven to nine years of schooling) surveyed in 1980 was 2.39 births at age thirty-five and 2.46 at age forty, compared with fertility rates of 1.78 and 1.95, respectively, for women with fifteen or more years of schooling. For women thirty-five years old in 1989, the fertility rate had declined to 2.06 children per woman with seven to nine years of schooling and 1.58 per woman with fifteen or more years of schooling (Kravdal 1992). According to Oystein Kravdal, "The lower average number of children born to women as their level of education increases is to a large extent due to differences in the proportion of childless women" (465). Nor does labor force participation have a significantly different effect on less and more educated Norwegian women's fertility rates.

9. The share of mothers in the United States whose children are under the age of six and who are employed climbed from 14 percent in 1950 to just over 60 percent in 1991.

10. In Japan, however, work for married women is a more controversial issue.

11. French and Italian teenagers scored higher in math than U.S. teenagers on the Third International Mathematics and Science Study (TIMSS) mathematics test.

Redefining Community
in a Flexible Economy

Men and women seek community beyond family. This is not surprising. Communities integrate individuals into a larger context, creating a broader sense of self, providing greater security than that offered by family alone but also demanding greater obligation and much more learning. Communities are complex organizations with rules, regulations, and multiple relationships. They are networks, friendships, and support systems, with insiders and outsiders. They are full of symbols, histories, and rituals. Those who succeed in communities are better at learning and manipulating these complexities. The reward of learning and belonging is that communities support individuals, often materially but mostly psychologically, giving them a sense of well-being, confidence, and connectedness fundamental to human existence.

As production, spatial living patterns, and political systems change historically, communities also change. Individuals have to learn new rules and regulations and develop new networks. Some do better than others in making this change. Those who do not do well often try to go back into the past to find communities that are more consistent with the kinds of rules, regulations, and relationships they understand. Others look for alternatives that attack the structure of a changing community that does not work for them. The cost to society of individuals' not finding community can be high. Isolation breeds alienation, and alienation breeds conflict. New communities tend to arise to respond to these new needs, but there is no iron rule that they will appear or, if they do, that they will engender socially constructive results. Two hundred years ago, the Industrial Revolution began to produce new organizations of work that, in Karl Marx's analysis, alienated workers from the means of production. New communities, built around industrial workers' search for collective identity, found expression in unions and revolutionary movements of various stripes. In some countries, these communities produced constructive, democratic responses to the alienation caused by industrialization (see Przeworski and Wallerstein 1982; Przeworski 1985); in others, communist revolutions produced responses that provided greater economic security at a tremendously high cost in human rights. The difference in these responses lay in each society's ability to react politically and socially to the change in human condition—to create new forms of community that expand rather than reduce basic rights (Skocpol 1979).[1]

We are again at such a historical watershed. Globalization is transforming the notion of community and the way individuals define their identities. A world in which Europeans, Americans, and Japanese consume the same products, coordinate economic policies, think environmentally on a global scale, and do not face an obvious military threat shifts identity from a national locus to a more international one. At the same time, flexible work individualizes and separates labor from the "job community"—workplace, union, and neighborhood. Because of concomitant changes in the social relationship between men and women, the family is not the same kind of community it used to be, either. Individuals are losing control over their environment. As the industrial system and its underpinnings erode, the various "communities" of identity and their support systems also erode. This creates a vacuum in terms of reintegrating "flexed" individuals into social networks and in recreating their identities as members of social organizations. Individuals who have difficulty fitting into the international market identities provided by the new global economy seek attachment of other kinds. They withdraw into specific identities built around religion, ethnicity, and gender.

The integrative power of national identity is redefined because globalization changes individual and collective conceptions of space and time. The local community is redefined because of worker individualization and the new spatial relations between work, residence, and leisure activities. Workers' organizations are in crisis because the traditional conception of a job upon which they are based has changed. The family's integrative capacity is also transformed by the stresses of democratized home life and by the legitimate claims of women for a paid-work identity outside the home.

This crisis in the meaning of community is important and unavoidable. "Identity is people's source of meaning and experience," writes Manuel

Castells. It is collective as well as individual, constructed from "history, from geography, from biology, and productive and reproductive institutions, from collective memory and from personal fantasies, from power apparatuses and religious revelations" (Castells 1997, 6–7). Because identity is shaped by institutions and by individuals' roles in institutions, changes in either alter the sense of self and the relation of the individual to others. With the reorganization of work and the fundamental transformation of the family, institutions that emerged out of the industrial labor system—the patriarchal consumption and investment family, the family wage, and a national conception of time and space—were bound to disintegrate.

At the same time, the stakes are high in the way communities reorganize themselves. Work disaggregation and family disintegration threaten to isolate and alienate individuals. That, in turn, threatens the development and education of the next generation of workers and increases potential political and social instability. Thus, ultimately, the very changes that are supposed to increase worker productivity can end up reducing societies' capacity to generate economic wealth.

What will the institutions that fill this void look like? What is the logical shape of the new communities, and what are the political conditions under which they may be realized? Where are isolated individuals likely to turn if their traditional sources of social integration and identity do not meet their needs?

The answer lies largely in existing communities and their capacity to react to globalization, competition, flexible labor, and the new conditions of family life. At the same time, new communities also appear, and old ones, long dormant, reassert themselves. I have already discussed the family; now I turn to the changing national and local communities, revisit the workplace as a community, and speculate about new forms of communities, including virtual ones.

National Identity in Decline?

Individuals construct multiple identities and multiple communities. This construction includes the community of "nationality." When a person in what Anthony Giddens calls a "late modern" society (Giddens 1991) is asked, "Who are you?" she or he is likely to answer, "I am an American," or French, or Japanese, as well as other things. Nationality has real meaning, but it is a constructed meaning, and it changes over time. It bonds individuals to others, usually those living in a particular territory, through a shared set of beliefs defined by historical symbols, political values, and language. Internal and external conflicts create new symbols and often change the interpretation of past history, redefining what it means to be German, Italian, French, or Australian.

An individual's national identity represents a real, not virtual or imagined, community.[2] It creates an ethical bond to others in the national community that is different from the bond to human beings in general or to family members or to others in the same ethnic group. Individuals belonging to that community do not necessarily know others in the community personally. Yet they feel that they have a lot in common with them, enough to fight collectively for their rights when threatened, respond similarly to historical symbols, and be comfortable with them when in another country. The bond to others who speak the same language, live in the same territory, are socialized in the same school system, and are raised in the same legal and political institutions is surprisingly strong. However, those of the same nationality may have deep conflicts with one another. Class, ethnicity, religion, and race are all potential sources of separation within the same nation. If nationality represents a real community, national institutions must reduce these feelings of conflict or risk delegitimation and disintegration.

These aspects of national identity combine to influence individuals' relations with and actions toward other individuals of the same nationality; that is, other individuals living within the same national boundaries.[3] National boundaries are at once a constructed reality and have long had real meaning to those who live within them, through power relations defined by the political institutions of the nation-state. National boundaries shape the ethical relations of the individuals who live within them toward those who live outside, just as other boundaries do. The most important of these in late-modern nations is the value that people who form a national community in the national territory should have the right to political self-determination (Miller 1995). The rights and rules of political self-determination—the essence of modern democracy—within geographic boundaries have become important aspects of identity in late-modern societies. Concurrently, they are sources of legitimacy for the institutional practices of the late-modern nation-states, distinguishing them from less "advanced" nations and competitors in the "morality wars," such as the Soviet Union.

Yet the citizens of a nation or region can use political self-determination continually to express and define their identity by defining and redefining the ethical bonds that tie one citizen to another within particular geographic boundaries. This may seem to be a stretch in defining national identity, but in modern democratic societies, rules of law and legal interpretations go far in simultaneously shaping and expressing national values. Even assuming that a particular group (big business or the capitalist class, for example) dominates the shaping of national values, liberal democracy makes it possible for subordinate groups to contest the dominant vision.

The direction these conflicts take historically produces different expressions of ethnic relations in different nations. Legal and political practices designed to enable Americans or Swedes, for example, to make collective decisions are strikingly similar when compared with the structures and practices of nations ruled by authoritarian regimes. Americans and Swedes, however, view their social commitment to their compatriots in different ways. These rights and the institutional frameworks developed to express them are an integral part of the national identity of an individual, which in turn shapes what each individual identifying with a particular nation is willing to do for the others sharing that identity. For example, certain religious values, historical conflict with the established church, homogeneous ethnicity, long-standing "neutrality" in world wars among nearby countries, and a social pact between capital and labor are part and parcel of Swedish identity as it has developed historically. That identity translates into a strong ethical commitment to material equality and individual equity, as expressed by democratically elected governments that enact such commitments into law—so much so that equality has itself become a symbol of Swedish national identity. Other Scandinavian nations have developed similar ethical relations within their boundaries for many of the same historical reasons. Americans, because of a much different history, one that has been shaped by colonization, immigration, the frontier, slavery, and ultimately, enormous economic and military power, have a somewhat different set of ethical bonds to one another, even though they, along with the Swedes, place great value on democracy and civic participation.[4]

National identities, as expressed by the ethical bonds that tie, for instance, one American to another, change over time. Only a few decades ago, Americans seemed more committed to the reduction of poverty and racial and class differences. In the late 1960s, income distribution in the United States was not much more unequal than that in Sweden. Today, the emphasis in the United States has shifted back to "individual merit," a euphemism for reduced collective responsibility for those who have difficulty succeeding materially and socially. Swedes, too, are apparently less convinced that they are ethically bound to help all those Swedes who have difficulty coping in postindustrial society. The shift to greater "individualism" in both societies, although starting at very different levels, marks an important trend throughout the OECD. It is bound to affect how people in each country relate to one another and form community.

Does globalization mean the gradual disappearance of national identity? Is national identity declining, or is it merely taking a different shape? The answer is not simple. Pollsters and political scientists have been measuring people's values for many years, but tying these changes to globalization is complicated. At best, we can infer what seems to be happening by examining the data available and determining the significance of the trends. The most obvious arguments for the decline of national identity lie in the current compression of time and space on a global scale. Markets for goods and services, including cultural products such as films, television programs, and books, are becoming increasingly global. Consumers who can, or believe that they will eventually be able to, afford these products identify less with a particular local or national way of life and more with a global conception of living. As people are more mobile, those in nations other than our own seem less foreign, less strange. "Insofar as our belief that we share a distinct national identity depends on a certain degree of ignorance about how people are actually leading their lives in other places, it is eroded by direct contact with those cultures" (Miller 1995, 156).

Results from various sources indicate the probability of a postnationalist era. Table 5.1 shows a sharp decline in national pride in major European Union countries since 1970, a very low level of pride in Japan by the 1980s, but a continuing high level in the United States. That said, most of the drop occurred in the 1970s in Europe, before globalization, and is most likely the result of European supranationalism. If so, the end of the cold war and further Europeanization in the 1990s—both related to globalization—should have reduced a sense of national pride even more. A more indirect way of measuring national identity, complicated by the way citizens identify with political institutions rather than community itself, is political involvement. Robert Putnam argues that one measure of community participation, although the community in question may not necessarily be a national or local one, is voter participation in national (and local) elec-

Table 5.1 National Pride, by Country, Various Years (Percentage)

Country	1970	1981	1990
Belgium	70	29	31
Denmark	—	30	42
France	66	31	35
Italy	62	40	40
Japan	—	30	29
Netherlands	54	20	23
Spain	—	51	45
United Kingdom	—	53	53
United States	—	76	75
West Germany	38	21	17

Source: Therborn 1995, table 14.3. See also Inglehart 1997.

Note: Percentage who answered that they were "very proud" of their nationality.

tions. Voter participation in the United States has decreased steadily among various generations of voters. The decline begins with those who turned eighteen in the 1930s and accelerates rapidly beginning with those who turned eighteen in the 1940s (Putnam 1996, 43). Globalization, which arrived much later, is not the culprit here. Voter turnout in Western Europe has been stagnant rather than falling sharply, but it is lower in many countries than it was two or three decades earlier (Inglehart 1990, 336).

The political scientist Ronald Inglehart, who traces the shift in values in Western society, argues that voter turnout rates are not a good measure of political activity. Some countries require citizens to vote (Belgium and Italy, for example), and voting is largely an "elite-directed form of participation, and constitutes a poor indicator of more active forms of participation, which are becoming increasingly significant. The process of cognitive mobilization gives rise to sophisticated electorates who are less closely linked to the political machines that bring voters to the polls but show a higher potential for issue-specific forms of participation" (Inglehart 1990, 342). In place of voter turnout, Inglehart uses as his data the answer to the question, "When you get together with your friends, would you discuss politics frequently, occasionally, or never?" The question appears on the Euro-barometer survey, the Political Action surveys, and the World Value surveys carried out in 1981 and 1990. The data suggest that in general, the more educated discuss politics more often than the less educated, and men more than women, with the gap particularly large in more "traditional" countries such as Italy, Spain, and Japan. Despite the worldwide trend of a higher-educated electorate and greater political participation by women, the average proportion of those who discuss politics fell sharply in the age cohort born from 1956 to 1965 after a steady rise among those in older cohorts (table 5.2). Because previous generations' discussion rates had risen, this measure of political participation increased in the 1980s in many European countries (table 5.3).

Rather than indicating stronger or weaker national identity or even willingness to participate politically, the data suggest that late-modern citizens are participating in national politics differently from those of the past. The combination of more, rather than less political discussion over time (despite declines among the youngest generation surveyed), other data that show gradual declines in political party loyalty, and a rapid shift to issue politics, in which citizens are much less likely to be "oriented by group ties . . . than by concerns for specific political decisions" (Inglehart 1990, 364) reflects a more politically sophisticated electorate that is more likely to consider each issue on its merits and less likely to follow party lines. The trend is toward more individualistic behavior, but it does not tell us whether the national identities of individuals have weakened.

Table 5.2 Political Participation in Ten Western Societies, by Age Cohort, 1973 to 1984 (Percentage)

Birth Years of Cohort	Actually Observed	Adjusted for Education	N
1956 to 1965	66	59	26,295
1946 to 1955	73	69	38,081
1936 to 1945	71	71	32,476
1926 to 1935	66	69	28,773
1916 to 1925	64	68	26,129
1906 to 1915	58	63	21,133
Before 1906	49	56	9,574

Source: Inglehart 1990, table 10.2. Inglehart combined the results of European Community 1973 Survey and Euro-barometer surveys 3-21 (from 1975 to 1984) carried out in Britain, France, Italy, West Germany, Netherlands, Belgium, Luxembourg, Ireland, Denmark, and Greece.

Note: Percentage who answered that they frequently or occasionally have political discussions. Adjusted across age cohorts for education differences; more educated respondents tend to discuss politics more frequently.

Table 5.3 Political Participation, by Country, 1973 to 1990 (Percentage)

Country	1973 to 1975	1976 to 1978	1979 to 1981	1982 to 1987	1990
Belgium	42	47	46	53	52
Denmark	70	72	70	74	—
France	62	68	61	63	63
Greece	—	—	66	74	—
Ireland	62	57	59	64	59
Italy	60	64	61	56	64
Netherlands	63	75	74	78	74
United Kingdom	66	66	68	68	66
United States	—	—	68	—	70
West Germany	78	76	78	83	83

Source: Inglehart 1990, table 10.7; Inglehart 1997, figure 10.8.

Note: Percentage who answered that they frequently or occasionally have political discussions.

Changing Local Community

The notion of local community is also undergoing major change. Both in the United States, where local community was traditionally defined by a strong sense of civic association, and in Europe, where community was traditionally defined by medieval conceptions of space and identity, local identity is being transformed (Ascher 1998, 51). The causes of this transformation are multiple, but the main ones are changing demographics, changing work, and the communications revolution. Equally important, local community in OECD countries after World War II was affected by the growth of the welfare state and the new kinds of social and political participation that developed around it, including the gradual shift to television as the main source of news and political organizing. Globalization, competition, and the gradual "de-welfarization" of the state also created new meanings for and constraints on local association.

The Industrial Revolution disassociated residential communities, workplaces, and social life in a historical movement that classical sociologists identified as the substitution of organic for mechanic solidarity. Today, with the loss of social relevance of the workplace and of work-based forms of social organization, a greater demand is placed on other organizational forms of sociability. Local communities and voluntary associations are foremost among such forms. However, available evidence in advanced so-

cieties suggests a serious erosion of membership in locality-based voluntary associations, a result of individualistic values, time constraints, and
the preponderance of two-job families (Putnam 1995). The resurgence of
local communities as social networks could provide a useful compensatory
mechanism for well-tempered individualism. Spatial development in the
past twenty years, however, has been characterized by widespread territorial sprawl, be it in high-rise banlieues or suburban, and then exurban,
single-family dwellings (Garreau 1991; Dogan and Kasarda 1987). The
functional separation between residence, work, and urban services, the increasingly lower density of new urban forms, geographic mobility, and decreasing participation in neighborhood social activities make rebuilding
social communities on a neighborhood basis difficult (Fischer 1984). Although community organizations do exist all over the urban geography
of advanced societies, fieldwork research by Manuel Castells and others
show the defensive and parochial character of most community organizations (Castells 1983; Borja 1988). According to these analysts, such organizations are mainly agents of "collective individualism," more interested in
preserving the status quo in their neighborhoods than in building new
kinds of supportive social relationships.

By and large, residence-based communities as forms of social interaction and collective undertaking are fading away in advanced societies. The
isolation and vulnerability of inner-city neighborhoods has been exacer-
bated by reduced investment from outside public and private institutions
(Halpern 1995). Europeans, Asians, and Americans have moved into what
François Ascher calls "metapoles" and Joel Garreau calls "edge cities"—urban and suburban metropolitan sprawls with multiple centers, in which
individuals move daily from one part to another as part of their "normal"
activities (Ascher 1998; Garreau 1991). According to Garreau, "two-thirds
of all American office facilities are in Edge Cities, and 80 percent of them
have materialized in only the last two decades" (Garreau 1991, 5). This is
more than simple suburbanization, which has been a feature of American
life since the late 1940s. Many middle-class and high-income suburbs had
their own coherence and sense of community. As service jobs moved out to
the suburbs, they gained even more coherence. However, the new urban
and suburban complex is defined by a different dynamic. Work is increasingly disaggregated from permanent, full-time jobs, and both husband and
wife are likely to work—and to work in different localities that change over
their work lives. As parents, these husbands and wives also have to arrange

for their children's day care and schooling. Community primary schooling is still the norm in Europe, Japan, and the United States. In the United States, this has meant that housing prices in communities with good public schools are high, in part because living there allows parents access to high-quality, free local educational services. Such schools may not be close to one or both parents' place of work, although professionals are more likely to live near their work and lower-skilled (and lower-paid) workers travel long distances. This is the inverse of the industrial organization of space. Those who cannot afford high-priced housing near service and job centers either have to settle for lower-quality schooling or send their children to private schools. They also tend to live in the distant margins of the metapoles. In Europe, public schooling or publicly financed but privately run schooling (such as in the Netherlands) is characterized by more choice, with parents allowed to send children to schools outside their immediate neighborhoods. Yet this means that parents who "choose" education outside their neighborhoods may have to transport their children a considerable distance to school.

Families also incur more economic and social risk because of increased global competition and reduced assumption of risk by the state. The quantity and quality of education pursued is more crucial to an individual's future possibilities than it was in the heyday of the national welfare state economy in the 1950s, 1960s, and early 1970s. This makes parents' educational choices for their children far more important now than in the past. When income distribution was more equal and jobs relatively secure, parents were content to settle for the schools that were convenient to their work location. This is much less true today. Parents are now more likely to do complicated spatial cost calculations that balance the cost of housing in particular locations with the distance to work and to high-quality schools.

In this new context, locality begins to have a different meaning. Individuals' networks shift from neighbors and fellow community members to contacts in "destinational" institutions such as work and schools. Because work associations become more precarious and children change schools as they grow older, social networks also become much less permanent.

Take Bruce Gerstman, for example. He worked at a search engine firm in Silicon Valley with such rapid turnover that after working there only a year and a half, he was considered an old-timer. He found that this situation discouraged friendships at work. "Why get close, I thought. He or she will probably be leaving soon anyway, or perhaps I will" (Ilana DeBare, "Keeping a Packed Bag at Work," *San Francisco Chronicle*, April 30, 1999).

This declining permanence of networks is not a result of greater spatial mobility, as might be supposed. Data on mobility within the United States, for example, suggest that spatial mobility has not increased and has probably decreased. These data include only the spatial mobility of those already residing in the United States, not that of new immigrants; hence, it underestimates total mobility. According to the U.S. Census Bureau, in the 1950s, 20 percent of Americans changed residence each year, and 6.9 percent annually changed county of residence. In the 1990s, only 17 percent moved, and 6.6 percent changed counties (Putnam 1996). One reason for less mobility is that the average age of individuals living in a particular place is increasing. A second is that when husband and wife both work, the freedom to move is constrained even when a change would be advantageous for one member of the couple. A third is that once an individual or family chooses a metapole to live in, a variety of work possibilities is opened, and individuals are willing and able to switch jobs within the vast boundaries of the metapole by altering their daily itinerary.

A major question is whether these spatial and relational changes lead to a "loss of community" or merely to its transmutation into other forms. Garreau gropes for the answer to this question in *Edge City:* "[Community] is entirely voluntary and thus fragile. If you don't like the ties that bind you to others—for even the most ephemeral or transitory or stupid reasons—you can and may leave. You are no longer forced to proclaim your identity as part of any inexorable membership in a larger whole. . . . People reach out in a myriad of directions for society and friendship, even family. Peer groups—community—are defined by job, avocation, church, or some other institution, far more than by location" (Garreau 1991, 278–79).

Individuals certainly do continue to try to build community, interact in their localities, and establish social networks. Based on data from the late 1970s and early 1980s, Castells argues that urban social movements situated in local communities dotted the landscape even as global processes began to dominate economic structures and thereby decreased identity with cities' spatial neighborhoods (Castells 1997, 61). These movements arose precisely because traditional national institutions, such as labor unions and political parties, failed to deal with the worst excesses of capitalism. Although largely "defensive identity," the movements were "integrated in the structure and practice of local government, either directly or indirectly, through a diversified system of citizen participation, and community development" (Castells 1997, 62). Suburbia, exurbia, and urbanized countryside produced their own movements, also largely at the local level, mainly for a cleaner, healthier environment.

Are these local movements on the rise or are they declining? Some analysts, such as Amitai Etzioni, see local community in the United States reviving in the age of globalization as individuals seek to reestablish local networks and identity to replace their declining confidence in national politics and sense of nationality (Etzioni 1993). Others, such as Robert Putnam, argue that "Americans who came of age during the Depression and World War II have been far more deeply engaged in the life of their communities than the generations that followed them" and that there is substantial evidence "for the decline of social capital [networks, norms, and trust that enable participants to act together more effectively to pursue shared objectives] and civic engagement" (Putnam 1996, 34; see also Putnam 1995). In earlier work, Putnam shows the importance of these social networks for effective local government by analyzing the large variation in local government performance in Italy. He argues, however, that such differences were imbedded historically in local social relations (social capital) rather than the product of recent changes. Participation in civic culture has long been much more pronounced in certain Italian regions—namely Emilia Romagna, Lombardia, and northern Italy in general—than in others—such as Puglia, Sicily, and southern Italy in general. Civic culture, in turn, is highly correlated with effective local government even when average education per capita is accounted for (Putnam 1993).

Putnam's recent claims that social capital in the United States is declining through decreased local participation in civic life goes far beyond his Italian regional comparisons. He now suggests that we may be witnessing a transformation in the nature of long established local networks as much as a rise or fall in civic association. Indeed, the two processes are probably happening at once. Putnam's data show that since the 1950s, "bowling alone," mainly, he believes, because they watch television instead of engaging in group activities (Putnam 1995, 70). Time spent on informal socializing and visiting is down by about one-fourth, and time devoted to clubs and organizations is down by one-half. Between 1973 and 1993, attendance of meetings on town or school affairs is off by 39 percent, and volunteer work for a political party is down 56 percent. He further cites the

General Social Survey as showing a drop of about one-fourth in group membership since 1974. "Slumping membership has afflicted all sorts of groups, from sports clubs and professional associations to literary discussion groups and labor unions." The Gallup Poll shows church attendance down by 15 percent in the 1960s and remaining low ever since, and the National Opinion Research Center suggests that this decline continued during the 1970s and 1980s, dropping to about 30 percent in the mid-1990s (Putnam 1996, 35). Putnam acknowledges that secondary and tertiary associations, such as the American Association of Retired Persons and the Sierra Club, as well as the Christian right and the National Rifle Association, have grown considerably, but he claims that they are less associations than political interest groups and provide little social connectedness.

One of the most interesting aspects of Putnam's claim is that although civic engagement in all forms, including social trust and membership in different types of groups, rises rapidly with education, particularly college education, and average education has risen over the past thirty years, civic group participation and social trust have both declined, implying that the shift in the curves at all levels of education must be large. Social connectedness eroded steadily among the generations raised after World War II, particularly as reflected in voter turnout, the number of newspapers read, and membership in group organizations. The major drop in social trust appeared later, among those who turned eighteen in the 1960s. The main culprit in fostering this decline, he concludes, is television. The average American actually watches about four hours of television daily, which means that this activity eats up a significant proportion of his or her leisure time. Historically, the growth of television viewing coincides almost exactly with the drop in membership in civic associations. At any point in time over the past twenty years, "each hour of television viewing is associated with less social trust and less group membership. . . . TV watching comes at the expense of nearly every social activity outside the home, especially social gatherings and informal conversations. . . . In short, television privatizes our leisure time" (Putnam 1996, 47–48).

Although others question Putnam's conclusions that civic life in America has declined since the "long civic generation" (Putnam 1996) that came of age in the 1930s and 1940s, as well as his explanation that television is primarily to blame for this phenomenon (see Schudson 1996; Skocpol 1996; and Valelly 1996), all agree that civic involvement has profoundly changed. Whether this change is partly toward more child-centered activities (sports leagues, for example), multiple activities in a single organization (such as a church), work-related professional activities, or more time-efficient political activities (such as high-clout national tertiary organizations), it seems indisputable that Americans are less likely to join in the same kind of civic activities as in the past. New patterns of group activities, Putnam's critics suggest, indicate a move away from community-based civic and political associations toward more time spent on child- or family-centered and professional networking and more relegation of local political activity to specialized national lobby groups.

For example, parents may be shifting their volunteer time to those organizations that more directly benefit their own children but are not counted as civic membership. For example, the American Youth Soccer Organization involves hundreds of thousands of school-age boys and girls, and almost as many parents, in California alone. Similarly, parent voluntarism in their children's classrooms would not count as belonging to an organization, whereas being a member of a school's parent-teacher association (PTA) would. Theda Skocpol (1996) mentions going bowling with a group of families rather than with a bowling league as another example of family-oriented informal associations not counted in the surveys used by Putnam.

Highly educated married women, who in the past devoted the most time to civic organizations, are now more likely to be working full time and more interested in networking for professional advancement. As Skocpol points out, the PTA, the local YWCA (Young Women's Christian Association), or the local church group may not be the most effective organization to join for this purpose. Indeed, there may be no formal civic organization today that works as well for professional advancement as some of those of the past. Instead, informal networks of the kind described by AnnaLee Saxenian (1994) among high-tech professionals may increasingly be the new "community" that serves this purpose most effectively.

Putnam readily admits that television is not the only reason that participation in formal civic associations is down, but his critics are correct in arguing that his focus on television viewing places the blame for reduced civic participation on individual behavior rather than much larger changes in politics and work (of which television is a part). "An association may decline," Skocpol writes, "not only because people with the wrong sorts of individual traits proliferate in the population, but also because opportunities and cultural models for that association (or type of organization) wither in the larger society and polity. An association may also decline because the defection of crucial types of leaders or members makes the enterprise less resourceful and relevant for others" (Skocpol 1996, 22). Changes in the family and the labor market for women, for example, probably drew large numbers of women out of associations even if they did not work. Women's identity has changed, and with it the kinds of activities in which they engage. The fact that women were and are crucial to associational activities means that a change in their role could have made these associations decline even if television had not come along. Politics are completely different as well, increasingly organized around media, high-stakes fundraising, and massive national write-a-check-and-join lobbying groups rather than local political clubs and people power. Is this because Americans are watching television, or is it because their day-to-day involvement is no longer an integral part of politics? The notion of community built around political work seemed to die with the 1960s and the shift to media-based politics. Individuals have responded rationally to this change by reducing their participation in local political associations. There are exceptions, of course. The Christian right revived locally based associational politics in the 1980s, mainly through fundamentalist churches but also through new mass-mailing techniques. The women's movement also created a number of locally based, issue-focused political organizations that did not exist thirty years ago, and so have some environmental organizations. All have had political success, but so have lobbying groups, such as the American Association of Retired Persons, that are not organized around local chapters.

Skocpol also points out that civic culture was promoted by a politics that engaged individuals in the belief that they could make a difference. This included a sense of nationality and of collective purpose. In the "long civic generation," associations were encouraged, not discouraged, by big government, brought on by the New Deal and World War II. The decline of traditional community in the post–World War II period, particularly in the generation that came of age in the 1960s, was spurred on by the welfare state's success in generating inclusive, equalizing, and stable economic growth. The welfare state simultaneously increased complacency and demands for even more inclusion by women and minority groups. In the present round, the welfare state's failure in the face of new global competition and computerization of political and social life impacts community once again, and civic associations and politics appear to be declining further.

The trend away from associational politics may not be a feature only of the U.S. political scene. It also seems to apply to Europe, although the discussion of these trends there is different from that in the United States. In the United States, which outranks most European countries in community involvement if not in political participation, the issue is whether Americans spend as much time and energy on civic associations and locally based membership organizations. In Europe, the issue is more the type of political participation ("it is not the degree of political participation that distinguishes civic from uncivic regions, but its character" [Putnam 1993, 109]) and neighborhood ties, including, for example, participation in sports and political clubs. Inglehart's (1990, 339) findings suggest that there is a rapid shift from group to issue politics, in response to which citizens are becoming less likely to be oriented by group ties and increasingly likely to make their political decisions as individuals independent of any political party line. Putnam also points out that in countries such as Italy (this could apply to France and Spain as well), "organized religion . . . is an alternative to the civic community, not a part of it. . . . [In Italy] at the regional level, all manifestations of religiosity and clericalism . . . are negatively correlated with civic engagement" (Inglehart 1990, 107). Thus, at least in Catholic Europe, a decline in religiosity could suggest greater civic engagement and more participatory and "effective" local community.

The two surveys on world values conducted by Inglehart from 1981 to 1984 and from 1990 to 1993 suggest that in addition to the increased individualization of political decisions and decline in religiosity (both of which could imply more civic community), civic culture in Europe does not seem to be declining; it may be simply changing. As illustrated in figure 5.1, the proportion of people who agreed with the statement, "Generally speaking, most people can be trusted," did not decline in most countries. Social trust was highly correlated with the cumulative percentage of people in each country who also said that they belonged to one or more of sixteen types of voluntary associations (figure 5.2) from 1990 to 1993, the one survey in which both questions were asked. This suggests that at least in the 1980s, membership in such associations probably did not decline significantly in the OECD. Civic culture in countries such as Japan, Italy, France, and Spain is low, but this appears only somewhat related to low national pride. It is not clear that national identity is shifting to local identity or that declining national identity finds a ready home in local identity. If anything, the main trend is probably one in which the same civic culture feeds into

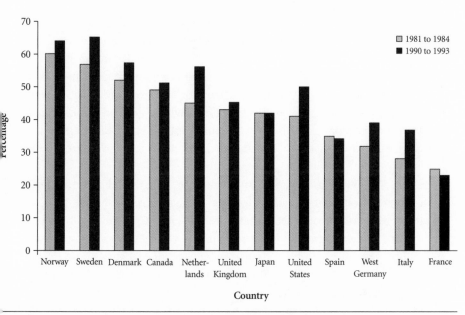

Figure 5.1 Social Trust, by Country, 1981 to 1984 and 1990 to 1993 *Sources:* Inglehart 1990, 1997.

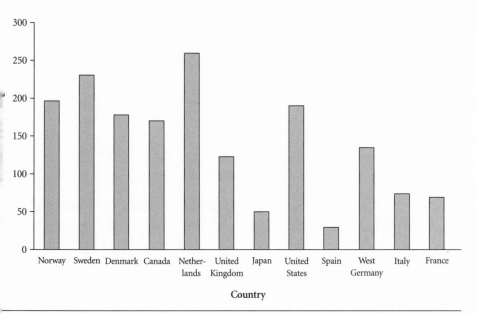

Figure 5.2 Civic-Mindedness, by Country, 1990 to 1993 *Source:* Inglehart 1997.

both local and national community, and both communities are changing simultaneously in the direction of greater individual expression and a prevalence of individually built networks. Change in community definition is fueled by new structures of families' community time and space and by the increasing focus by individuals on acquiring information and knowledge. It is also fueled by media politics, which is aimed at individuals rather than groups, by declining class consciousness, and by an educational system and labor market that stress individual competition over group solidarity.

The data point to a major transformation in local identity and the meaning of local community. The transformation began before globalization, but globalization exacerbates it. The civic association, which has provided a high degree of social trust in the United States, is apparently eroding. This may also be occurring in Europe and Japan. The new individualization of civic and political behavior may be more sophisticated and discriminating, however, than the old. It seems to be producing participation in new forms, focused on issues rather than traditional group or class interests. It may also be producing new forms of association or at least a willingness to engage in such associations. Thus we have two sides to the story: Globalization contributes to increased individualization and an erosion of the communities and civic structures that helped integrate industrial and service workers during the industrial age. Yet this same individualization, when accompanied by more education and more information, may mean that emerging communities can form politically and socially effective groups with new, cohesive identities that satisfy individual needs in the information age. The main question, then, is what these new "communities" of the globalized future will be like.

New Notions of Community

The decline in Europe, America, and Japan of community structures built around the "republican" movements of the nineteenth century, followed by the decline of the twentieth century's welfare state and patriarchal, "consumption," single-employee family, raises the issue of whether other communities are emerging that might fill this void. Keep in mind the trend toward individualization wrought by workplace changes, the media revolution, and women's redefinition of the family. New communities will have to incorporate workers who are more educated, more choice-oriented, more "flexible," more time-conscious, and more eager to influence their environment.

The new bond that holds these individuals together in the global information age is the search for knowledge. Knowledge is much more important today for social mobility, the raising of children, and self-understanding than it was in the past. It makes sense that individual identity and the search for community will flow out of this need for knowledge and information. Three major types of such communities are emerging, all organized around the increased role of knowledge and information in economic and social life. I call them the self-knowledge community, the knowledge-use community, and the knowledge-production community.

The Self-Knowledge Community: Ethnicity, Gender, and Cultural Identity

Self-knowledge has always played a role in identity. The very essence of being human is the individual's capacity for self-reflection and self-understanding. An individual's identity has therefore always been rooted in knowledge of self. "Getting in touch with your feelings" is now a hackneyed expression, but it is a good description of self-knowledge, especially when it means developing an understanding of who one is historically and emotionally.

Self-knowledge is highly contextual. A child with black skin living in the United States cannot help but learn that he or she, as a black person, has a particular history in American society. Similarly, gypsies in Europe cannot avoid being tagged with their history. This produces an inevitable self-knowledge that then plays a role in black or gypsy identity. Think of the complications for U.S. Latinos who are black: part of their self-knowledge is that they do not share the same history with U.S. blacks, yet they are often forced to do so in the context of a dominant white society that may not distinguish one black skin from another. Not every African American has a strong identity with African American culture. It is virtually impossible, however, in the context of U.S. society for a person with black skin not to deal with his or her relation to European white culture. Neither can people of gypsy heritage avoid seeing themselves as "different" in the cultural space of most European nations, more different in some than in others.

For many in the economically developed areas of the world, their source of identity is the market and its notions of merit, material reward, and local and global networks based on professional (market) interests. National identity increasingly becomes linked with the nation's "market power"— the nation-state's capacity to provide employment and rising wages to individuals living within its borders. Such a new global concept of identity has important national and local elements and gives new meaning to both the state and local communities. In that sense, ethnic, gender, and cultural identities as well as nationality are subsumed in an individual-centered global identity. Knowledge also has a particular meaning in that notion of identity: identity is tied to an individual's market worth, and that worth is established globally. This explains the enormous pressure many parents feel regarding the quality of education for their children or the pressure that employees feel to build up their résumés with certain kinds of skills, even when they already have what they consider a good job. Disaggregated labor is always "in formation."

Thus for many, if not most, individuals in highly developed OECD countries, their "roots" in ethnic or religious identity is added to global, market identity. Individuals in any society have multiple identities. For some, ethnic or religious identity is strong and may provide community, but neither the individual nor his or her community views itself as a primary source of identity. Many individuals attend religious services regularly but have a strong sense of national identity and a strong sense of market identity. Many identify with some ethnic group; others are feminists. The tendency in most OECD countries is toward greater individualism, both economically and politically. Religious observance is in steady decline, spatial communities are transformed, workplaces are desocializing, and political allegiances to traditional parties and traditional class alliances are disintegrating. When most men and women in the developed countries seek ethnic, gender, or religious identity in today's globalizing market environment, they seek it individually. These secondary identities are politically important, but they are not dominant. When they conflict with the individual's market identity, serious personal problems may arise, and these may reveal themselves politically, as individuals vote from self-knowledge rather than market "interest."[5]

The market does not work well as a source of identity for everyone. Markets also increase material differences among individuals. Thus, even if the market creates a sense of community among those who share the same professional networks, it also continuously destroys communities, isolating individuals until they are able to find new networks. With the individualization of workers and their separation from permanent jobs, even the identities individuals have with respect to their workplaces become more tenuous and subject to more frequent change. Today's co-workers are not necessarily tomorrow's friends. To be successful in the marketplace requires that one develop more extensive, cross-firm, shallower networks rather than close ties in any particular work organization. For less successful global marketers, the search for identity turns in other directions and does so more intensely than in the past. Cross-class local organizations in which local elites take leadership roles, such as the PTA and the American Legion in the United States and the local political party organizations in Europe and the United States, have been abandoned in favor of interest-group organizations and movements of the "weak" marketers.

In this context, many search for other identities. When these do not coincide with existing national territories, they also seek to redefine nationality. Ethnic identity is certainly one such identification. In sociologist Göran Therborn's words, "Affirming an ethnic identity amounts to discounting the present and the future for the past, to thinking and saying that the past is more important than the present. . . . Who your parents were is more important than what you do, think, or might become. . . . So, the less value the present appears to provide, the more important ethnicity, other things being equal" (Therborn 1995, 231). Religious identity is another. Religious fundamentalism is on the rise worldwide. It rejects the market as authority, and although fundamentalist groups have targeted the nation-state as a power base, there is an inherent contradiction between religious fundamentalism and a territorially defined nation. The same contradiction does not exist when it comes to local communities or to globalized movements for religious identity. Religious localism necessarily means communities based on exclusion. Even ethnic movements move away from their inclusionary focus. Rather than centering on nation-state legislative and financial intervention (for example, the civil rights movement or the bilingual education movement in the United States) that includes the particular ethnic or racial group in the national project, they now focus on cultural identities independent from the national project or seek recognition in global terms, beyond nationality. The fastest-growing self-identity group among U.S. blacks, for example, is Muslims. Although Muslims represent a small percentage of all African Americans, they provide a sense of exclusive community based on moral rather than market success. Christian fundamentalism follows a similar line for whites, Latinos, and Asians toward providing a new self-knowledge that stands above market success: all the information you need to lead a fulfilling life is in the Bible. Fundamentalist beliefs do not exclude success in the marketplace, but the appeal of fundamentalism is strongest for those who feel simultaneously threatened by the inclusiveness of a multiculturalist version of the welfare state, which offers a racial-equality vision of nationality, and the inclusiveness of the global market, which serves the power of money and complex information systems.

Cultural identity—whether religious, ethnic, racial, or gender related, whether local, regional, or global—is an antidote to the complexity and harshness of the global market as the judge of a person's worth. For white nationalists, it is also an antidote to the multicultural welfare state. Such a trend could, however, mean increased social conflict. If some local, ethnic, or religious groups feels increasingly excluded from the high end of the market, a weakened nation-state incapable of reincorporating them socially could mean less stability. We see this in the varied politics of the National Front movement in France, white nationalist movements in the United States, and Quebecois separatism in Canada, among others.

The market itself has never been sufficiently inclusive. Because strong undemocratic and nonegalitarian nation-states existed before the economic systems were dominated by the free market, many believe that states are no guarantee of inclusion. The modern capitalist state, however, has developed into a successful market "softener." The decline of that role in the face of powerful global marketization of national economies pushes the dispossessed to seek refuge in new and more exclusive collectives. These collectives generally have neither the power nor the funds to help the dispossessed financially or to help them develop the skills and knowledge valued by global markets. They can help develop self-knowledge and therefore self-confidence. They can provide community and therefore a sense of belonging. They often do so by defining others as outsiders without the "true" self-knowledge or the "right" ancestors. At the extreme end, these communities are often highly undemocratic. If the nation-state does not have the financial capability or the political legitimacy to dissipate such movements by incorporating its members into much broader notions of community and values, societies unable to maintain market success may face serious, irreconcilable divisions.

The story is an old one: establishing self-identity for groups that feel powerless often means asserting their separateness; but that, in turn, gives space for conflict that emphasizes this very separateness. Such ethnic conflicts occur at the bottom of the global market totem pole, where the movements for cultural identity are most likely to occur.

Cultural identity movements do not only thrive among those dispossessed by globalization. Some cultural identity movements also develop around a positive relation between globalization and the particular ethnic or regional group. The Catalans' push for greater autonomy from Spain, the Lega's (northern Italians) demands for separation from Italy, and Slovenia's for independence from Yugoslavia emerge partly from these regions' (and their people's) sense that they are better global marketers than those in the rest of the country. They want to be freed from financial and political responsibility for their less capable compatriots. The three regions mentioned feel closer to the economies of northern Europe and the new global economy than to the rest of the country of which they are (or were) a part. The fact that they also have a different "culture" is the political basis for greater autonomy but not necessarily the underlying reason. Globalization gives a new space to such movements because the locus of economic power and identity shifts away from the nation-state to regional and global economies. This allows for the reemergence of cultural identities that are ancient and local, rooted in tribal affiliations, and postmodern and global.

The Knowledge-Use Community: Professional Identification and Work Networks

One of the main effects of increased competition in a global economy is the disaggregation of labor from lifetime jobs and the redefinition of a worker from an employee to a productive asset. This redefinition means that employers have a different social relationship to their workers. Employers are less likely to feel responsible for the training, social wages, and continued employment of their workers, and workers are less likely to feel "attached" or loyal to their firms but more likely to be fearful of losing their jobs. The redefinition also means that the knowledge enhancing the value of a worker's existing skills changes. Just as any community, the firm is a complex organization with rules, regulations, and multiple relationships. When jobs were perceived to be more permanent, no matter what the skill levels or roles of individual workers, workers found it to their advantage to build close relationships inside the firm and to acquire detailed knowledge about the firm and their particular jobs (or the jobs just above them in the hierarchy). If the firm was unionized, it also made sense to develop close relationships in the union local. The most useful work knowledge was therefore knowledge specific to the firm, including learning how to manipulate the symbols, histories, and rituals of the firm (and the union local). Those who did best at that were rewarded with promotions, higher wages, and the support of fellow workers, even in a highly competitive environment.

It still benefits employees to acquire knowledge specific to the firm. Such specific knowledge helps people keep their jobs longer, and firms still do promote people from within the firm. Much of firm-specific knowledge can also be generalized to other jobs in other companies. If an engineer working on a product at one company learns a lot about the culture of that company, he or she already knows what to look for in learning about the culture at another company.

However, one effect of the movement to disaggregate labor is that employees and workers need to learn a lot more about the market for their skills beyond the particular company in which they happen to be working. This includes the culture of other firms, the kinds of jobs available in other firms, and the kinds of skills that will make them more attractive in the broader market. This is the kind of knowledge that people used to try to acquire when first looking for a job, or for their first "career job" (following a period of part-time work while they completed their educations). Now, with the possibility of repeated episodes in the job market, the information and networks needed for a first job are becoming a permanent feature of a worker's process of knowledge acquisition. At the same time, union locals and firms become less important for employees as knowledge-use communities, even if they identify closely with the union or the firm while they are working in that job.

INFORMAL WORK INFORMATION NETWORKS   How does this networking play out? Let us look at the networking appropriate to two levels of workers: professionals and semiskilled workers. Professionals working in one firm establish networks with professionals in their area of expertise who work at other firms in many different ways. College connections are one. An important reason for going to particular colleges and graduate(or professional) schools is to develop relationships with people who may play a significant role later in life. The more elite the institution, the better the connections made there. Professionals also belong to associations. These have been important in the past, and although some, such as the American Medical Association, are in decline, new professional associations are springing up all the time. With the internet, professional association takes on new meaning.

Before exploring professional association in the era of telecommunications, however, I want to focus on the more informal knowledge-use networks that professionals build up around workplaces. Although Silicon Valley is hardly typical of most work regions, it represents a globally integrated site that has thrived because of networking. It also represents a model intimately connected with new information and communications technologies: innovation and new knowledge. Innovation and new knowledge are becoming crucial elements across all industries, so the Silicon Valley model is one that many other work regions worldwide would like to emulate, and probably will. In other words, Silicon Valley is a "frontier" region. The way people work there now is the way people in other regions will work in the future.

In her study comparing Silicon Valley with Route 128 around Boston, AnnaLee Saxenian (1994) argues that Silicon Valley prospered whereas Route 128 fell behind largely because of the close ties that firms and professionals developed in California, which did not exist in the East. Innovation, she claims, requires such "collaboration" even in the context of intense competition. Popular bars in Silicon Valley serve as important poles for exchanging information about "competitors, customers, markets, and technologies." Saxenian chronicles a culture of social relations organized around work knowledge, in which relationships and "even gossip" are crucial to successful conduct of business (Saxenian 1994, 32–33).

Because professionals in Silicon Valley tend to be highly mobile, labor market information is crucial to career success. Saxenian reports that during the 1970s, "average annual employee turnover exceeded 35 percent in local electronics firms and was as high as 59 percent in small firms. . . . An anthropologist studying the career paths of the region's computer professionals concluded that job tenures in Silicon Valley averaged two years" (Saxenian 1994, 34–35). I interviewed vice presidents in charge of personnel in larger Silicon Valley companies in the 1990s, and the comments were almost identical. An executive at one company commented, "Twenty percent of skills become obsolete every few years, so there is a lot of turnover. We give opportunities for retraining and try to reengineer people to keep them aboard, but there is a lot of turnover. . . . I would characterize the trajectory of someone in the company as 'blows and goes fast.' Five years maybe in the company. Learn a lot, go out and get a great job somewhere else." The situation at another was remarkably similar: "The job market for engineers is extremely volatile at the moment. People are moving from job to job and can gain tremendous offerings from new places. The majority of our engineers have been with the company for two years or less. It was somewhat lower three years ago, but still high."

Thus, the networks and the meeting places "also function as efficient job search networks . . . as informal recruiting centers as well as listening posts; job information flowed freely along with shop talk" (Saxenian 1994, 34). Search networks not only pervade Silicon Valley professional life, they are also part of its social life. This goes beyond the lunchtime and after-work "watering holes." A typical Silicon Valley professional and his professional wife go out to dinner on Saturday with other couples in the "business"; more often than not, this is part of their job networking as well as socializing. New companies are developed around such friendships and professional associations. Innovative ideas and socializing are part and parcel of a professional community that transcends a single firm and in which the boundaries between work and play become blurred. As late as 1980, this was almost exclusively a male club, but by 1990, more than one-fourth of the professionals and managers in the San Francisco Bay Area's electronics industry were women (Carnoy and Gong 1996). Women too now use the informal job-networking system to move from firm to firm. Employability security is based not just on skills but also on reputation and connections. Those who can make their abilities known through a network of firms are in a better position to find employment (Kanter 1995).[6]

The information networks developed among professionals serve to enhance both the production of knowledge and the value of knowledge embodied in individuals, by helping them move to the best paying, most satisfying jobs. Such networks are genuine new community forms. What distinguishes them from civic associations and political activities is that they combine leisure activities with innovation and work life rather than with social concerns. The new community is an extrafirm but intrawork community. Silicon Valley professionals are notoriously apolitical (many are libertarians) and relatively unconcerned with the larger community outside their profession. Other features that distinguish these networks from traditional civic associations are that they are largely restricted to highly educated professionals and are based on use of knowledge.

Such information networks are much scarcer among Silicon Valley's production workers, and when they do appear they have a different form. Assembly workers, secretaries, and technicians never had the kinds of knowledge skills that are in short supply in the valley; hence they have had to develop other kinds of networks to maximize the value of the knowledge they do have and to acquire new kinds of knowledge of higher value. In industry and the construction trades, the traditional forum that provided this information and this knowledge was the labor union. Unions have generally been kept out of the electronics industry, however, so they do not serve as networks for Silicon Valley workers.[7]

TEMPORARY AGENCIES AS KNOWLEDGE-USE NETWORKS   The fastest-growing networking organizations in Silicon Valley are temporary agencies. Just as professional networking is the product of the highly mobile labor market for skilled engineers and programmers, temp agencies are booming because a growing proportion of Silicon Valley employees are on temporary contracts. There are at least 250 different offices of temporary help agencies operating in Silicon Valley. They range from major multinational companies, like Manpower or Adia, to small firms operating only in the local labor market. Unlike the informal networks among professionals, which are controlled by the professionals themselves, temp agencies are large corporations that charge workers high fees for networking services. Although they may provide benefits to workers, these are generally restricted to those who work a minimum amount of time each year. The main function of the agencies is to provide access to jobs for workers who have limited networking capability. These are not just low-end jobs: some professionals also avail themselves of temp networking.

Neither do temp agencies serve as new communities for networking individuals. The networks are not controlled by the workers who use them. They are not the result of social interactions based on knowledge use; hence, they are qualitatively different from the informal professional networks in Silicon Valley. Indeed, it is in the interest of the temp agencies to keep workers from forming temp worker communities. The agencies' economic existence depends on the individualization and separation of workers seeking jobs. The agency has the information the worker needs; it often provides specific training to individuals to make them more employable and then charges fees for providing those services. If communities form among such workers, they form in ethnic enclaves, in extended family units, and among friends from school and from church. In other words, less skilled workers network precisely through those communities that are declining, whereas the new networks are controlled by private companies antithetical to the formation of worker networking communities.

This leaves a major opening for unions to become a new networking community for contract workers. The precedent for this is unions' role in the construction trades. Construction workers are, in effect, "temp" workers: they move from one job to another, but they are allocated to jobs by unions who negotiate on behalf of their membership. By getting into the temp agency business, unions can help lower-skilled workers develop the kind of interfirm, knowledge-use communities now largely restricted to professionals and managers.

COMPUTER NETWORKS AS KNOWLEDGE-USE COMMUNITIES   Internet and e-mail have enhanced knowledge-use networking. They are transforming the amount of information easily accessible to individuals and the speed at which it moves. They are boons for small business entrepreneurs, who can now communicate in real time with entrepreneurs all over the world and can do so without ever leaving their offices or, for that matter, their homes. Most of the people using the internet and e-mail appear to be "politically conservative white men, often single, English-speaking, residing in North America, and professionals, managers, or students" (Wellman et al. 1996). Surveys conducted in the mid-1990s found that only 20 percent of users were women, but those women tended to be highly educated professionals and students. Computer networking is currently, therefore, mainly an activity for professionals and secretaries (because they have everyday access to computers), not production workers or retail clerks.

According to Barry Wellman and his associates, who have done the best syntheses of research in this field, much of the communication on-line consists of information exchange, and some of that information helps those on-line in their work and professional communities; but that is not the only function of what they call computer-supported social networks (CSSNs). "People find social support, companionship, and a sense of belonging through the normal course of CSSNs of work and community, even when they are composed of persons they hardly know" (Wellman et al. 1996, 220). These "virtual" knowledge-use communities, composed of bulletin boards, chat rooms, and the social part of e-mail communication, expand the physically fixed-in-space "watering holes" of Silicon Valley into a worldwide informal network operating around the clock. Thus, virtual and real communities have many of the same characteristics. For example, the virtual-community part of CSSN participation is voluntary. Members of the virtual community, like professionals meeting at social gathering places, base their feelings of closeness on shared interests rather than shared personal characteristics. "This is a technologically supported continuation of a long-term shift to communities organized by shared interests rather than by shared neighborhoods or kinship groups" (Wellman et al. 1996, 224). Finally, many on-line relationships are between people who see each other off-line, either at work or in the local community. On-line relations at work are more than knowledge-use communities or support groups; they can and do play an increasingly important role as knowledge-production communities within and sometimes across firms.

At the same time, virtual communities are different from communities involving face-to-face contact. Many who participate in on-line relationships do so with people about whom they know little, and may actually want to know as little as possible, beyond having conversations and social support. They like to keep the costs of participation in these networks as low as possible, and they give limited social cues to the network. This encourages communication among different social classes, gender and ethnic groups, and people of different ages, even though it is unclear, given the relative homogeneity of those who use the internet, how much of this cross-group communication there is. It also encourages weak ties. Yet the research seems to suggest reciprocal supportiveness on CSSNs, even between people with weak ties.

The main questions regarding virtual communities are whether they produce the trust needed to recommend someone for a job, and whether people rely on the information and knowledge provided outline as much as on that coming from someone they know through various face-to-face encounters. For individuals intent on protecting their "space" and controlling their time and commitment to others, virtual communities have the great advantage of distance. This distance, so useful to individuality, may, however, detract from communities of engagement and trust. Wellman and his associates claim that there is enough evidence of reciprocity to suggest that virtual communities work pretty much like "real" communities based on shared interests rather than participants' social characteristics. This is probably enough for knowledge-use communities, in which some trust is important.

Not everyone agrees with this assessment, however. As one Australian political scientist puts it, "Virtual communities are celebrated as providing a space and form for a new experience of community. This experience is depicted as multiple, liberating, equalizing, and thus providing a richer experience of togetherness. However, a critical examination of these understandings reveals, paradoxically, a 'thinning' of the complexities of human engagement to the level of one-dimensional transactions and a detaching of the user from the political and social responsibilities of the 'real space environment'" (Willson 1997, 159).

Scattered observations, both for France and for the United States, also suggest that electronic interactive networks are ephemeral forms of social relationships, except when they are anchored in ongoing professional activity or become the extension of family and friendship networks. Although it is certainly too early to assess the emerging phenomenon of interactive electronic communication, it is likely that it will reinforce existing social networks rather than substitute for them (Benson 1994).

The Knowledge-Production Community: Schools as Community Centers

The computer and informal, face-to-face professional networks in Silicon Valley are not just knowledge-use communities; they also serve to create knowledge through the interchange of ideas among innovators. Many individual firms are knowledge producers, and to the degree that they create the conditions for cooperative work and for worker training, they produce innovation and new knowledge.[8] Workers often choose to work for firms that are known to provide an environment in which they can pick up useful knowledge that will enhance their future employability or simply make work more stimulating and fun. Hewlett-Packard has long been known around the San Francisco Bay area as that kind of company; so have Xerox, IBM, and Sun Microsystems, and there are many others.

Although employers cannot predict which workers will be more flexible, flexibility has consistently been associated with higher levels of general education and general job training (Schultz 1975). Individual workers with more education are more able to adjust to new situations, learn new tasks, and adopt new methods of performing old tasks. At the same time, firms that provide relatively large amounts of general training tied to workers' taking on multiple tasks and to wage incentives are more likely to show larger gains in productivity than firms that follow traditional, inflexible production methods (Brown, Reich, and Stern 1993).

This complex interplay between more highly educated workers who are prepared to learn more quickly, to take on new tasks, and to move from one job to another, and best-practice firms that promote increased flexibility through general training, multitasking, and employee decision making, is at the core of high-productivity work in the information age. Flexible work organizations are necessarily learning organizations, and new technologies—including the art of flexible organization itself—make their greatest contribution to productivity when they are based on learning and teaching as an inherent part of the work process. When firms operate as learning organizations, they also create learning communities, although flexibility implies that workers may not be long-term members of these communities.

More productive or not, most workers do not work in learning organizations, even in Japan, Germany, the Netherlands, and Scandinavia, the countries with the firms that provide the most on-the-job training. The main knowledge-production centers in most towns and cities are still schools and universities. Historically, communities structured around the place of residence have been the locus of such knowledge production. However, current conditions of urbanization and the transformation of sociability have reduced the potential of neighborhoods as integrative devices. Neighborhoods are also ceasing to be the organizing space for knowledge production.

Knowledge-production centers themselves can be the organizing space for new communities. Individuals and families may no longer be linked socially to a particular neighborhood, but those with children are increasingly linked to child-care centers, preschools, and elementary schools. Working parents in Europe and now the United States are spending more of their time choosing day care and schools for their children inside or outside their immediate residential area and transporting them there. Children and parents build friendships and social and civic activities around their children's care and learning, wherever it takes place. Thus, their community "space" is defined by their children's day care and schooling rather than by where they live. At the same time, if residence and learning center coincide, that location is the main basis for neighborhood ties.

Parents and children are not the only ones focusing their activities on

learning institutions. Adults going back to postsecondary schools for career changes or job retooling, immigrants who need language training and
other education to assist in their assimilation and social mobility as well as
training in how to help their children succeed in school, and seniors wanting to keep intellectually active and searching for community through
learning are all groups that see knowledge-production centers as a primary
locus of their social lives.

Two important implications emerge from this concept of community.
The first is that social movements seeking to rebuild community make
knowledge-production centers the focus of their organizing activity. If
learning is what parents and adults care about, social movements cannot
hope to be successful if they ignore knowledge production. The second im-
plication is that schools change. Schools are in the process of being transformed into community centers because schools are at the center of the
"new community" described here. Recent experiences with social services
and community centers are discouraging. They are instruments of social
work and counseling but hardly sites of stable social networks. Without
precluding the positive role of community centers, the central organizing
points in OECD towns and cities are elementary and secondary schools
and child development centers. Because schools' location patterns are pervasive and residence based, and because sociability is made easier through
children's connections, schools become the platforms from which to deal
with a variety of issues in neighborhoods, towns, and metapoles.

A good example of community movements' shifting their focus to
schools is the Industrial Areas Foundation (IAF) in the southwestern
United States. The IAF, originally founded in Chicago by Saul Alinsky, is
a community-based organization that mobilizes low-income groups to
improve their living conditions through direct political action on local institutions. "The central role of the IAF organizations is to build the compe-
tence and confidence of ordinary citizens and taxpayers so that they reorganize the relationships of power and politics in their communities in
order to reshape the physical and cultural face of their neighborhoods"
(COPS 1994, 11). In the Southwest, the IAF began by organizing around infrastructure investment and public utility rates, but by 1983 it was pushing
for public education reform, mainly to get legislators to raise the amount
that Texas spent on schools in low-income communities. The success of
that effort (championed by Ross Perot) changed the shape of education
in Texas. It also put the IAF permanently in the business of education re-

form. In 1989, one IAF organization in Austin, Texas—Austin Interfaith—launched a community-wide effort to lower dropout rates in Austin's schools. It organized a partnership among its congregations, the business community, and the school district. In 1990, Austin Interfaith pushed for and won passage of a bond issue to rehabilitate and replace school buildings throughout the city. Since then, Austin Interfaith and other Texas IAF associations have organized parents in poor and predominantly Hispanic and African American neighborhoods to get involved in their children's education and influence what goes on in schools.

Why is education a focus of community organizing? The answer is fairly simple, and it is key to the future of the meaning of community in the information age. Education is an important issue for low-income parents, just as it is for high-income parents. The IAF organizes through activist religious organizations intent on improving the conditions in which their members live and will live in the future. The IAF works on issues that capture the political imagination of the local population it hopes to serve. In the words of Ernesto Cortes Jr., the IAF's regional director for the Southwest, "Organizing is a fancy word for relationship building. No organizer ever organizes a community. What an organizer does is identify, test out, and develop leadership. . . . But you don't organize people around your agenda. If I want to organize you, I don't come and sell you an idea or proposal. What I do, if I'm smart, is try to find out your interest. What's your situation? What are your dreams?" (Texas IAF Network 1990, 38). Organizing around dreams means getting access to resources, and in most low-income communities, education is the most important public resource. Schools are often the largest employer, and education the biggest public investment, in the community. In the information age, they are a major source of high-value information. Exerting some control over schools not only empowers parents, it also builds community around high-value resources.

The efforts of the IAF to organize in schools require parent participation. Much of the writing about educational reform emphasizes parent participation as key to improved learning (Darling-Hammond 1997). High-income parents not only pass along more "cultural capital" to their children, they are also generally more outspoken in dealing with schools and are more likely to get involved. Their expectations tend to be higher, and they have more knowledge about what constitutes quality education (Carnoy, Benveniste, and Rothstein 1998). So it makes sense that schools impacted by the IAF organizing in predominantly Hispanic and black low-income neighborhoods mobilize parents to participate in school reform with a real sense of power to change the schools. The IAF also provides technical assistance to parents and school personnel on how to improve local schools (Murnane and Levy 1996). Parent participation alone is not the key here. If the school gets low-income parents to come to teacher conferences or open house or even school site council meetings, that is obviously better than no participation at all, but it is not the same as IAF-organized parent participation. "You see, part of what makes this different from parent-teacher associations led by their own lay membership is that the organization [IAF] has trained organizers who know how to go about creating an organization, who know how to go about infusing it with values and ideas" (Austin Interfaith organizer, interview with author, Austin, Texas, November 10, 1997). The IAF builds these organizations outside the schools, in church congregations, and the schools become both objects and subjects of this larger movement for political community. The difference between parents' involvement in educational matters at the invitation of school personnel and the IAF's organizing activities lies in the political power and technical expertise that accompany community organizing. In effect, the IAF turns low-income parents with little knowledge of the educational system into the equivalent of vocal, politically powerful upper-middle-class parents. Yet in order to achieve this equivalent to the knowledge-production community that upper-middle-class parents create autonomously by networking individually around their children's school activities, the IAF creates the knowledge-production community by first empowering parents collectively around school improvement.

When schools are viewed and utilized as knowledge-production communities, they change from specialized educational institutions to community centers responding to a complex of knowledge-production needs. Schools usually act as community centers by combining the traditional function of teaching youth during the day and adults at night. For example, U.S. high schools often provide evening classes in English as a second language to immigrants. Community colleges have since their founding provided vocational education to adults. They have also served American women with an educational platform from which to reenter the labor market after raising children to school age. Lifelong education is part and parcel of schools' and colleges' community service functions.

Through the school, other social networks organized at the municipal level can also come into contact with one another. For instance, the Municipality of Bologna, Italy, has developed an interesting experience of social exchange between classrooms and associations of the elderly, whereby groups of children and the elderly adopt one another. The elderly visit the school to tell the children their life stories, thereby transmitting oral history, and also baby-sit when parents need such services. The children, in turn, befriend and energize the elderly. The individualization of society, which gradually erodes the traditional role of grandparents vis-à-vis their grandchildren, is counteracted with the organization of intergenerational networks on a local basis.

These functions are expanding in both higher- and lower-income communities throughout the OECD but in somewhat differing forms. For example, in high-income communities in the United States, privately run child development centers are increasingly located next to public elementary schools so that parents can drop off children at the center before school begins; school personnel then bring the children to classes at the start of school and return them to the center at the end of the school day, where they remain until their parents arrive to bring them home. This seamless procedure allows working parents maximum flexibility and provides a reasonably rich educational environment for young children while their parents work. Parent-run sports leagues also use the same school grounds after school, allowing yet another activity to be organized at the school.

In low-income communities in the United States, those schools lucky enough to have Head Start programs also take preschoolers, usually in the same school building. Few such schools have day care in addition to formal schooling, however. This will most likely happen in the future. However, more and more middle schools and high schools are developing after-school programs to keep unsupervised preteens and teenagers off urban streets. The programs channel them into sports and other activities designed to build a sense of civic duty and self-esteem. The programs also integrate schools into communities that tend, often with good reason, to see schools as an arm of the law rather than educational sites. When he was principal of a middle school in Santa Fe, New Mexico, the late Ed Ortiz transformed the school's relationship with low-income Hispanic parents by allowing them to use the school site for weddings and other family events on weekends. Parents stopped seeing the school as an institution that punished their children as truants and poorly behaved young people.

Instead, the school became their community center, with legitimate educational authority. In the same way, the Beacon program in San Francisco provides after-school activities for teenagers, focusing on extracurricular activities as an alternative to the street-corner drug culture and teen gangs. Because parents fear the violence associated with teenagers' street activity, Beacon has support from parents, which in turn builds support for the schools.

Yet another way of recreating the school as a knowledge-producing community center is demonstrated by Score!, which provides after-school computer-assisted tutoring in subjects learned in school. Although Score! caters mainly to upper-middle-class students and provides these services privately at storefront drop-in centers, it has begun to collaborate with public high schools in Los Angeles. The after-school tutoring programs it provides to low-income urban youth at the school sites are intended to make learning standard math, reading, and writing more enjoyable. The programs have been highly successful.

In these examples of encouraging knowledge production as a community-building activity—in one case, by building community outside the school and making the school a community's project, and in the other by making the school relevant to the community's needs—communities have "taken back" their school sites and rebuilt them into institutions that help build sociability and self-reliance. They are the material bases for the formation of networks between families of different types, all concerned with the future of their children. Family, community, and the future worker (the child) are brought together in a system of interaction that blends instrumental goals (child care, development, and education) with expressive and emotional social interaction. This requires an effort, both from government and from community organizations such as the IAF, to transform the school, to make it more open to the community, and accordingly to provide the public school system with more resources to hire better-trained personnel and more innovative management.

---

1. The ultimate failure of communist state solutions to the search for community shows that most individuals want the security of collective support systems but also want the freedom to choose and the human rights associated with democracy and other liberal values.

2. Benedict Anderson (1983) argues that nations are "imagined communities,"

meaning that national identity (like all identity) is culturally constructed. On the one hand, identity is clearly a cultural construction. On the other, it is based on shared experience, common language, and common socialization that binds those living in the same nation, regardless of their separate or collective relations to the national state. In that sense, it is hardly imagined and represents emotions that shape social behavior in the real, observable world.

3. In today's world, this gets even more complicated by the increased practice by immigrants of holding two passports, one from their country of origin and one from their adopted country. If passports represent some sense of national identity, such dual citizenship means that a small but growing percentage of "nationals" have dual identity, even in the sense of political participation. For example, one candidate for the presidency of Serbia was a U.S. citizen, and the current president of Latvia is a U.S. citizen.

4. I refer to those living in the United States as Americans, even though other nationalities, such as Canadians, Mexicans, and residents of the many countries of Central and South America and the Caribbean, can also claim that identification.

5. A good example in the United States is that many fairly wealthy African Americans and women continue to vote Democratic even when their market interest might incline them toward the Republican Party. On the other hand, many low-income whites vote Republican because of their religious or racial views, even when their economic interests might lie more with the Democrats.

6. See also Mark Granovetter's 1995 classic study, *Getting a Job,* in which he presents strong evidence correlating higher income levels with workers who got new jobs through personal contacts rather than through formal mechanisms.

7. Union organizing of janitorial services are an exception. Janitors are organized primarily through social ties in immigrant Latino communities, with industry-wide organizing aimed at multiemployer bargaining agreements rather than organizing on the basis of individual work sites.

8. For a recent summary of such knowledge-production networks, see OECD 1996c.

6

Sustaining the New Economy

Work is being transformed worldwide because of global competition and the explosion of information and communication technologies. By making production more flexible, the transformation helps firms compete in the new economic environment. It enables them to respond to fast-paced, global-scale product change, customized marketing, and just-in-time deliveries. However, flexibility also disaggregates workers from the social institutions that sustained past economic expansion. Unless new integrative institutions emerge to support new work organizations, and do so quickly, the social development and cohesion needed for longer-term economic growth could be threatened.

What are the new integrative institutions of the new economy going to be, and where will they come from? Will some communities react more effectively to the new conditions than others? The response to the crisis of industrialization in the 1930s was the national welfare state, which set out to protect the jobs and incomes of (male) workers and their families during and after their work lives. That form of reintegration assumed job permanence and a male wage earner as the head of a nuclear family. It also assumed well-defined local and national communities. With the profound changes taking place in work, family, and community, the new integrative institutions will have to be different. Although income guarantees are still important as a means of avoiding the reproduction of poverty from generation to generation, the heart of a more equitable and integrated society in today's global economy is access to knowledge, skills, and information.

Traditionally, the public sector has subsidized both the transmission of existing knowledge and the development of new knowledge. Governments build and staff educational systems. They finance and often manage scientific research and development. In the early stages in the development of new products, governments are also the main buyers. This marriage between public policy and the production of knowledge, unlike many modern marriages between individuals, will undoubtedly last. On the whole, despite its ups and downs, it works. Many argue, however, that government involvement is too great and that other, nongovernmental knowledge and networking institutions must play a greater role. Community organizations, privately managed (usually religious) educational institutions, and unions are powerful political actors in most postindustrial societies.

The transmission of knowledge and information needs to be redefined in the context of flexible production and families in which both parents are employed. This is true for all groups in society, but there is a particular need to focus on those who have traditionally been marginal to the knowledge-production and information system. Such knowledge-marginalized groups will no longer be easily reintegrated through an industrial economy of "permanent" jobs, company or union social structures, and income safety nets as they have been in the past. The days of dropping out of high school and getting a lifetime, high-paying union job in the auto factory are long over. A good school, a solid college education, a good job and training network after college, and a developed sense of self are the new social anchors in a flexible environment. Well-organized knowledge communities will themselves be key to reintegration, and making them successful integrators needs to be a major public goal.

As in past transitions, many of these new knowledge and information institutions will appear spontaneously, in response to market demand, social movements, and visionary leadership. As in the past, the most rapid and effective change will occur spontaneously for those at the top of the pecking order. Private markets are highly sensitive to change and respond quickly. In Silicon Valley, networking is already a way of life, especially for professionals and managers. Informal job networks and new forms of just-in-time customized business management courses available through the internet are already actualities or in the works. Certain obstacles to spontaneous growth in networking and knowledge face those who are nearer the bottom of work hierarchies, however. Most employers are not willing to pay to expand the general knowledge base of their workers. Current institutions such as labor unions, churches, and other voluntary organizations resist change because they have a vested interest in conducting business according to past practices.

Furthermore, most of the new institutions will require public financing to reintegrate isolated individuals and stressed families. This is also problematic. Current public policy is built on models of social integration that assume permanent jobs, held predominantly by men, and traditional families, and political interests hold those models in place: they fight for them even when they make little sense in terms of most citizens' everyday lives. For countries and regions concerned about development and cohesiveness, however, hanging on to such models is bound to be costly. Waiting for existing nongovernmental organizations to change or new ones to appear is also a risky strategy. So public sector entities—whether nation-states, regions, or local governments—able to develop the appropriate public policies for sustaining flexibility will have a distinct advantage over those that cannot.

In this chapter I focus on how the knowledge and information institutions needed in today's emerging flexible work environment will develop. My argument hinges on three main premises. The first is that although nongovernmental intermediaries can be important, government will continue to play a key role in social integration. The role will be transformed, both spatially and in the kinds of programs that are relevant to sustaining new work and family organizations. Publicly financed and managed services as such will still be crucial, however, to restructured communities in the information age. The second premise is that social integration in the competitive, flexible work environment of the information age will take place mainly through knowledge-related activities, including those that enhance people's capacity to learn and innovate, such as basic health care and early child development. Even with the continued existence of social safety nets—mainly providing retirement security—government and nongovernmental organizations will shift their activities toward knowledge building. It is these activities that will be most responsive to sustaining workplaces, families, and new integrative community forms. The third premise is that those societies that are unable or unwilling to develop coherent public policies and to build relevant, socially integrative institutions will suffer economically. I assume that flexible production is one pillar of economic success in the global information age. The other pillar is public policy that effectively sustains flexibility. Not only will some societies be more pleasant, cohesive, interesting places to live, but in the longer run those that have their public act together will do better economically as well.

Before turning to the nature of public knowledge and information policy and the possible roles of nongovernmental organizations, we need to discuss briefly the current debate on the role of public policy itself in the context of current transformations. Government's role is changing, and it is viewed very differently in different parts of the developed world. The starting points for public policy differ by country and region. Such varying initial conditions create many possibilities but also many possible dead ends.

Reconstructing Networks in a Global Environment: Free Market, Public Intervention, or Government Intermediaries?

Communities reconstruct social integration in response to new conditions in the workplace and the family, a process that is worked out through political conflict. Today, reconstruction is being contested politically at three levels: The first level is ideological, between market and public sector intervention approaches to reconstruction. Neither the neoconservative free market approach nor the traditional welfare state approach fits the new conditions. Nevertheless, proponents of such traditional approaches are slow to give up on deeply entrenched policy models. Business groups, unions, retired workers, and other groups have vested interests in keeping them. The second level of conflict is over policy itself: What are the appropriate institutions needed to respond to the new conditions? Where should resources flow, and how much should be spent on different kinds of responses? In the free market model, this is a less compelling issue. The market itself allegedly produces the institutions most relevant to collective needs and allocates resources according to client demand and suppliers' willingness to invest. Even then, however, public policy decisions have to be made, because many of the "market" solutions for delivering schooling, health care, and transportation and communication infrastructure need to be financed, and probably regulated, by government. The third level of disagreement—assuming some role for public intervention—is spatial, a dimension contested among supranational, national, regional, and local policy makers. Different parts of the public bureaucracy, such as national, state or regional, and local governments, have political legitimacy and therefore can gain access to resources and successfully implement policy programs. Each level, and the members of its community, may try to expand its responsibility for institutional responses to the new conditions.

Initial Conditions

Globalization brings with it the seeds of transformation in nation-states. Public intervention in OECD countries over the past seventy years developed primarily around central governmental institutions. In part because they demanded mass mobilizations, the twentieth-century wars between mature industrialized countries and their aftermath (which includes a worldwide economic crisis in the 1930s) forced governments in Europe and the United States to offset the negative effects of capitalist industrial development. They did so through economic arrangements that reduced poverty, income inequality, and the economic risks associated with losing a job, growing old, and getting sick. Governments also used their financial power to generate economic growth and jobs, often through military spending and preparation for war against the nation's "enemies." Over the past sixty years, then, governments in the highly industrialized countries took major responsibility for full employment and assuring that economic growth produced higher standards of living for their citizens. Aside from guiding the economy with monetary and fiscal macroeconomic policies and "planning" economic development through zoning and environmental controls, the state was successful in supporting industrial expansion. It supplied infrastructure investment, such as those needed for transportation, research and development, mass general and specialized vocational and university education, and direct and indirect subsidies to industry and agriculture (including tariff protection and direct public ownership).

The state also entered directly into relations between labor and management. It mediated accords with labor unions and employers that steadily increased real wages, established increasing minimum wages, and created jobs through public employment. In Europe, public employment has accounted for almost the entire increase in jobs since the 1970s (OECD 1994a). The state directly and indirectly supported family security and the family's capacity to invest in its children. Government taxed payrolls (and individuals) to provide a series of social wages that increased families' standard of living through social "guarantees" (health care, old-age pensions, child care, welfare, unemployment insurance, public housing, and direct family subsidies). This "traditional" social-democratic strategy of state-sanctioned and state-financed support networks helped industrial countries to achieve high levels of productivity, wages, and social services. The model worked in a post–World War II global economy dominated by a few highly industrialized countries, all with national or regional markets (such as the European Union) large enough to sustain rapid growth in productivity and wages. That global economy was also marked by small differences in ratios of productivity to wages among the industrial countries. Competitors could trade without undermining each other's basic growth of wages and employment. Most important, national economies could mobilize rising tax revenues to achieve many social and economic goals at the same time. Public funds were used to increase the productivity of capital, expand the demand for goods and services, invest in the family- and school-based education (and health) of future workers and citizens, and assure community and family stability with a social safety net of insurance and pensions. In brief, the democratic nation-state that eventually emerged in the capitalist countries was a welfare state built on the reduction of class conflict.[1] The post–World War II welfare nation-states were largely successful in greatly reducing class identifications among individuals and enhancing the social and ethical bonds among them. To a varying degree, they did so through massive social spending that reduced poverty and the reproduction of class from generation to generation.

However, the welfare state, partly because of an aging population and partly because of a highly competitive world economy with many new actors, is stretching its financial limits. The state can no longer be the "last resort"—the guarantor of full-time incomes or fulfilling jobs—mainly because populations in the OECD have aged so much and because pensions and subsidies in many countries are incredibly generous. For example, Sweden's budget deficit surged to 13.5 percent of gross domestic product in 1993, forcing the government to abandon much of its subsidized youth employment and helping to drive unemployment rates up to record levels. The government also reduced contributions to family incomes for each child (from twelve hundred to one thousand dollars per child annually) and its maternity leave subsidy (from 80 to 75 percent of the woman's salary), and more cuts are down the road (Richard Stevenson, "A Deficit Reins in Sweden's Welfare State," New York Times, February 2, 1995). Italy, France, and Germany, in which government spending hovers close to (or above) 50 percent of gross national product (GNP) (compared with 34 percent in the United States in the 1990s), all had to make an enormous effort to bring deficits down below 3 percent of GNP to meet the self-imposed requirements of the European Monetary Union, which kicked off with the introduction of the euro in January 1999. Germany was in an especially tough position because it had committed so much public spending to subsidizing the former German Democratic Republic (East Germany). At the beginning of the new millennium, Germans face the specter of major reductions in social spending to preserve fiscal integrity within the framework of the Maastricht Accord. Part of Italy's strategy to bring down government spending is to gradually raise the age of retirement from fifty-five to sixty years of age, but Italy, too, continues to face fiscal problems that will be resolved only with a restructured social welfare policy.[2]

The main problem for all these states lies in what happens to spending on retirement pensions in the not very distant future. The big rise in social security spending in most OECD countries begins in the year 2005. A generation later, unless retirement is gradually delayed from age fifty-five or sixty until a person's mid-sixties, pension spending will reach gigantic proportions: Italy's will rise to 20 percent of GDP, France's to 14 percent, and those of the United Kingdom, Canada, and the United States to 9 or 10 percent. All this assumes, of course, that voters in these countries would be willing to pay the same level of taxes that they do today.

Increasing the age at which European workers plan to retire seems to make little political sense in today's relatively high-unemployment context. Given the current drastically low European fertility rates, however, and a definite aversion by Western Europeans to major increases in foreign immigration, lengthening work life may not be so unreasonable by the year 2005 and later, when the social security squeeze really begins to be felt. With increased deregulation, increased flexibility in financial markets, and a moderate to strong rate of economic growth, unemployment rates could continue to drop and reach much lower levels by that time. Just as in the tight labor market of the mid-1990s in the United States, Europe could face a "natural" increase in labor market participation by older workers, making pension reform that much easier.

The direction taken by the Netherlands can serve as a model, at least for Europe. To follow the Dutch model would require union cooperation in rewriting the "social pact." It would also mean changing the social security system over the next seven or eight years and writing new laws that encourage nonstandard and full-time employment. Although most European countries are already making these changes, they are not going to be easy in a political climate in which most Europeans continue to fight for a way of life whereby the nation-state sharply reduces the risks associated with living in a market system.[3] Nevertheless, the unsavory task of the now predominantly social-democratic governments controlling European parliaments will have to be the transformation of welfare provision, and no government will be able to avoid it. That does not mean that continental European and Scandinavian public sector spending will become like that of the United States, as the Dutch and Swedes have shown. Voters in Europe do not have the same set of tastes as Americans regarding public sector involvement, and there is no reason to expect that to change in the future. European public spending will have to adjust, nonetheless, especially if governments plan to deliver more "knowledge services" in the future.

A Free Market Alternative?

The decline of capacity and legitimacy of nation-states raises valid questions about the ability of central bureaucratic institutions to resolve crucial issues of work and family in a globalized economic environment. Some analysts simply question whether central government is the appropriate public site to develop and administer new approaches to social integration. However, the financial problems of nation-states have opened the door to a larger debate: should the public sector be in the business of social integration at all? For free market advocates, government intervention at any level is inherently inefficient unless it solves a problem of "market failure." Yet the meaning of market failure is subject to interpretation, and increasingly proponents of the free market model tend to exclude broad categories from the discussion of market failure, including unequal income distribution, environmental degradation, high levels of poverty in otherwise wealthy societies, and labor market discrimination based on race and gender. These are precisely the categories that justified government action in the past. By insisting that no level of income distribution consists of "market failure" or that racial and gender differentiation results from "correct" market evaluation of differential productivity, market proponents delegitimate government intervention.

Although free market advocates' assault on government social programs is not new, globalization—particularly fast-moving flows of private capital and the renewed strength of the free-market-oriented U.S. economy in the 1980s and 1990s—has added muscle throughout the OECD to arguments for deregulating national economies and reducing public spending. Furthermore, financial limitations on governments' expanding social services and the perception that the quality of health services, education, and other programs is declining have made market approaches more attractive and legitimate to a wider constituency. Ironically, because the poor count on high-quality public services even more than in the past but are least likely to get them, in frustration they are embracing free market approaches to delivery of these services. Existing evidence suggests that private management of these services for the poor are no more effective than public management, and distribution is more unequal.[4] Yet given the exigencies of current trends in labor markets, low-income parents and workers justifiably want action, and free market advocates are more than willing to promise enormous improvement, even as they urge cuts in social spending, especially for the poor.

The market deregulation approach correctly posits that new information technologies are compatible with more jobs. The argument that in today's competitive environment, societies have to rely primarily on a dynamic private sector to create jobs is also persuasive. Private sector dynamism may not depend so much on totally deregulating labor markets, however, as many market deregulators claim. A study by the McKinsey Global Institute, for example, concludes that product market restrictions are more important than labor market rigidities in explaining unemployment. Thus, removing barriers to forming new companies or breaking into markets may be more important for raising European employment than lowering the social wage (McKinsey Global Institute 1994). This confirms OECD studies that show no relation between labor market rigidity and overall employment (OECD 1999b).

Free marketers argue, on the other hand, that even under present conditions of world economic competition, market deregulation will unleash sufficient economic energy to increase employment and wages. They also assume that wage increases will be high enough to make politically acceptable the rise in wage inequality that ensues whenever deregulation policies are implemented. This was the argument for the deregulation policies in the United States and the United Kingdom in the 1980s under Reagan and Thatcher. In England, wages and employment did rise together, but in the United States, Australia, and New Zealand, where such policies were also implemented, they did not, at least not for the vast majority of male workers. More deregulated economies do have lower average unemployment rates than more regulated ones; but many highly regulated economies (for example, those of Austria, Switzerland, Norway, the Netherlands, Denmark, and now Sweden) have unemployment rates as low as or lower than those in relatively deregulated economies, such as the United Kingdom, Australia, and New Zealand. Increased wage inequality has marked all four economies that pursued a deregulated market strategy, including England's. Moreover, the strategy privatizes many of the social costs of private production, such as environmental protection. For a public becoming increasingly aware of the effects of social costs on their individual lives, privatization of such costs can create the sense that things are getting worse even when real earnings are constant.

The United States in the 1990s is often used as a positive example of the free market version of social reintegration. The model arguably works politically because of greater job availability, relatively high rates of economic growth, and increased participation of small investors in rising stock markets. For Americans in the 1990s, "employment inclusion" and (for some) increased wealth, if not real income, seem to provide a collective sense of optimism. Yet higher economic inequality and individual vulnerability are also part of this model. Wages remain stagnant, and family incomes rise through more hours worked rather than higher wages per hour worked. The less educated are employed but face a dearth of family support services and frequently fall below the poverty line. Americans are anxious about keeping a job, dissatisfied with lack of family time (or absence of family), and have rising stress from living in a high-risk, individualized environment.

Free market advocates' assault on the legitimacy of government intervention creates another long-term problem. To justify market solutions to social integration, the model's advocates deride government's role as such. This may have the salutary effect of increasing government efficiency by pushing those committed to welfare state policies to dismantle anachronistic, inefficient spending; but concerted attacks on government spending as inherently illegitimate increases public cynicism toward government interventions, even those that make society more livable and equitable. It can also reduce government's ability to attract talented professionals.

The attack on the public sector belies the role that public activities and public employees play in the smooth functioning of markets, not the least of which is to shape a set of collective values under which public concerns can override individual interests. Just as in the immediate past, an efficient public sector and dedicated, highly productive public sector workers are crucial to sustaining private production in the new global environment. That said, public sector employees (such as teachers) themselves have to be conscious of the fact that they are in an ideologically contested situation in which market advocates are pressing for the privatization of public services. In their own self-interest and in the interest of the public for whom they work, public employees must be proactive in improving the services they deliver.

However, in addition to private provision or direct government intervention in knowledge and information services, nongovernmental intermediaries—unions and community movements, for example—can also play a role. There are constraints on such nongovernmental organizations; some are financial, some because they are not "universal" in the same way as either the market or government. In Europe, however, where many workers are members of labor unions (for example, 90 percent in Sweden, 70 percent in Belgium), unions that paid more attention to becoming temporary labor agencies, worker retraining organizations, and job-training information networks could become major reintegrative institutions in the flexible work environment. Community and social movements would be especially important in redefining knowledge production and information diffusion in ways that would protect marginalized groups and the environment.

The bottom line is that between pressures of aging populations on budgets and of global competition and the process of globalization itself on revenues, the level of financial support provided to workers in the Scandinavian and continental European versions of the welfare state will have to decline over the next generation, even if economic growth is stimulated by monetary union. That is why the surge in Swedish growth rates at the end of the 1990s evokes caution among Swedes about the future: "Partly because of the strong social programs, Sweden's economy often swings from feast to famine. When the economy is strong, government revenue rises much faster than expenses. But when conditions turn bad, the country is hit by a double punch of added social costs and shrinking capital investment" (Edmund Andrews, "A New Swedish Prosperity Even with a Welfare State," *New York Times,* October 8, 1999, p. C4). That welfare system will eventually have to be further modified to maintain growth.

At the same time, the model of ever increasing deregulation, such as championed by the Anglo-Saxon societies, may not work either. Increased work time, continued poverty, and the likelihood that millions of children will remain marginalized from the mainstream society because of poor education and tough conditions at home are antithetical to achieving the good life in a flexible economy.

Shifting Public Policy Toward Building Knowledge Communities

The idea that knowledge should be seen as the basis for creating communities is not new. For example, since the nineteenth century, industrializing nation-states have made the ideas of schools being central to the socialization of children into national norms and values, and much of knowledge production in basic education focused on community values (including basic literacy and numeracy in a national language) and behavior norms. In the contemporary world, in which scientific knowledge, communication skills, and information of all kinds are becoming increasingly valuable, it is logical that communities would begin to define themselves by their capacity to provide those kinds of knowledge in addition to the traditional focus on community values.

How can public policy and intermediary organizations contribute to this definition and thereby to social integration in the new global environment? Three examples can illustrate major public policy discussions around knowledge communities: immigration and multiculturalism, the promotion of knowledge-use communities, and the redefinition of schools.

Immigration and Multiculturalism

All the major postindustrial societies have recent immigrants or long-time resident groups with cultures very different from the dominant local culture. In terms of percentages, their numbers are relatively small in most countries, but politically speaking, minorities pose problems far beyond their proportion in the population. Because of low current birthrates among dominant Europeans or, in Japan, Japanese, immigration of non-Europeans or non-Japanese and higher birthrates among these immigrants mean that future populations within national or regional boundaries will look very different from what they are now. Thus the very existence of what may now be small minority groups symbolizes a potential challenge to the dominant culture.

Historically, immigrant groups have tried simultaneously to assimilate into their host societies and to maintain elements of their native culture. Knowledge institutions such as schools have been important vehicles for both efforts, and language policy in schools a symbol of how societies choose to deal with the conflicts between dominant and immigrant notions of the self-knowledge community. In the United States, a society that absorbed tens of millions of immigrants in the thirty years before 1914, self-knowledge policy was assimilationist, with English-only the main form of instruction in public schools. The dominant self-knowledge community was defined as national and distinctly northwestern European. Yet many examples existed even during that period of public school districts and religious (private) schools that fostered instruction in immigrants' native languages (Rothstein 1998, 103).

In a period of intense nationalism and nation building, it made sense to push for a unified sense of collective self by proselytizing immigrants into one dominant culture—even if in practice it did not work as well as popular myth would have us believe. Today's more globalized notion of national identity in a period of declining state power, however, makes it less logical to impose a narrow sense of national, regional, or local culture. Because markets are increasingly global, an individual's economic value is determined by broader criteria than acceptability in his or her local community. Furthermore, the state's declining capacity to impose norms creates political space for counterdominant concepts of self-knowledge. In practice, groups that do not assimilate well into the global market knowledge culture have political options—greater today than even a generation ago—of forming relatively autonomous cultural groups with their own knowledge institutions. This is true for fundamentalist religious groups as well as particular immigrant groups wanting to preserve their native language and culture.

In terms of public policy, this suggests approaches to the self-knowledge community that are very different from those of the past. Two models come to mind. The first is one in which the state allows any community group to create a knowledge institution with public funds as long as it meets minimum legal criteria. In this model, each community in a society can therefore socialize its children and transmit knowledge in the way it chooses. This implies a vision of society in which groups with widely different beliefs are held together by market relations but not necessarily by other common bonds. Those who support educational vouchers and charter schools tend toward this approach. The second model is one in which the state uses multicultural self-knowledge to socialize all young people in the public system. This multicultural approach differs from totally autonomous definitions of self-knowledge on the part of each group.[5] It also abandons the imposition of a single dominant culture but does make all children attending publicly funded institutions learn about the variety of cultures in the community (and their points of view). In that sense, the state (that is, the national, regional, or local community) continues to impose an ideological perspective, but it is one that reflects the diversity of today's postindustrial societies.

The first model assumes that market relations (in particular, the profit motive) are enough to keep increasingly diverse societies working together successfully. To build social capital, however, diverse communities need to share common social experiences. In a knowledge-based society, a common school experience, in which children and parents are exposed to at least some diversity in background and values, serves this function. The second model, the multicultural approach to socialization, does more: it allows children of various groups to gain an understanding of their own history and culture but also allows them to think critically about it. This makes it consistent with the higher-order problem-solving skills needed for an innovative, democratic society.

The multicultural approach is also consistent with a positive, constructive vision of what postindustrial societies are becoming, a vision distinctly opposed to the parochial and defensive antiglobalism of the nationalist right. Anyone who was in France during the 1998 soccer World Cup tournament felt the liberating effect on French society of this positive vision of France's new multicultural reality. A diverse team made up of French players of European, North African, Caribbean, and African origin brought victory and the cup to France for the first time in history. Jubilant and tearful, the team wrapped itself in the French flag, seizing its symbolic power from the ultranationalist, whites-only Front Nationale. The celebration that followed was the most inclusive and joyful since the country's liberation by the Allies at the end of World War II. The French were mainly celebrating their ability to win, but in so doing, they affirmed the positive effects of immigration and multiculturalism. The United States and some European societies, such as the Netherlands, have had an easier time with their multiculturalism, but for France the event was an awakening to their new place in the world. It created political space for innovative public policy approaches to self-knowledge in a French educational system long dominated by narrow views of French values and norms. The soccer team and the World Cup soccer federation that helped create this new self-knowledge were, strictly speaking, nongovernmental organizations, yet they were able to alter national conceptions of identity and even national politics.

Public Policy and Knowledge Use

Knowledge-use communities form spontaneously, especially among professionals, and private businesses organize their own knowledge-use communities for profit. Temp agencies are the chief example, but proprietary schools selling secretarial and computer training and access to jobs are another. By becoming knowledge-use communities, labor unions would become more attuned to new organizations of work and would better serve workers in flexible labor markets (as suggested in chapter 5).

The Santa Clara Central Labor Council, with its Silicon Valley bailiwick, is not a hotbed of union organizing. The absence of much unionism in Silicon Valley, however, means less power for individual unions and more autonomy and freedom for the council itself. Amy Dean, the council's creative director, has used this freedom to develop a temp agency run by the labor unions as part of the council's Temporary Worker Employment Project. In the Working Partnerships Staffing Group, as the agency is called, union dues, not steep agency commissions, pay for the agency's overhead. The agency also provides immediate social benefits to temp workers, unlike Manpower, Inc., and other private agencies. It also affords workers a professional association that brings temporary employees together to work on a variety of issues in which they share a common interest. Working Partnerships is, in effect, a networking organization run for workers by workers (Benner and Dean 1999).

If Dean and her organization can create a union-run temp agency in the heart of a relatively unionless environment, powerful union federations in European countries should be able to do the same. This means, however, that these organizations need to accept new realities and protect younger workers and women in new ways. It is not surprising that in Sweden, private temp agencies have seized quickly on the new reality to become fast-growing businesses. But where is the competition from unions to keep temp workers in the union fold? Swedish unions could easily be the base for such knowledge-use communities.

There is also an important role for public policy in building knowledge-use communities. Regional and local governments in central northern Italy, in Germany, and in Catalonia, just to name a few cases, have taken major responsibility for connecting local life and the collective conditions for new economic development. Local centers for training, information, productivity development, and management counseling have been critical in revitalizing a flexible network of small- and medium-size enterprises; but in so doing, they have also revitalized local society by demonstrating the advantages of belonging to the community and creating an antidote to the whirlwind of capital mobility so disruptive to community life.

In the 1980s, I visited the municipality of Poggibonsi in Tuscany, not far from Florence, an office furniture manufacturing center. The municipal government had taken an active role in stimulating the furniture industry by supporting its small and medium-size enterprises with a publicly financed and managed marketing organization. It also provided them technical assistance in closing international sales. None of the firms in Poggibonsi was large enough to sustain its own marketing division, but by marketing the products of all the firms collectively, the municipality provided them with a global market. Much of Poggibonsi's furniture was sold in Japan. As sales increased, the municipality gained from increased tax revenues. Thus, in contrast to many U.S. states and cities that try to attract prospective employers with tax concessions, municipalities and regional governments in Italy tend to provide services that make small and medium-size enterprises much more profitable.

In Baden-Württemberg, Germany, home to Daimler-Benz, the regional government has played a similar role on a larger scale. There, government policy focuses on coordinating labor relations policies among firms and works with firms to supply the kinds of worker education and training most relevant to job openings and future product mix. These policies have made Baden-Württemberg a particularly attractive place to do business (Cooke and Morgan 1994). Although relations between business, labor, and government in Germany operate in the context of a long-standing cooperative social compact, the policy lesson is transferable to other OECD countries: namely, government can help develop knowledge-use communities around groups of firms by linking skill production to job intermediation. The more flexible the labor market, the more general the skills provided in training centers and educational institutions, and the more important the task of intermediation.

In both these examples, the key to success is social trust in government on the part of both employers and labor. If local government is to play a role in helping small and medium-size businesses, entrepreneurs have to consider public officials as fair and reliable service providers. Knowledge-use communities are particularly reliant on trust because they are based on the exchange of information, and information providers have to be trusted by information users. A simple illustration is that employers will tend to hire on the basis of information about job applicants provided by current employees or from educational institutions whose previous graduates have done well in the firm. The German apprenticeship system has functioned well, in part because German employers generally trust the evaluations of potential apprentices by their secondary school teachers. This is in sharp contrast to the absence of any knowledge-use community between U.S. employers and public secondary schools.

Expansion of Knowledge Production in Community Schools

Public education faces two major policy challenges in the age of global flexible production. The first is how to provide high-quality problem-solving skills to the mass of students in school, and the second is how to do this in a way that does not increase inequality between disadvantaged and advantaged students. The two challenges are becoming closely linked as an increasing proportion of students in OECD schools come from less educated families in which both parents work full time. For communities to bring up educational quality increasingly means that they must do so for children with few available resources at home.

Evidence suggests that over the past generation, public secondary education in the OECD has expanded enormously, incorporating many of these young people from less educated families, with little, if any, decline in average academic performance.[6] Yet in every OECD country, children from the lower social classes perform less well academically, and schools for low-income children are generally not as well equipped, expectations for them are much lower, and teaching is often not of the same quality as in schools for higher-income children.

Market advocates, notably, in the English-speaking countries, have succeeded in convincing the public that their public education systems are to blame for this poor performance: they overspend, are inefficient, and are incapable of meeting quality standards required for the information age. In the United States, for example, polling data shows that the vast majority of parents are satisfied with their own children's schooling but think that the educational system as a whole is in serious trouble (Rothstein 1998, 29). In place of the current public management of schools, market advocates propose increasing private management through educational vouchers, publicly financed but usable in any school, public or private. Their argument is that vouchers would introduce competition into educational delivery, which would simultaneously increase choice and school efficiency, mainly by breaking the hold of the public bureaucracy and teachers' unions over education (see Friedman 1955; Chubb and Moe 1990). The empirical support for these claims is scanty at best (see Carnoy and McEwan 1997; McEwan and Carnoy 1999a), yet this does not stop market advocates from steadily hammering on this largely popular case for government's involvement in people's daily lives. Because there is no evidence that privately managed schooling is more effective or more efficient in delivering education, one can only conclude that market advocates are less interested in the quality of schooling than in dismantling public values that might interfere with general market notions of efficiency and equity.

The downside of this strategy is threefold: first, it denigrates an institution that was created mainly to socialize children into a publicly defined (by local community or national) notion of society. This public notion of society is the antithesis of market competition because it is intended to develop a common collective experience and social trust—cooperation rather than competition.[7] By making schools competitive units and privatizing them, the common experience and values inherent in the very publicness and commonality of education are eliminated. With choice and privatization, families will tend to identify with individual schools and their approaches to education but not with the broader communities that provide their public financing. Social trust is narrowed to more immediate environments, such as the private school, and even then, parents are encouraged to abandon that environment for another one should it fail to satisfy their immediate needs. Notions of exercising voice to improve broader or longer-term political or institutional conditions fall prey to immediate, individual goals.

Second, although the strategy appears to be justified in attacking the public sector because it relies heavily on the "traditional" family as the basis for reproducing citizens and employees, it ignores the underlying conflict the family faces as male earning potential declines. In effect, parents are being asked to choose between limiting their material consumption or forfeiting time with their children. For many low-income families—indeed, the very families the privatization strategy is supposed to help—there is little choice, because they earn hardly enough to provide the basic necessities for their children in the first place. The strategy creates the possibility of even greater inequality in future generations, as home environments deteriorate in low-income families but are maintained in high-income families able to provide better child care and early education privately.

Third, in going after teachers' unions (and often, teachers themselves) the strategy cannot help but denigrate the professionals on whose commitment school improvement ultimately depends. In public or private schools, teachers are largely unsupervised in their classrooms. Educational quality depends heavily on their internalized norms and standards, even when states use student testing to hold teachers accountable (Abelman and Elmore 1998; Carnoy, Benveniste, and Rothstein 1998). The privatization strategy claims to liberate teachers from public bureaucracy yet simultaneously claims that their collective efforts to improve working conditions and remuneration is the main obstacle to improving education. A sustained campaign against public education and public sector teachers' unions certainly does little to raise teacher morale or to make teaching a more attractive profession. This is the case even if some fraction of the teaching force does not identify with unions or may agree with efforts to privatize education. It is particularly the case because one of the subtexts of educational privatization is to reduce teachers' collective bargaining power in the workplace.

For all these reasons, I believe that the solution lies not in privatizing education but in transforming schools from their traditional role in late industrialization as knowledge-production partners of families and communities into a much broader notion of a center that serves families and communities as well as children. This expands the concept of education to include multiple services, from early childhood development to after-school youth programs to evening adult education classes. As noted in the previous chapter, this is already happening in some communities. Yet the transformation occurs only sporadically in most places because it explicitly requires a major commitment of public resources, and these resources are hard to find. Providing universal preschool to all children from two to five years old, even at partial public expense, is costly, as data from France and Scandinavian countries show. Even so, there is at least some evidence of a high payoff to early education (Myers 1996), and universal preschool and widely available day care are among the most politically popular public programs in the countries that provide them (Marlise Simons, "Child Care Sacred as France Cuts Back the Welfare State," New York Times, December 31, 1997, 1).[8]

Given changes in family structure and the increasing centrality of high-quality education, it is logical to expect that communities change schools to meet the new reality. Making formal education available earlier (even if on a voluntary, rather than compulsory, basis) also makes sense pedagogically if we really expect (as seems to be the case) all children, no matter what their home background, to learn to read by the end of first grade. In many OECD countries, pupils from middle-class families have had up to four years of preschool before entering first grade, but children from low-income families only one, and sometimes none. Yet all are expected to perform up to national (and now international) standards once they enter primary school. By the end of that first year, no matter what the child's previous educational experience, "les jeux sont fait" (the dice are fixed), to use the title of Jean-Paul Sartre's play.[9] One way public policy can begin to equalize opportunity is to supply the educational investment less educated families lack.

Even were public spending on education to be increased, however, many communities in OECD countries would still have problems with the quality of their primary and secondary schooling. Again, public policy has an important role to play here. Our previous studies on the Chilean voucher plan (Carnoy and McEwan 1997; McEwan and Carnoy 1999a, 1999b) and Cecilia Rouse's work on Milwaukee schools (1998) suggest that in improving students' academic performance, privatizing education is no substitute for well-organized public interventions. The main nagging issue in educational reform remains: what should these interventions be? The most recent consensus is that academic gains require better teaching, and better teaching requires a policy focus on classroom practices, including clearly defined student performance objectives (Darling-Hammond 1997). School directors well trained as managers and instructional leaders and teachers with high levels of content knowledge also help. So too does a tight, trustful relationship between school personnel and parents.

These elements suggest that local knowledge-production community centers also need to be tied into public policies beyond the local community. In the United States, where school and community colleges are already set up organizationally to function as local knowledge-production communities, states have taken on increasing regulatory functions, including equalizing financing among community schools and setting performance standards at a statewide level. In a review of the recent Italian educational reforms, an OECD team recommends increased school autonomy within the overall context of increased school accountability to national and regional student performance standards (OECD 1998d). Thus, one way of assuring that all knowledge-production communities deliver high-quality services is to set clear standards at regional, national, and international levels, measure how each knowledge-production community is doing in terms of those standards, and provide assistance those that are not doing well to improve.

Improvement is also likely to come from greater flexibility in service delivery. If knowledge-production centers are to redefine themselves to provide a combination of early childhood development, formal schooling, supplemental academic and nonacademic activities, and adult education, they will have to be flexible in using personnel resources and will have to subcontract part of the work to nongovernmental organizations and private providers. Centers can then more easily vary their services, depending on demand. Subcontracting can also lead to more experimentation and risk taking, because centers can contract with external providers on a short-term basis. For example, it may be far more efficient for a center to hire a nongovernmental organization or a private business to supply its after-school programs or day care than to provide them using in-house staff.

Besides expanding downward, knowledge production will also expand upward in OECD countries. Historically, communities have increased knowledge in the labor force not so much by improving the quality of what is taught in each year of schooling but by increasing the number of years young people stay in school. University enrollment as a proportion of the age cohort has shot up rapidly in the past generation and will continue to rise. New groups, such as women returning to the educational system after stints as workers and full-time mothers, are major new members of university communities. Tertiary education is simultaneously becoming mass education and is globalizing, especially at the graduate level, where almost one-half of the doctoral students in the sciences and engineering in the universities of the United States, France, and Great Britain are from foreign countries (Carnoy 1998).

This raises important issues about public policy toward universities as knowledge-production communities. On the one hand, universities have increasing meaning as centers of community learning and innovation. They are becoming broadly inclusive—so inclusive, some argue, that governments cannot afford to bear the cost of that much public education. On the other hand, they are producing knowledge that is, in some cases, leaving the community for other regions and nations and also attracting knowledge from communities in other regions and nations. Who, then, should pay for knowledge production in each university community? To what extent should the university charge for knowledge produced there? To what extent should the university focus on activities that serve localities and regions, and to what extent should they be global? In the case of new knowledge gained from publicly sponsored research, who should get the benefits if the university does charge? The answers to these questions go far in defining the university as a knowledge-production community.

The greater inclusiveness of colleges and universities and their gradual transformation into community centers also means that higher education will have to become more accountable to the community it serves. Despite the enormous pressure on kindergarten through twelfth grade education to improve in all OECD countries, higher education is still allowed to claim exception from such scrutiny. Colleges and universities retain their status as selective institutions, but this will change, and even elite universities will need to show that they are successful in serving traditionally marginalized groups (Carnoy 1999).

Where Should Public Policy Be Made?

With globalization, logic tells us, control over the economic environment and political legitimacy both move away from the nation-state. The locus of the economic environment shifts to globally mobile, transnational capital and innovative ideas, and the locus of political legitimacy to regional and local governments. If this is the case, nation-states are increasingly powerless to develop genuinely national economic programs, and local authorities should increasingly be responsible for social policy making.

Many argue that shifting policy making to the local level would make government programs more efficient and more democratic. That is one major reason that when the nation-state seems to lose financial power as the employer and provider of last resort, as in the current transition, it also loses political legitimacy. The citizenry turns its attention naturally to more local forms of government. The standard case for decentralization is that local government is more accessible to the citizenry and that local politicians can respond more quickly and accurately to their constituencies than can officials in the far-off national capital. Because the local citizenry can see more clearly the effects of local government services, they are also more willing to pay local taxes.

Differences in the quality of local government put in stark relief the advantages and limitations of localizing policy. Robert Putnam's study of Italian regions shows that those regions (mainly in the North) with well-run local governments are also those with high levels of civic involvement, and that civic involvement has its roots in the distinct histories of northern and southern regions (Putnam 1993). Thus, when Italians reformed their government management system in the 1970s to give more responsibility to regions, those in the North did far better than those in the South. Regions in the North such as Emilia Romagna, Tuscany, and Lombardia were able to create local institutions that supported local economic development, whereas local regions in the South continued to stagnate, with little growth in autonomous economic activity.

Putnam's work suggests that local governments with the capacity to manage well generally operate in contexts that resonate well with public interventions. Although differential financial resource availability is not an issue in the Italian case because almost all regional funding comes from the central government, in other decentralized systems, such as that in the United States, for example, localities (states, counties, cities, and school districts) also have differential taxing capacity because of widely different levels of community income and wealth. Thus, capacity to govern can vary tremendously among regions and localities, both because of the distribution of management skills (including the relationship between constituency and government officials) and because of differential capacity to tax.

In theory, local government is more representative of local interests and is therefore much more closely connected to its constituency. In practice, however, local governments in communities with highly differentiated groups of residents often represent only part of the community, excluding minorities from any kind of representation and providing them with a much lower level of services. The archetypal case is counties and states in the South after 1876, when Southerners, with support from the nation-state, reestablished control over local government. Once achieved, local government in the South became a vehicle for excluding blacks from public resources and channeling almost all spending into the white community. This is a blatant case, but more subtle forms of resource exclusion occur often at the local level. At least in late modernity, locally excluded groups such as blacks in the South have sought recourse at the national level and counted on national government to gain them local participation.

For both reasons—differential local capacity to govern and local exclusion of minority groups—during the past century higher levels of government involvement were increasingly brought into policy making by local citizens. To the degree that these distributional problems continue to exist, certain activities, particularly those that meet distributional concerns, will be argued out at the national and supranational levels. Other public activities are also more logically national or supranational, even if they do not have redistributional implications. For example, different localities could set up pension plans for all local residents in place of national social security taxes, and these plans could be managed by professionals based on the risk preference of the majority of local residents. Because many individuals do not maintain residence in one community or region all their working lives, however, it makes more sense to run pension plans nationally. In Europe, it might make sense in the near future to develop plans that are supranational, allowing citizens of the European Union, who can already work anywhere in the EU, to pay into a European social security system. At the same time, it is possible for national governments to assist localities in building capacity to deliver social services. This indeed is an important function of nation-states in an era in which their own legitimacy and financial capacity will decline.

However, taking careful stock of capacity differences among local communities, OECD societies would greatly benefit from a major shift in power, resources, and responsibility to active, innovative local governments that will redefine democracy more precisely for the majority of citizens. Strong local governments; active citizen participation; and formation of networks of solidarity and reciprocity around local community institutions such as health care, schools, family support centers, and business support services could all help rebuild community, strengthen the new family, and contribute to the education and employment of future high-quality labor. Health care and education are already decentralized in most OECD countries, or at least headed there. Better-organized regions in Europe are also actively assisting local businesses in a host of activities, from negotiating cooperative arrangements between unions and employers to providing marketing services. Given the shift to knowledge-based public services, it makes real sense for public policy to be made and implemented at the local level, with higher levels of government playing a more regulatory role and equalizing the quality of delivery through technical assistance and compensatory financing.

A Concluding Note: Flexibility and Public Interventions

Explicit in the arguments that I have made for a continued public sector role in socially reintegrating flexible labor is the increased flexibility of the public sector itself. The last thing the public sector needs at any level of government is a large bureaucracy hired "permanently" to do tasks that are constantly changing. Such bureaucracies tend to find work to do to justify their employment rather than simply do the work that needs to be done. Part of increased flexibility can come from decentralizing responsibility for service delivery to the local level. Part can come from subcontracting activities to nongovernmental organizations or private providers on a project-by-project basis.

If public sector flexibility is an asset and knowledge communities the integrative institutions of the future, the United States would seem to have an advantage over many nations in confronting the labor disaggregation problem. Knowledge use and production in the United States is highly decentralized, schools and universities have a great deal of autonomy, and educators are expected to be innovative and ready to change. The system is also already flexible in defining the community it serves. Knowledge-production institutions have long been willing and able to incorporate youth and adults of all ages and at different stages of their lives. Everyone is given a second, third, or even fourth chance to acquire knowledge. The U.S. model has also adapted well to demands for new kinds of self-knowledge communities and to new ways of incorporating immigrants into knowledge-production institutions.

Beyond flexibility, however, my arguments for successful reintegration also make explicit the requirements for a strong commitment by the citizenry, particularly at the municipalities and regions level, for public spending on expanded knowledge communities. Because of much greater historical distrust of government in societies such as the the United States, Great Britain, and Australia, and the ideological conflicts this has produced in the past three decades, they are at a disadvantage in meeting the challenges of the current transition. France, Germany, and Scandinavia all start into the transition much more willing to have the public sector engage directly in building new knowledge communities and to devote the public resources needed for social cohesiveness. In Italy and parts of Spain, regional commitment to public sector intervention is also high.

The breakdown of the industrial employment system means a redirection of state monies from job-centeredness toward learning-centeredness: family educational investments in adults and children, municipal spending for small-business management support services, public services at the local level organized around adult teaching and learning, and new bridges between private sector job training and public secondary and higher education.[10] Countries such as Sweden are already a long way down the road to such education and training policies because of their welfare state environments. Sweden has invested a larger part of its gross domestic product in knowledge—research, development, training, and education—than any other country in the world (Andrews, "New Swedish Prosperity"). Thus, even if the public sector cannot afford to continue to spend at current levels in these countries or regions, the commitment to provide high-quality knowledge institutions is distinctly greater there than in the United States, Australia, and even Great Britain. This makes it much more likely that in the continental European countries, Japan, and Scandinavia, ways will be found to maintain existing programs and expand into others. Whether Europe and Japan find it easier politically to become more flexible in the way they approach social reintegration, or whether the United States and the United Kingdom find it easier politically to develop a greater public commitment to social cohesion, are questions that can only be answered with the passage of time.

---

1. Even the Soviet Union and the European nation-states it controlled politically after World War II can be seen as capitalist welfare states, in which state bureaucracies were simultaneously capitalists and political apparatuses.
2. In Sweden, Italy, and Germany, as well as some other OECD countries (though not all), public spending as a percentage of GDP has declined since the early 1990s, owing in part to mild economic growth but also to efforts to cut back on pensions and other social spending (table 6.1).
3. "Therefore the nation-state is increasingly powerless in controlling monetary policy, deciding its budget, organizing production and trade, collecting its corporate taxes, and fulfilling its commitments to provide social benefits. In sum, it has lost most of its economic power, albeit it still has some regulatory capacity and relative control over its subjects" (Castells 1997, 254).
4. For an analysis of Chile's national educational voucher plan implemented almost twenty years ago, see Carnoy and McEwan 1997; McEwan and Carnoy 1999a, 1999b. Fully subsidized private schools in Chile are more likely to be located in higher-income communities, and, despite legal prohibitions against

Table 6.1 Total Government Spending as Share of GDP, by Country, Various
Years (Percentage)

Country	1981	1985	1990	1993	1995	1997	1999[a]
Australia	31.3	35.1	32.1	35.4	35.1	33.5	32.6
Denmark	—	55.3	56.0	60.5	59.3	56.6	54.4
France	48.6	52.1	49.8	55.0	54.3	54.2	54.1
Germany	48.7	47.0	45.1	49.5	49.8	47.9	47.1
Italy	46.3	51.3	54.0	57.4	52.7	50.2	49.2
Japan	32.8	31.6	31.3	33.7	35.6	35.0	39.2
Netherlands	57.6	57.1	54.1	55.1	51.3	48.7	47.8
Spain	34.9	40.2	42.5	47.8	45.5	42.2	41.2
Sweden	62.6	63.3	59.1	71.0	65.6	62.3	60.2
United Kingdom	44.2	44.0	41.8	45.4	44.4	41.0	40.8
United States	35.7[b]	35.5	35.2	35.9	34.9	33.6	32.3

Source: OECD 1998a, annex table 28; OECD 1999a, annex table 28.
[a]Projection.
[b]1982.

selecting students, most private schools find ways to reject low-performing
students.

5. Critiques of multicultural approaches to self-knowledge focus on their flight
   from the classics of Western civilization and the new "fascism" of political cor-
   rectness. It is ironic that neoconservatives critique multiculturalism in the
   form that could certainly occur under a voucher system or charter schools—
   educational alternatives pushed by neoconservatives. I agree that there is some
   validity in these criticisms. They are primarily aimed at minorities' and wom-
   en's attempts to define culture in new ways; but to be consistent, I would also
   have to critique Christian fundamentalists who want to use public funds to socialize their children into values and norms inconsistent with the European
   Enlightenment. It is also ironic that in their fear of the multicultural future,
   neoconservatives push for the alternative implicit in these critiques—namely,
   using the state to impose an assimilationist view of language, history, and culture on groups that seek their own interpretation of history and culture—at
   the same time that they want highly localized autonomy over school curricula,
   teacher hiring, and modes of socialization.

6. For a good study of achievement over time in the United States, see Rothstein
   1998. There is little doubt that similar historical studies of achievement in
   France or Germany would produce similar conclusions: that the secondary
   school system has expanded enormously without significant declines in aver-

age achievement, even though the average student finishing secondary education today comes from a relatively less elite background than most of those who completed high school thirty or fifty years ago. The point is that the education level of the average parent has also gone up in the meantime, and despite all the complaints about the quality of teaching and curricula, those have probably continued to rise as well.

7. As Adam Smith argued in *The Theory of Moral Sentiments,* written twenty years before his market bible, *The Wealth of Nations,* some value system external to the market's competitive individualism is needed to keep people's "natural" greed and aggressiveness in check (Smith 1907).

8. The lack of extensive public day care in Holland may have contributed to many women's working only part time. If that is the case, more spending on child development centers could pay for itself, if a significant percentage of mothers chose to work longer hours. There is also the question of what Dutch families prefer in terms of spending more time with their children or at work. The absence of public day care almost certainly affects the choices for lower-income parents more than for higher-income parents.

9. In the early 1980s, we interviewed first-grade teachers in two schools in a high-income California community. Although the students in the two schools came from families separated by only a short social distance, teachers had clear differences in expectation for the two groups, based on first-grade test scores. See Carnoy and Levin 1985.

10. Sweden has long organized its unemployment compensation system around retraining and reemployment and continues to focus on spending for child development (day-care centers), education, and job training. With some increased cost recovery for education and child care, plus a continued reduction of income subsidies to families that do not "need" them, the government deficit could be sharply reduced and a learning-centered public investment policy could still be promoted. In contrast, the current welfare reform debate in the United States is being pushed steadily toward greater job-centeredness and away from learning- and work-centeredness. Neoconservative legislators tend to ignore the fact that jobs available to most hard-core welfare recipients are dead-end ones. See Spakes 1992.

References

Adler, Paul S. 1992. *Technology and the Future of Work*. New York: Oxford University Press.

Alberdi, Ines. 1994. *Informe Sobre la Situacion de la Familia en Espana*. Madrid: Ministerio de Asuntos Sociales.

Allen, Steven. 1993. "Technology and the Wage Structure." Unpublished paper. North Carolina State University, Raleigh.

Amin, Ash. 1998. "Globalization and Regional Development: A Relational Perspective." *Competition and Change* 3(1–2): 145–66.

Amsden, Alice. 1989. *Asia's Next Giant: South Korea and Late Industrialization*. New York: Oxford University Press.

Anderson, Benedict. 1983. *Imagined Communities: Reflections on the Origin and Spread of Nationalism*. London: Verso.

Appelbaum, Eileen, and Rosemary Batt. 1994. *The New American Workplace*. Ithaca, N.Y.: ILR Press.

Appelbaum, Eileen, and Ronald Schettkat, eds. 1990. *Labor Markets, Adjustments to Structural Change, and Technological Progress*. New York: Praeger.

Aries, Phillippe. 1962. *Centuries of Childhood*. New York: Knopf.

Aronowitz, Stanley, and William DeFazio. 1994. *The Jobless Future*. Minneapolis: University of Minnesota Press.

Arthur D. Little. 1992. *Executive Caravan TQM Survey*. Boston: Arthur D. Little.

Ascher, François. 1998. *La Republique contre la ville*. Paris: L'Aube.

Atkinson, Anthony, Lee Rainwater, and Timothy Smeeding. 1995. *Income Distribution in OEDC Countries*. Paris: OEDC.

Aznar, Guy. 1993. *Travailler moins pour travailler tous*. Paris: Syros.

Bailey, Paul, Aurelio Parisotto, and Geoffrey Renshaw. 1993. "Multinationals and Employment." Paper. Geneva: International Labour Organization.

Barnet, Richard. 1993. "The End of Jobs." *Harper's* 287(1720): 47–52.

Barnet, Richard, and Ronald Muller. 1974. *Global Reach*. New York: Simon and Schuster.

219

Bartel, Ann P., and Frank R. Lichtenberg. 1987. "The Comparative Advantage of Educated Workers in Implementing New Technology." *Review of Economics and Statistics* 69(1): 1–11.

Batt, Rosemary, and Eileen Appelbaum. 1995. "Worker Participation in Diverse Settings: Does the Form Affect the Outcome, and If So, Who Benefits?" *British Journal of Industrial Relations* 33(3): 354–78.

Bell, Daniel. 1973. *The Coming of the Post-Industrial Society.* New York: Basic Books.

Benner, Chris, and Amy Dean. 1999. "Labor in the New Economy: Lessons from Labor Organizing in Silicon Valley." Unpublished paper. Working Partnerships, San Jose, California.

Benson, Rob. 1994. "Computer Mediated Communication: A Literature Review." Unpublished paper. University of California, Berkeley.

Berman, Eli, John Bound, and Zvi Griliches. 1993. "Changes in the Demand for Skilled Labor Within U.S. Manufacturing Industries: Evidence from the Annual Survey of Manufacturing." Working Paper 4255. Cambridge, Mass.: National Bureau of Economic Research.

Berndt, Ernst, Catherine Morrison, and Larry Rosenblum. 1992. "High-Tech Capital Formation and Labor Composition in U.S. Manufacturing Industries: An Exploratory Analysis." Working Paper 4010. Cambridge, Mass.: National Bureau of Economic Research.

Bernstein, Jared, Edith Rasell, John Schmitt, and Robert Scott. 1999. "Tax Cut No Cure for Middle Class Economic Woes." Briefing Paper, September. Washington, D.C.: Economic Policy Institute.

Bessant, John. 1989. *Microelectronics and Change at Work.* Geneva: International Labour Office.

Bielenski, Harold, ed. 1994. *New Forms of Work and Activity: Survey of Experiences at the Establishment Level in Eight European Countries.* Dublin, Ireland: European Foundation for the Improvement of Living and Working Conditions.

Blazejczak, Jurgen, George Eber, and Gustav Horn. 1990. "Sectoral and Macroeconomic Impacts of Research and Development on Employment." In *The Employment Impact of New Technology: The Case of West Germany,* edited by Egon Matzner and Michael Wagner. Aldershot, England: Avebury.

Bluestone, Barry. 1995. "The Inequality Express." *American Prospect* 20(Winter): 81–95.

Bluestone, Barry, and Stephen Rose. 1997. "The Growth in Work Time and the Implications for Macro Policy." Working Paper 204. New York: Jerome Levy Economics Institute of Bard College.

Borja, Jordi. 1988. *Estado y ciudad.* Barcelona: Promociones y Publicaciones Universitarias.

Bound, John, and George Johnson. 1992. "What Are the Causes of Rising Wage

Inequality in the United States?" *Federal Reserve Bank of New York Economic Policy Review* 1(1): 9–17.

Bowles, Samuel, and Herbert Gintis. 1985. *Democracy and Capitalism.* New York: Basic Books.

Bowles, Samuel, David Gordon, and Thomas Weiskopf. 1983. *Beyond the Wasteland.* New York: Doubleday.

Braudel, Fernand. 1979. *The Wheels of Commerce.* Vol. 2 of *Civilization and Capitalism.* New York: Harper and Row.

Braverman, Harry. 1974. *Labor and Monopoly Capital.* New York: Monthly Review Press.

Brown, Clair, and Michael Reich. 1989. "When Does Cooperation Work? A Look at NUMMI and G.M. Van Nuys." *California Management Review* 31(4): 26–44.

Brown, Clair, Michael Reich, and David Stern. 1993. "Becoming a High-Performance Work Organization: The Role of Security, Employee Investment, and Training." *International Journal of Human Resource Management* 4(2): 247–75.

Bruce, Judith, Cynthia Lloyd, and Ann Leonard. 1995. *Families in Focus.* New York: Population Council.

Bushnell, P. Timothy. 1994. *The Transformation of the American Manufacturing Paradigm.* New York: Garland Publishing.

Calhoun, Arthur. 1919. *Social History of the American Family.* Vol. 1 of *Since the Civil War.* Cleveland: Arthur Clarke.

Campbell, Duncan. 1994. "Foreign Investment, Labor Immobility, and the Quality of Employment." *International Labour Review* 133(2):185–203.

Cappelli, Peter. 1993. "Are Skill Requirements Rising? Evidence from Production and Clerical Jobs." *Industrial and Labor Relations Review* 46(3): 515–30.

———. 1997. *Change at Work.* New York: Oxford University Press.

Card, David. 1996. "The Effect of Unions on the Structure of Wages: A Longitudinal Analysis." *Econometrica* 64(5): 957–79.

Carnoy, Martin. 1993. "Multinationals in a Changing World Economy: Whither the Nation-State?" In *The New Global Economy,* edited by Martin Carnoy, Manuel Castells, Stephen Cohen, and Fernando H. Cardoso. University Park: Pennsylvania State University Press.

———. 1994. *Faded Dreams.* New York: Cambridge University Press.

———. 1998. "The Globalization of Innovation, Nationalist Competition, and the Internationalization of Scientific Training." *Competition and Change* 3(1–2): 237–62.

———. 1999. "Education in 2010." Unpublished paper. Stanford University School of Education, Stanford.

Carnoy, Martin, Luis Benveniste, and Richard Rothstein. 1998. "Private and Public School 'Effectiveness': A Reappraisal." Unpublished paper. Consortium for Policy Research in Education, Philadelphia.

Carnoy, Martin, Manuel Castells, Stephen Cohen, and Fernando H. Cardoso. 1993. *The New Global Economy in the Information Age.* University Park: Pennsylvania State University Press.

Carnoy, Martin, and Fred Fluitman. 1994. "Training and the Reduction of Unemployment in Industrialized Countries." Report prepared for the International Labour Office, Geneva.

Carnoy, Martin, and Weimin Gong. 1996. "Women and Minority Gains in a Rapidly Changing Local Labor Market: The San Francisco Bay Area in the 1980s." *Economics of Education Review* 15(3): 273–87.

Carnoy, Martin, and Henry Levin. 1985. *Schooling and Work in the Democratic State.* Stanford: Stanford University Press.

Carnoy, Martin, and Patrick McEwan. 1997. "Public Investment or Private School? A Reconstruction of Educational Improvements in Chile." Unpublished paper. Stanford University School of Education, Stanford.

Carnoy, Martin, Seth Pollack, and Pia L. Wong. 1993. "Labor Institutions and Technological Change: A Framework for Analysis and Review of the Literature." Report prepared for the International Labour Office, Geneva.

Carnoy, Martin, Derek Shearer, and Russell Rumberger. 1983. *The New Social Contract.* New York: Harper and Row.

Castaño, Cecilia. 1994. *Tecnologia, empleo, y trabajo en Espana.* Madrid: Alianza Editorial.

Castells, Manuel. 1983. *The City and the Grassroots.* Berkeley: University of California Press.

———. 1996. *The Rise of the Network Society.* London: Blackwell.

———. 1997. *The Power of Identity.* London: Blackwell.

Cherlin, Andrew. 1981. *Marriage, Divorce, Remarriage.* Cambridge: Harvard University Press.

Chubb, John, and Terry Moe. 1990. *Politics, Markets, and America's Schools.* Washington, D.C.: Brookings.

Cohen, Stephen S. 1994. "Competitiveness: A Reply to Krugman." Berkeley, Calif.: Berkeley Roundatable on the International Economy, Research Note 1.

Coleman, James. 1988. "Social Capital in the Creation of Human Capital." *American Journal of Sociology* 94(supp.): S95–S120.

Communities Organized for Public Service (COPS). 1994. *Investing in People: The Story of Project Quest.* San Antonio, Texas: Metro Alliance.

Cooke, Philip, and Kevin Morgan. 1994. "The Regional Innovation System in Baden-Württemberg." *International Journal of Technology Management* 9(3–4): 394–429.

Croissandeau, Matthieu, and Thierry Philippon. 1999. "Trente-cinq heures: A la researche du temps perdu." *Nouvelle Observateur* July: 86–88.

Daniel, William. 1990. *Workplace Survey of Industrial Relations.* London: Policy Studies Institute.

Danmarks Statistik, Socialforskningsinstituttet. 1992. *Living Conditions in Denmark: Compendium of Statistics 1992.* Copenhagen: Danmarks Statistik.

———. 1997. *Statistical Yearbook 1997.* Copenhagen: Danmarks Statistik.

Darling-Hammond, Linda. 1997. *The Right to Learn.* San Francisco: Jossey-Bass.

Dean, James W., Se Joon Yoon, and Gerald I. Susman. 1992. "Advanced Manufacturing Technology and Organization Structure: Empowerment or Subordination." *Organization Science* 3(2): 203–29.

Derber, Charles. 1994. "Contradictions: Clinton, Cooperation, and the Contradictions of Capitalism." *Tikkun* 9(5): 15.

Development Dimensions International. 1990. *Self-Directed Teams: A Study of Current Practice.* Pittsburgh, Pa.: Development Dimensions International.

DiNardo, John, Nicole Fortin, and Thomas Lemieux. 1996. "Labor Market Institutions and the Structure of Wages, 1973–1992: A Semiparametric Approach." *Econometrica* 64(5): 1001–44.

DiNardo, John, and Jorn-Steffen Pischke. 1996. "The Returns to Computer Use Revisited: Have Pencils Changed the Wage Structure, Too?" Working Paper 5686. Cambridge, Mass.: National Bureau of Economic Research.

Dogan, Mattei, and John Kasarda. 1987. *The Metropolis Era.* 2 vols. London: Sage Publications.

Downs, Alan. 1995. *Corporate Executions.* New York: AMACON.

Economic Report of the President. 1999. February. Washington: U.S. Government Printing Office.

Ehrenreich, Barbara. 1983. *The Hearts of Men.* New York: Anchor Press.

Abelman, Charles, and Richard Elmore. 1998. "When Accountability Knocks, Will Anyone Answer?" Research Report. Philadelphia: Consortium for Policy Research in Education.

Etzioni, Amitai. 1993. *The Spirit of Community: Rights, Responsibilities, and the Communitarian Agenda.* New York: Crown Publishing.

Eurostat. 1997a. *Statistics in Focus: Population and Social Conditions,* no. 10, *1970–1990.* Luxembourg: Office for Official Publications of the European Communities.

———. 1997b. *Yearbook: A Statistical Eye on Europe, 1986–1996.* Luxembourg: Office for Official Publications of the European Communities.

———. 1999. *Demographic Statistics.* Luxembourg: Office for Official Publications of the European Communities.

Evans, Peter. 1995. *Embedded Autonomy: States and Industrial Transformation.* Princeton: Princeton University Press.

———. 1997. "The Eclipse of the State?" *World Politics* 50(1): 62–87.

Farber, Henry. 1993. "The Incidence of Job Loss: 1982–1991." In *Brookings Papers on Economic Activity: Microeconomics.* Washington, D.C.: Brookings.

Fischer, Claude. 1984. *Dwelling Among Friends.* Chicago: University of Chicago Press.

Flanagan, Robert. 1983. *Unionism, Economic Stability, and Incomes Policies.* Washington, D.C.: Brookings.

Fortin, Nicole, and Thomas Lemieux. 1996. "Labor Market Institutions and Gender Differences in Wage Inequality." Unpublished paper. University of Montreal.

Freeman, Chris, and Luc Soete. 1994. *Work for All or Mass Unemployment?* London: Pinter Publishers.

Freeman, Richard. 1993. "How Much Has De-Unionization Contributed to the Rise in Male Earnings Inequality?" In *Uneven Tides: Rising Inequality in America,* edited by Sheldon Danziger and Peter Gottschalk. New York: Russell Sage Foundation.

Freeman, Richard, and Lawrence Katz. 1995. *Differences and Changes in Wage Structures.* Chicago: University of Chicago Press.

Freeman, Richard, and Karen Needels. 1991. "Skill Differentials in Canada in an Era of Rising Labor Market Inequality." Working Paper 3827. Cambridge, Mass.: National Bureau of Economic Research.

Friedman, Milton. 1955. "The Role of Government in Education." In *Economics and the Public Interest,* edited by Robert Solo. New Brunswick: Rutgers University Press.

Fukuyama, Francis. 1995. *Trust.* New York: Free Press.

Fuller, Bruce, Casey Coonerty, Fran Kipnis, and Yvonne Choong. 1997. *An Unfair Head Start.* Berkeley: Policy Analyses for California Education (PACE).

Garreau, Joel. 1991. *Edge City.* New York: Doubleday.

Giddens, Anthony. 1991. *Modernity and Self-Identity: Self and Society in the Late Modern Age.* Cambridge, England: Polity Press.

Gould, Susan B., Kerry Weiner, and Barbara Levin. 1998. *Free Agents: People and Organizations Creating a New Working Community.* San Francisco: Jossey-Bass.

Granovetter, Mark. 1995. *Getting a Job: A Study of Contacts and Careers,* 2d ed. Chicago: University of Chicago Press.

Grant Thornton Accountants and Management Consultants. 1991. *Grant Thornton Survey of American Manufacturers: A National Study of Executive Attitudes and Opinions Towards Quality and Global Competition.* Chicago: Grant Thorton.

Griliches, Zvi. 1969. "Capital-Skill Complementarity." *Review of Economics and Statistics* 51(4): 465–68.

Grossman, John. 1998. "You're Fired." *Sky* (October): 102.

Gruppo Onda. 1991. *Lavori di donne.* Milan, Italy: Franco Angeli.

Guillaume, Marc. 1983. *Partager le travail.* Paris: Presses Universitaires de France.

Guillemard, Anne Marie. 1993. "Travailleurs vieillissants et marche du travail en Europe." *Travail et Emploi* (September): 60–79.

Hall, Robert. 1982. "The Importance of Lifetime Jobs in the U.S. Economy." *American Economic Review* 72(4): 716–24.

Halpern, Robert. 1995. *Rebuilding the Inner City: A History of Neighborhood Initiatives to Address Poverty in the United States.* New York: Columbia University Press.

Hammonds, Kevin Kelly, and Karen Thurston. 1994. "The New World of Work." *Business Week,* October 17, 1994, p. 76.

Harrison, Bennett, and Barry Bluestone. 1988. *The Great U-Turn.* New York: Basic Books.

Hewitt, Patricia. 1993. *About Time: The Revolution in Work and Family Life.* London: Rivers Oram Press.

Hewlett, Sylvia Ann. 1991. *When the Bough Breaks.* New York: Basic Books.

Hirschhorn, Larry. 1984. *Beyond Mechanization: Work and Technology in a Postindustrial Age.* Cambridge: MIT Press.

Hochschild, Arlie Russell. 1996. *Time Bind.* New York: Metropolitan.

Hofferth, Sandra. 1989. "What Is the Demand and Supply of Child Care in the United States?" *Young Children* (July): 28–33.

Howell, David, and Susan Weiler. 1996. "Explaining the Collapse of Low-Skill Earnings: Implications for Education and Training Policy." Unpublished paper. New School for Social Research and Columbia University, New York.

———. 1998. "Skill-Biased Demand Shifts and the Wage Collapse in the U.S.: A Critical Perspective on the Conventional Wisdom." *Eastern Economic Journal* 24(3): 343–66.

Howell, David, and Edward Wolff. 1991. "Trends in the Growth and Distribution of Skills in the U.S. Workplace, 1960–1985." *Industrial and Labor Relations Review* 44(3): 486–502.

Inglehart, Ronald. 1990. *Culture Shift in Advanced Industrial Society.* Princeton: Princeton University Press.

———. 1997. *Modernization and Post-Modernization.* Princeton: Princeton University Press.

Institut National de la Statistique et des Études Economiques (INSEE). 1996. *Données Sociales 1996: LaSociété française.* Paris: INSEE.

Institute for Health and Policy Studies. 1999. *The Work and Health of Californians—1999.* San Francisco: University of California.

Instituto Nacional de Estadística Geografica e Informatica (INEGI). 1998. *Annuario Estadíctico de los Estados Unidos Mexicanos 1998.* Mexico: INEGI.

International Labour Office (ILO). Various years. *Statistical Yearbook.* Geneva: ILO.

———. 1990. *ILO Yearbook of Labour Statistics, 1989–1990.* Geneva: ILO

———. 1996. *World Employment, 1996–1997.* Geneva: ILO.

———. 1997. *ILO Yearbook of Labour Statistics, 1997.* Geneva: ILO

International Telecommunications Union (ITU). 1995. *ITU Statistical Yearbook.* Geneva: ITU.

———. 1998. *World Communications Development Report.* Geneva: ITU.

Jaynes, Gerald, and Robin Williams, eds. 1990. *A Common Destiny*. Washington, D.C.: National Academy of Sciences.

Johnson, Chalmers. 1982. *MITI and the Japanese Miracle: The Growth of Industrial Policy, 1925–1975*. Stanford: Stanford University Press.

Kalleberg, Anne, Edith Rasell, Ken Hudson, David Webster, Barbara Reskin, Naomi Cassirer, and Eileen Appelbaum. 1997. *Nonstandard Work, Sub-Standard Jobs*. Washington, D.C.: Economic Policy Institute.

Kamo, Yoshinori. 1990. "Husbands and Wives Living in Nuclear and Stem Family Households in Japan." *Sociological Perspectives* 33(3): 397–417.

Kanter, Rosabeth Moss. 1995. "Nice Work If You Can Get It: The Software Industry as a Model for Tomorrow's Jobs." *American Prospect* 23(Fall): 52–59.

Kaplinsky, Raphael. 1987. *Microelectronics and Work: A Review*. Geneva: International Labour Office.

Kelley, Maryellen R. 1990. "New Process Technology, Job Design, and Work Organization: A Contingency Model." *American Sociological Review* 55(2): 191–208.

Kochan, Thomas, Harry Katz, and Robert McKersie. 1986. *The Transformation of American Industrial Relations*. New York: Basic Books.

Kravdal, Oystein. 1992. "The Emergence of a Positive Relationship: Education and Third-Birth Rates in Norway with Supportive Evidence for the United States." *Population Studies* 46(3): 459–75.

Krueger, Alan. 1991. "How Computers Have Changed the Wage Structure: Evidence from the Microdata, 1984–1989." Working Paper 3858. Cambridge, Mass.: National Bureau of Economic Research.

Krugman, Paul R., and Robert Z. Lawrence. 1994. "Trade, Jobs, and Wages." Working Paper 4478. Cambridge, Mass.: National Bureau of Economic Research.

Lawler, Edward, Susan Mohrman, and Gerald Ledford. 1992. *Employee Involvement and Total Quality Management: Practices and Results in Fortune 1,000 Companies*. San Francisco: Jossey-Bass.

Leal, Jesus. 1993. *La desigualdad social en Espana*. Research Monograph. Madrid: Universidad Autonóma de Madrid, Instituto de Sociología de Nuevas Tecnologías.

Leontief, Wassily, and Faye Duchin. 1985. *The Future Impact of Automation on Workers*. New York: Oxford University Press.

Maharidge, Dale. 1996. *The Coming White Minority*. New York: Times Books.

Mander, Jerry. 1978. *Four Arguments for the Elimination of Television*. New York: Morrow.

Marcotte, Dave E. 1995. "Declining Job Stability: What We Know and What It Means." *Journal of Policy Analysis and Management* 14(4): 590–98.

Martinotti, Guido. 1984. *Odissea Informatica: Alle soglie della nuova era: Itinerario nelle societa informatiche*. Milan, Italy: Gruppo Editoriale Jackson.

Matthews, T. J., and Stephanie J. Ventura. 1997. "Birth and Fertility Rates by Educational Attainment: United States, 1994." *Monthly Vital Statistics Report* (of the National Center for Health Statistics, Centers for Disease Control and Prevention) 45(10, supp.): 11–20.

McCourt, Frank. 1996. *Angela's Ashes.* New York: Scribner.

McEwan, Patrick, and Martin Carnoy. 1999a. "The Effectiveness and Efficiency of Private Schools in Chile's Voucher System." Unpublished paper. Stanford University, Stanford.

———. 1999b. "The Impact of Competition on Public School Quality: Longitudinal Evidence from Chile's Voucher System." Unpublished paper. Stanford University School of Education, Stanford.

McKinsey Global Institute. 1994. *Employment Performance.* Washington, D.C.: McKinsey Global Institute.

Miller, David. 1995. *On Nationality.* Oxford, England: Oxford University Press.

Miller, Steven M. 1989. *Impacts of Industrial Robotics: Potential Effects on Labor and Costs Within the Metalworking Industries.* Madison: University of Wisconsin Press.

Millett, Kate. 1970. *Sexual Politics.* New York: Doubleday.

Mincer, Jacob. 1991. "Human Capital, Technology, and the Wage Structure: What Do Time Series Show?" Working Paper 3581. Cambridge, Mass.: National Bureau of Economic Research.

Mishel, Lawrence, and Jared Bernstein. 1994. "Is the Technology Black Box Empty? An Empirical Examination of the Impact of Technology on Wage Inequality and the Employment Structure." Working Paper. Washington, D.C.: Economic Policy Institute.

Mishel, Lawrence, and Ruy Teixera. 1991. *The Myth of the Coming Labor Shortage: Jobs, Skills, and Incomes of America's Workforce 2000.* Washington, D.C.: Economic Policy Institute.

Mitchell, Juliet. 1971. *Women's Estate.* New York: Pantheon.

Murnane, Richard, and Frank Levy. 1996. *Teaching the New Basic Skills.* New York: Free Press.

Myers, Robert G. 1996. "Pre-School Education in Latin America: 'State of the Practice.'" Washington, D.C.: Programa de Promoción de la Reforma Educativa en América Latina y El Caribe (PREAL) .

Nomura, Naoki, et al. 1995. "Family Characteristics and Dynamics in Japan and the United States: A Preliminary Report from the Family Environment Scale." *International Journal of Intercultural Relations* 19(1): 59–85.

Office of Population Census and Surveys. 1991. *General Household Survey, 1990.* London: Office for National Statistics.

Okimoto, Dan, and Thomas Rohlen. 1988. *Inside the Japanese System: Readings on Contemporary Society and Political Economy.* Stanford: Stanford University Press.

Organisation for Economic Co-operation and Development (OECD). 1992a. *Employment Outlook,* July. Paris: OECD.

————. 1992b. *Information and Technology Outlook 1992.* Paris: OECD.

————. 1993a. *Employment Outlook,* July. Paris: OECD.

————. 1993b. *Main Economic Indicators: Historical Statistics, 1962–1991.* Paris: OECD.

————. General Secretariat. 1994a. "Employment/Unemployment Study: Policy Report." Document prepared for Council at Ministerial Level, Paris (May).

————. 1994b. *OECD Jobs Study: Facts, Analysis, Strategies.* Paris: OECD.

————. 1995. *Labour Force Statistics, 1974–1994.* Paris: OECD.

————. 1996a. *Employment Outlook,* July.

————. 1996b. *Information Technology Outlook, 1995.* Paris: OECD.

————. 1996c. "The Knowledge-Based Economy." Paper. Paris: OECD.

————. 1997a. *Employment Outlook,* July. Paris: OECD.

————. 1997b. *Historical Statistics, 1960–1995.* Paris: OECD.

————. 1998a. *Employment Outlook,* June. Paris: OECD.

————. 1998b. *Labour Force Statistics, 1977–1997.* Paris: OECD.

————. 1998c. *OECD Economic Surveys: The Netherlands, 1998.* Paris: OECD.

————. 1998d. *Reviews of National Policies for Education: Italy.* Paris: OECD.

————. 1999a. *Economic Outlook,* July. Paris: OECD.

————. 1999b. *Employment Outlook,* June. Paris: OECD.

Osterman, Paul. 1994. "How Common Is Workplace Transformation, and Who Adopts It?" *Industrial and Labor Relations Review* 47(2): 173–88.

Ozaki, Muneto, et al. 1992. *Technological Change and Labour Relations.* Geneva: International Labour Organization.

Paltridge, Sam. 1996. "How Competition Helps the Internet." *OECD Observer* 201(August–September): 25–27.

Peters, Tom, and Robert Waterman. 1982. *In Search of Excellence.* New York: Harper and Row.

Pfeffer, Jeffrey. 1998. *The Human Equation: Building Profits by Putting People First.* Cambridge: Harvard Business School Press.

Piore, Michael, and Charles Sabel. 1984. *The Second Industrial Divide.* New York: Basic Books.

Polivka, Anne E., and Thomas Nardonne. 1989. "On the Definition of 'Contingent Work.'" *Monthly Labor Review* 112(12): 9–16.

Portes, Alejandro, and Robert Barach. 1990. *Immigrant America.* Berkeley: University of California Press.

Przeworski, Adam. 1985. *Capitalism and Social Democracy.* New York: Cambridge University Press.

Przeworski, Adam, and Michael Wallerstein. 1982. "The Structure of Class

Conflict in Democratic Capitalist Societies." *American Political Science Review* 76(2): 215–38.

Putnam, Robert. 1993. *Making Democracy Work: Civic Traditions in Italy.* Princeton: Princeton University Press.

———. 1995. "Bowling Alone: America's Declining Social Capital." *Journal of Democracy* 6(1): 65–78.

———. 1996. "The Strange Disappearance of Civic America." *American Prospect* 24(Winter): 34–48.

Rifkin, Jeremy. 1995. *The End of Work.* New York: Putnam.

Rosen, Sherwin. 1996. "Public Employment , Taxes, and the Welfare State in Sweden." *In The Welfare State in Transition,* edited by Richard B. Freeman, Brigitta Swedenborg, and Robert Topel. Chicago: University of Chicago Press.

Rosencrance, Richard. 1996. "The Rise of the Virtual State." *Foreign Affairs* 75(4): 45–62.

Rothstein, Richard. 1997. "Union Strength in the United States: Lessons for the UPS Strike." *International Labour Review* 136(4): 469–91.

———. 1998. *The Way We Were? The Myths and Realities of America's Student Achievement.* New York: Century Foundation Press.

Rothstein, Richard, Martin Carnoy, and Luis Benveniste. 1999. *What Can Public Schools Learn from Private Schools.* Washington, D.C.: Economic Policy Institute.

Rouse, Cecilia. 1998. "Private School Vouchers and Student Achievement: An Evaluation of the Milwaukee Parental Choice Program." *Quarterly Journal of Economics* 113(2): 553–602.

Rumberger, Russell. 1981. *Overeducation in the U.S. Labor Market?* New York: Praeger.

Russell, Thyra K. 1994. *Job Sharing: An Annotated Bibliography.* Metuchen, N.J.: Scarecrow.

Saboulin, Michel de, and Suzanne Thave. 1993. "La Vie en couple marie: Un modele qui s'affablit." In *Données Sociales 1996: LaSociété française.* Paris: INSEE.

Saez, Felipe, et al. 1991. *Tecnologia y empleo en Espana: Situacion y perspectivas.* Madrid: Ministerio de Economia.

Saxenian, AnnaLee. 1994. *Regional Advantage.* Cambridge: Harvard University Press.

Schettkat, Ronald, and MichaelWagner, eds. 1990. *Technological Change and Employment Innovation in the German Economy.* Berlin: Walter de Gruyter.

Schudson, Michael. 1996. "What If Civic Life Didn't Die?" *American Prospect* 25(March–April): 17–20.

Schultz, Theodore W. 1961. "Investment in Man." *American Economic Review* 51(1): 1–17.

————. 1975. "The Value of the Ability to Deal with Disequilibria." *Journal of Economic Literature* 13(3): 827–46.

Shaiken, Harley. 1985. *Work Transformed: Automation and Labor in the Computer Age.* New York: Holt, Rinehart and Winston.

————. 1993. "Beyond Lean Production." *Stanford Law and Policy Review* 5(1): 41–52.

————. 1994. "Research Report on Technology and Work in the GM's Saturn Plant in Tennessee." Unpublished paper. University of California, Berkeley.

Skocpol, Theda. 1979. *States and Social Revolution: A Comparative Analysis of France, Russia, and China.* New York: Cambridge University Press.

————. 1996. "Unravelling from Above." *American Prospect* 25 (March–April): 20–25.

Smith, Adam. 1907. *The Theory of Moral Sentiments.* London: G. Bell.

Spakes, Patricia. 1992. "National Family Policy: Sweden Versus the United States." *Affilia* 7(2): 44–60.

Spenner, Kenneth. 1985. "The Upgrading and Downgrading of Occupations: Issues, Evidence, and the Implications for Education." *Review of Educational Research* 55(2): 125–54.

Stella, Gian Antonio. 1996. *SCHEI: dal boom alla rivolta: Il mitico Nordest.* Milano: Ed. Baldini & Castodoli.

Stevens, Barrie, and Wolfgang Michalski. 1994. "Long-Term Prospects for Work and Social Cohesion in OECD Countries. An Overview of the Issues." Secretariat's Report to the OECD Forum for the Future. Organisation for Economic Co-operation and Development, Paris.

Taylor, Frederick Winslow. 1911. *The Principles of Scientific Management.* New York: Harper and Brothers.

Texas Industrial Areas Foundation (IAF) Network. 1990. *Vision, Values, Action.* Austin: Texas IAF Network.

Therborn, Göran. 1995. *European Modernity and Beyond.* London: Sage Publications.

Tilly, Chris. 1996. *Half A Job: Bad and Good Part-Time Jobs in a Changing Labor Market.* Philadelphia: Temple University Press.

United Nations Conference on Trade and Development (UNCTAD). 1993. *World Investment Report 1993: Transnational Corporations and Integrated International Production.* New York: United Nations.

U.S. Congress. House Committee on Government Operations. 1988. *Rising Use of Part-Time and Temporary Workers: Who Benefits and Who Loses? Hearing Before the Committee on Government Operations.* 100th Congress, 2d sess. May 19.

U.S. Congress, Office of Technology Assessment (OTA). 1984. *Computerized Manufacturing Automation: Employment, Education, and the Workplace.* Washington, D.C.: U.S. Government Printing Office.

————. 1986. *Technology and Structural Unemployment.* Washington, D.C.: U.S. Government Printing Office.

U.S. Department of Commerce, Bureau of the Census. 1981a. *Census of Population and Housing, 1960: Public Use Sample: 1/1000 Sample.* Ann Arbor, Mich.: Inter-University Consortium for Political and Social Research.

————. 1981b. *Census of Population and Housing, 1970: Public Use Sample: 1/ 1000 Sample.* Ann Arbor, Mich.: Inter-University Consortium for Political and Social Research.

————. 1984. *Census of Population and Housing, 1980: Public Use Sample: 1 Percent Sample.* Ann Arbor, Mich.: Inter-University Consortium for Political and Social Research.

————. 1993. *Census of Population and Housing, 1990: Public Use Sample: 1 Percent Sample.* Ann Arbor, Mich.: Inter-University Consortium for Political and Social Research.

————. 1996. *Composition of American Households.* Washington, D.C.: U.S. Government Printing Office.

————. 1988. *Current Population Survey, March 1988.* Washington, D.C.: U.S. Department of Commerce, Economics and Statistics Division, Bureau of the Census.

————. 1990. *Current Population Survey, March 1990.* Washington, D.C.: U.S. Department of Commerce, Economics and Statistics Division, Bureau of the Census.

————. 1995. *Current Population Survey, March 1995.* Washington, D.C.: U.S. Department of Commerce, Economics and Statistics Division, Bureau of the Census.

————. 1998. *Current Population Survey, March 1998.* Washington, D.C.: U.S. Department of Commerce, Economics and Statistics Division, Bureau of the Census.

————. 1999. *Current Population Survey, March 1999.* Washington, D.C.: U.S. Department of Commerce, Economics and Statistics Division, Bureau of the Census.

————. 1992. *Households, Families, and Children: A 30-Year Perspective.* Series P23–181. Washington, D.C.: U.S. Government Printing Office.

U.S. Department of Labor, Women's Bureau. 1988. *Flexible Workstyles: A Look at Contingent Labor.* Washington, D.C.: U.S. Department of Labor, Office of the Secretary, Women's Bureau.

U.S. General Accounting Office (GAO). 1987. *Survey of Corporate Employee Involvement Efforts.* Washington, D.C.: GAO.

————. 1994. *Child Care: Promoting Quality in Family Child Care.* GAO/HEHS-95–36. Washington, D.C.: U.S. General Accounting Office.

Valelly, Richard. 1996. "Couch-Potato Democracy?" *American Prospect* 25 (March–April): 25–26.

Warme, Barbara D., Katrina L. P. Lundy, and Larry A. Lundy, eds. 1992. *Working Part-Time: Risks and Opportunities.* New York: Praeger.

Watanabe, Susumu. 1986. "Labour-Saving Versus Work-Amplifying Effects of Microelectronics." *International Labour Review* 125(3): 243–59.

———. 1987. *Microelectronics, Automation, and Employment in the Automobile Industry.* Chichester, England: John Wiley and Sons.

Welch, Finis. 1970. "Education in Production." *Journal of Political Economy* 78 (1): 35–59.

Wellman, Barry, Janet Salaff, Dimitrina Dimitrova, Laura Garton, Gulia Milena, and Caroline Haythornthwaite. 1996. "Computer Networks as Social Networks: Collaborative Work, Telework, and Virtual Community." *Annual Review of Sociology* 22: 215–16.

Willson, Michele. 1997. "Community in the Abstract: A Political and Ethnical Dilemma?" In *Virtual Politics: Identity and Community in Cyberspace,* edited by David Holmes. London: Sage Publications.

Wilson, William J. 1987. *The Truly Disadvantaged.* Chicago: University of Chicago.

Wood, Adrian. 1994. *North-South Trade, Employment, and Inequality.* Oxford, England: Clarendon Press.

Wood, Stephen, ed. 1989. *The Transformation of Work?* London: Unwin and Hyman.

World Bank. 1993. *The East Asian Miracle: Economic Growth and Public Policy.* New York: Oxford University Press.

———. 1997. *World Development Report: The State in a Changing World.* New York: Oxford University Press.

Young, Michael, and Peter Willmott. 1973. *The Symmetrical Family.* New York: Pantheon.

Zaldivar, Carlos Alonso, and Manuel Castells. 1992. *Espana fin de siglo.* Madrid: Alianza Editorial.

Zuboff, Shoshana. 1988. *In the Age of the Smart Machine.* New York: Basic Books.

Index

Boldface numbers refer to figures and tables.

Adler, Paul, 43
Akre, Daniel, 57
Alinsky, Saul, 184
Allen, Steven, 88
Anderson, Benedict, 188*n*2
Appelbaum, Eileen, 102*n*8
Ascher, François, 7, 161
Austen, Jane, 6
Austin Interfaith, 185
Australia: employment, 77; job creation, 21; unemployment, 23; use of information technology, 34–36; wages and flexible labor markets, 85–86; women in the work force, 30–32
Austria, and flexible production, 65

Barnet, Richard, 15, 20
Batt, Rosemary, 102*n*8
Beacon program, 188
Belgium, use of information technology, 34–36
Bell, Daniel, 43
Bernstein, Jared, 89
Bessant, John, 17
birthrates, OECD countries, 116–17
Blazejczak, Jurgen, 38
Bluestone, Barry, 39, 136
Bowles, Samuel, 115
Braverman, Harry, 54*n*13
Britain. *See* United Kingdom
Burke, Alan, 1–3

Canada: job creation, 21; labor markets and differences from the U.S., 10; unemployment, 23; wages and flexible labor markets, 85–86; women in the work force, 30–32
Cappelli, Peter, 45
Carnegie, Andrew, 18
Castaño, Cecilia, 36, 43
Castells, Manuel, 60, 153–54, 161, 163
child care: in France, 139–40, 146–47; in the Netherlands, 217*n*8; in Scandinavia, 146
children: conditions in the United States, 142; growing up in poverty, **132**; social activities organized around, 166
China, People's Republic of, job creation, 22
civic life: changes in, 7; civic-mindedness by country, **169**; decline in, 164–70; social trust by country, **169**
communities: and change, 152–54; civic life, changes in, 7; emergence of new, 170–71; knowledge, building, 201–11; knowledge-use, 204–6; local, 160–70; national, 154–60; schools, 182–88; self-knowledge, 171–75; virtual, 180–82; work, 175–82
computers: and networking, 180–82; use of and income, 88. *See also* information technology
computer-supported social networks (CSSNs), 180–81

233